# BLIZZARD'S

✦ ✦ ✦ BOOK OF ✦ ✦ ✦

# WOODWORKING

# BLIZZARD'S

### ✦ ✦ ✦ BOOK OF ✦ ✦ ✦

# WOODWORKING

HarperCollins*Publishers*

First published in 1991 by
HarperCollins Publishers
London

**A CIP catalogue record for this book is available from
the British Library**

ISBN 0 00 412645/9

Designed and produced by Julian Holland
Photography by Howard Gimber
Diagrams by Peter Farley and Mervyn Hurford
Line drawings by Martin Smillie
Edited by Miranda and Martin Smith
Typesetting by Minster Typesetting

Printed and bound in China

**Author's acknowledgements**
Anyone who gets involved in writing a book will know that
although the author gets his name prominently displayed on
the cover, there are a great many other people who have
helped to bring the book to completion.

I should like, therefore, to personally thank the following
companies and individuals who have made this book possible:

Merlin Unwin, Robin Wood, Polly Powell and Miranda and
Martin Smith, for their editorial support

Peter Farley and Mervyn Hurford for all the exploded
isometric drawings

Julian Holland and Martin Smillie for their drawings and design of
the book

Margaret Ward for having typed up all my untidy notes

Makita Power Tools. In particular Gary Morikawa, George
Yamamota, Derrick Marshall, Carol Chant and Bruce Smith for
having sponsored the book and provided machines for the projects

Howard Gimber for having taken all the photographs

Davis & Son for moving all the furniture so very carefully

Mr Peter Grimsdale and Mr Jack Baird of the Finnish Swedish
Timber Council for their advice in the choice and supply
of Nordic redwood for the projects in this book

# Contents

# Introduction

I BELIEVE that within every human being there is a creative instinct. In different people this expresses itself in a variety of ways – painting, knitting, flower arranging, gardening, pottery, weaving, wood turning, carving etc. It is important not what you make, but that you actually get down to making something.

In every craft there has to be a starting-point; someone or something is needed to show you how to get started, to give that initial confidence to get you under way. We are blessed with libraries, books, videos and TV – all these play their part in both educating and entertaining us.

Woodworking is always seen as rather daunting, and so many people are "put off" by their first bad experience with a 152mm (6in) nail (never to be used unless you are constructing a roof) and a hammer with a wobbly head that belonged to Great Grandfather.

I have, therefore, tried in this book to give you not just projects, working drawings and cutting lists, but the techniques of how to hold saws, chisels and even electric tools correctly. Woodworking tools are not dangerous to use if you know how to hold them.

I suppose one basic rule always holds good for whatever craft you want to learn – start with something fairly simple, get a feel for the craft, develop your confidence and you will be surprised at what you can achieve.

I hope this book will be a source of both pleasure and inspiration.

*Richard B. Blizzard*

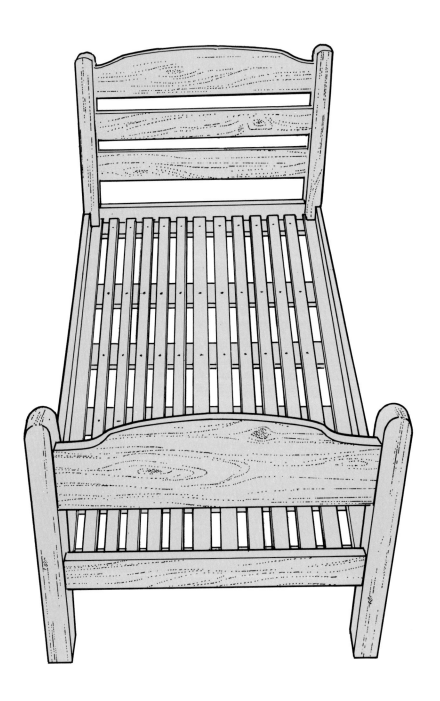

# The projects

THE SEVENTEEN projects in this book blend the best traditional methods of working wood with modern techniques made possible by the recent development of powered machinery. This does not mean, however, that power tools have taken over in the workshop. Many hand tools – such as the coping saw and spokeshave – are very efficient and still a joy to use.

The projects have been chosen not only because they are fine examples of the woodworker's craft but also because they illustrate the use of certain woodworking techniques. All the techniques in the book are useful for a variety of tasks – many both practical and decorative.

The featured techniques are highlighted at the beginning of each project. There is also a list of tools that are essential for the construction of that particular piece of furniture. Some techniques are used for several of the projects. Use the contents list or index to establish where in the book these are described in detail.

On pages 195 – 204 there is a comprehensive description of tools and materials referred to in the projects, with tips and recommendations on what to purchase and how each can be used most effectively and safely.

# Corner shelf unit

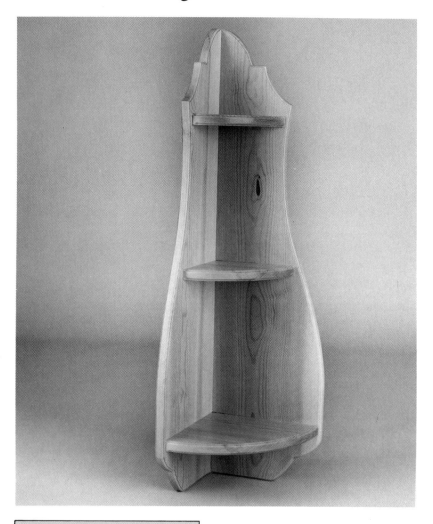

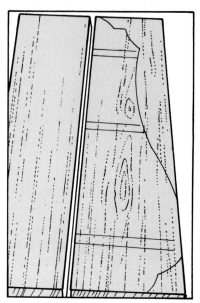

1 *When the pieces of timber are placed back to back, mark out the position of the joints with a pencil.*

2 *Insert the tip of the tenon saw into the hole at the stopped end of the joint and saw along the line carefully.*

*Essential tools*
Hand held or electric router
Coping saw or jigsaw
Spokeshave
Rebate plane

This small corner shelf unit is ideal for the display of treasured ornaments. A wide range of softwoods would be suitable for use here. Just two jointing techniques are used – the stopped housing joint and the rebate joint. The housing joint is "stopped" before the front edge of the shelf unit, thus preventing the joint from being seen.

## The housing joints

Make a start by cutting to length two pieces of timber. Place them back to back and mark out the position of the stopped housing joints. (**1**) Make sure that you mark out both pieces and that all the pencilled marks on housing joints line up. Do not start by working on the shaping – that is always the last job to be done.

There are two ways of cutting out the housing joint: the traditional way with a chisel, or the modern method with an electric router. For the traditional method, cut a small oblong hole at the stopped end of the joint with a firmer chisel and mallet. Then

saw back along the line with a tenon saw. (**2**) The same procedure is followed on the other side of the housing.

Once both sides of the housing have been cut down, use either a firmer or bevel edged chisel to chop out the waste. Start at the stopped end and work carefully along. Do not be tempted to make a deep cut to start with; it is far better to make a series of shallow cuts. (3) The shape of the chisel is designed to raise the wood, and after the first pass with the chisel the chippings are easily removed by reversing the chisel and tapping gently with the mallet. Then, to ensure that a uniform depth is achieved, use a hand router. This has a cutter projecting through its base which removes any high spots that the chiselling process has missed. (4)

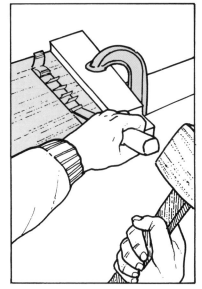

**3** *Chopping out the waste wood should be done by a series of shallow cuts.*

**4** *Remove "high spots" from the bottom of the housing with a hand held router.*

The modern technique for cutting this joint is to use an electric router. The cutter on this rotates at a very high speed and saves a great deal of time. The cutting action of the router takes away the need to cut the small oblong hole. However, it is necessary to cramp an offcut of wood onto the side, so positioned that the base of the router and the path of the cutter will remove the waste wood in the housing. (5)

**5** *If using an electric router, cramp a waste piece of wood onto the side.*

### Shaping

The traditional method for cutting the curved front edges was to use either a bow or coping saw. The coping saw is a very efficient hand tool, and although much slower than its modern counterpart, the jigsaw, shapes wood well. (6)

When all the sawing has been completed, use a spokeshave to remove all the saw cut marks. A well sharpened spokeshave is a joy to use as it will remove a very fine shaving from the timber. (7) Glasspaper can be used to finish off the curves.

### The shelves

The curved edges of the shelves are cut either with a coping saw or a

**6** *To achieve a smoothly curved shape, it is best to use a coping saw.*

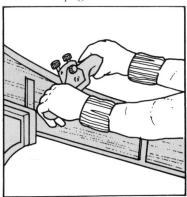

**7** *Now remove all saw marks with a spokeshave. All spokeshaving jobs must be done with the grain, or the tool will tear the wood.*

jigsaw. Once again, the spokeshave is used to remove the saw cuts. Then cut a small notch out of each of the shelf front edges. (8) This will allow the shelves to fit into the housing and hides the joints at the front edge.

At the back edge, two pieces of timber are held together by a rebate. This can be done using the traditional tool, a rebate plane, or the electric router. The rebate plane has adjustments for both width and depth. Start cutting at the front edge and work backwards down the plank. (9) The rebate is cut only on one side piece. The modern tool for producing rebates is the electric router. (10)

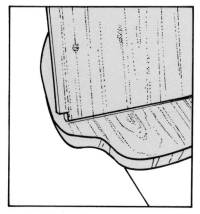

**8** *Now cut a small notch out of each of the shelf front edges.*

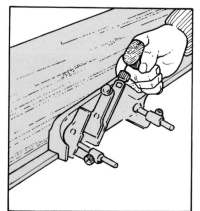

**9** *The rebate plane produces a first class rebate.*

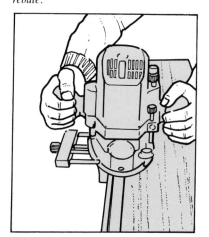

**10** *The electric router is used with a side fence fitted so that the machine cuts a rebate parallel with the side.*

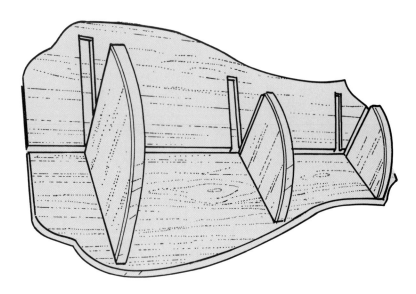

**11** *Before glueing up, make sure that everything fits together snugly.*

Once the sides have been shaped, the shelves cut to shape and the rebates cut out of the back, a fine moulding cutter is fitted in the router and all the edges moulded. There are many different shaped cutters available for routers, but probably the best to use are those fitted with a small ball bearing on the bottom which prevents the cutter pilot nose from burning the edges.

**Finishing off**

Make sure that everything fits together well. (**11**) Then, before glueing up, clean all the pieces of wood. The process of glueing up requires great care because most of the surfaces are curved. A variety of cramps can be used, but Stanley web cramps are particularly helpful. Cramps fitted with nylon heads are better than the traditional "G"

cramps, because steel cramp heads will damage the edges. Now you can apply a coat of varnish for a smooth finish. (**12**)

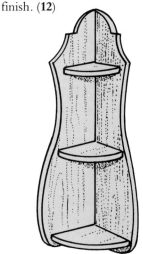

**12** *The finished shelf unit.*

| COTTAGE CORNER SHELF UNIT CUTTING LIST | | |
|---|---|---|
| Sides | 2 off | 914 × 279 × 22mm (36 × 11 × 7/8in) timber |
| Top shelf | 1 off | 152 × 152 × 22mm (6 × 6 × 7/8in) timber |
| Middle shelf | 1 off | 178 × 178 × 22mm (7 × 7 × 7/8in) timber |
| Lower shelf | 1 off | 248 × 248 × 22mm (9¾ × 9¾ × 7/8in) timber |

**Left** *The fine moulding created by a router fitted with a small ball bearing.*

**Below** *Fine moulding adds greatly to the visual appeal of the unit.*

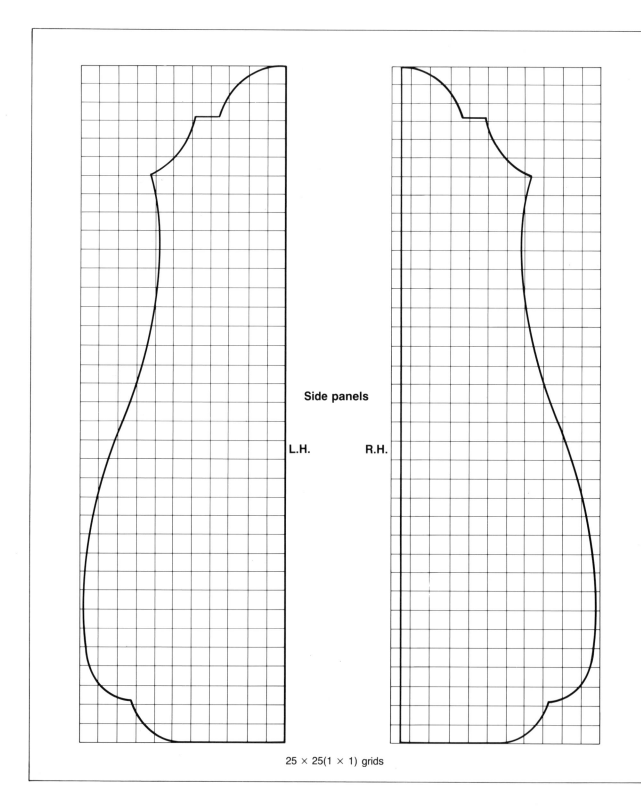

**Side panels**

L.H.          R.H.

25 × 25(1 × 1) grids

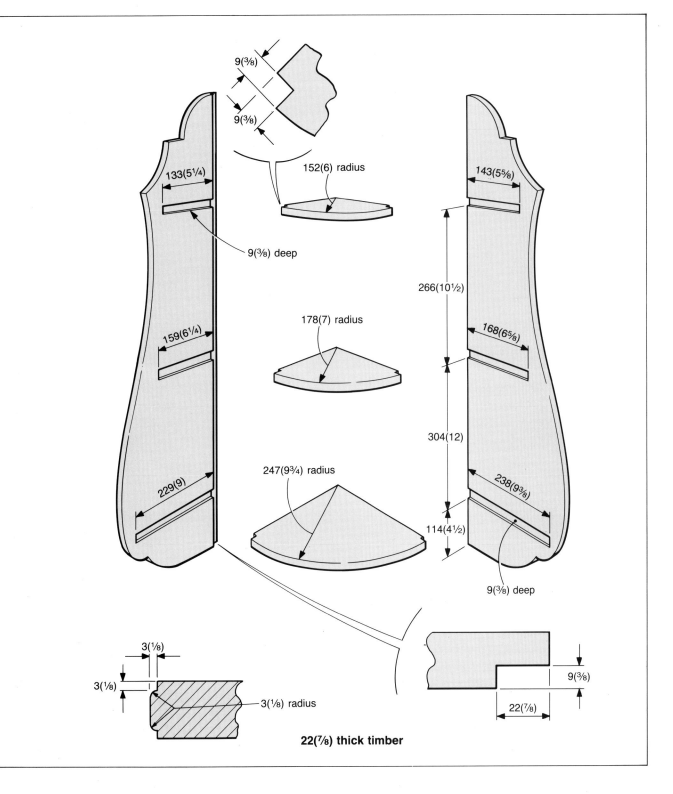

9(³/₈)

9(³/₈)

152(6) radius

133(5¼)

9(³/₈) deep

143(5⁵/₈)

266(10½)

159(6¼)

178(7) radius

168(6⁵/₈)

304(12)

247(9¾) radius

229(9)

238(9³/₈)

114(4½)

9(³/₈) deep

3(⅛)

3(⅛)

3(⅛)

3(⅛) radius

9(³/₈)

22(⁷/₈)

**22(⁷/₈) thick timber**

# Cottage stools

*Essential tools*
Sliding bevel gauge
Electric router
"G" cramps
Electric drill

Whatever your woodworking ability, it is sometimes very satisfying to tackle a job that can be completed in a day or weekend. Some of the original cottage style furniture is very easily made and suits most home settings. And although the cottage stools can be made with traditional woodworking tools, the design lends itself well to a more mechanised approach.

## Marking out

First mark out the legs and the sides. (**1**) Use a sliding bevel gauge to mark the angles to be cut on both the top and the bottom of the leg.(**2**) Set the bevel gauge at 10° and mark the angles very clearly on the timber. For accuracy, I always use the thickness of

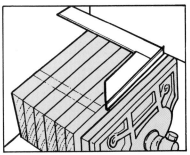

**1** *Make a start by marking out the legs and sides. Use the actual thickness of the wood to mark out the housing joints.*

**2** *Set the leg angles using a sliding bevel gauge, then score the marked out lines heavily with a Stanley knife to sever the wood fibres.*

the wood to mark the housing joints. In this case, take the leg, place it on the side of the stool and make a mark on either side of it with pencil. This method of marking out ensures good, tight-fitting joints.

**Cutting the housing joint**
Once the marking out is finished, score the pencil lines heavily with a Stanley knife, ensuring that all the wood fibres are severed. Now you can start to cut. The electric router has changed working methods and speeds jobs along. It is important to fit a batten onto the side of the stool to guide the router base as it cuts along the housing.(**3**) Spend a few minutes setting this up and checking that the cutter will run parallel along the housing. Use a pair of "G" cramps on the batten and adjust both until the correct setting is achieved.

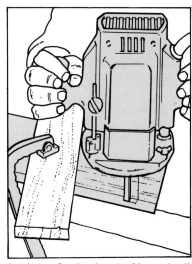

**3** *A batten fixed to the side of the stool will guide the router.*

The electric router takes out the wood in one pass. It is then necessary to re-position the batten to allow the router cutter to remove the remainder of the timber in the housing. You will find that scored in lines mean that the housing remains very tidy and clean at the edges. Many simple woodworking projects are spoilt at the early stages, and a failure to pencil and knife in the marking out lines is one of the most common faults. (**4**)

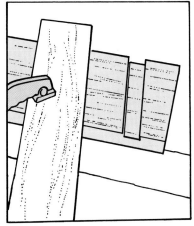

**4** *The finished housing joint.*

### The housing joint
Traditionally, a housing joint was cut with chisel and router. After scoring the pencil lines, use a tenon saw to saw down the lines until the right depth is reached. Take a sharp chisel and mallet and gradually and carefully chop out the housing between the saw cuts. The depth of the housing is very important; unless it is even throughout its length, the stool legs will not fit properly or "square up" when you try to assemble the stool. The hand router is therefore vital because its cutter ensures that the bottom of the housing is flat and uniform throughout its length.

### The legs
Cutting a 10° angle onto the end of a piece of timber is not easy, it is much simpler to use a plane. It is still quite difficult to hold a plane at a steady 10° and remove end grain. So make a small wooden block from waste wood and plane one side to 10°.(**5**) With this block firmly against the side of the chair leg, the plane sole will be set at 10° and, as the plane blade starts to cut, the bottom of the leg will

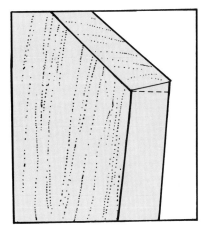

**5** *Hold the plane at a 10° angle to shape the ends of the legs.*

automatically be planed at 10°. However, it is important to remember that if you plane straight across, the plane will "split out" the timber when it reaches the end. To prevent this happening, work from both ends.

Now check the legs for fit into the housing joints.(**6**) Planing is necessary on both top and bottom of the legs. Once this is done, assemble the legs into the housing joints.

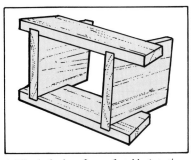

**6** *Check the legs fit comfortably into the housing joints.*

### Decorating the stools
If you study pictures of old furniture you will discover that cabinet makers and carpenters used several standard decorative patterns, and nice decorative features for these stools are holes bored in the legs. Traditionally, a brace and bit would be used to cut

the holes. Today, there are a number of choices of tool, but perhaps the most familiar is the flat bit.

The flat bit was produced for use in electric drills and it provides the woodworker with a relatively cheap method of boring a large diameter hole cleanly in wood. It is vital to drill through only partially from one side first.(**7**) This is easily achieved because the flat bit has a leading spike that comes through the timber before the main cutter breaks through. Once the leading spike has gone through, stop drilling and reposition the drill and flat bit on the other side of the timber, making sure that the flat bit spike is carefully positioned in the small hole it has already made. By drilling through from both sides you will prevent the ugly splinters that always accompany a flat bit drill breaking through.

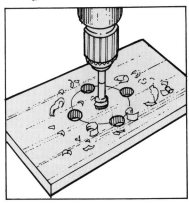

**7** *Create a neat decorative effect by boring holes with a flat bit on an electric drill.*

To give the stool legs and sides a smooth line, use a small router moulding cutter on the edges. This rounding off removes the square look of the stools but does not detract from the chunky design.

### Glueing up
Now glue the legs and sides together. Do not be too generous with the glue; with tight housing joints, too much glue will only prevent the joints

fitting together easily. Make sure that the housing joints pull up tight; you will find a pair of "G" cramps most useful for this job. Check that the leg tops are parallel with the sides before the final clamping.

The top is made from either two pieces of wood glued together, or you can buy parana pine boards which are available in the right widths. Parana pine can give a very interesting colour combination, as the boards often have a lovely red or deep rich brown stripe. Glue the top to the frame.(**8**) Use the router to round and smooth the edges of the top and remove all sharp edges from the sides.

### Finishing off

There are two methods of fixing the tops. The top can be glued straight onto the frame. If you adopt this method, make sure that you use a knife to provide the glue with a key on both the underside of the stool and the frame. A criss-cross knife pattern will give more glueing surface and a stronger join.

If you prefer, a matching set of countersinks and plug cutters can be bought. Counterbore a hole to take the screws, then finish off with a wooden plug glued over the top. Do not be tempted to use dowel rods to fill in the screw holes – the dowel rod leaves end grain and will always show on the top. The plug cutter allows you to cut plugs of wood from offcuts which will match the stool tops perfectly. Use glue to fix the plugs over the screws. Once the glue has dried, cut off the waste with a sharp chisel.

Now apply a polyurethane varnish or one of the new acrylic varnishes for a smooth finish. (**9**)

**8** *The top can be glued straight onto the frame. Note the two "G" cramps holding the top to the frame while the glue dries.*

**9** *The stools are varnished for a smooth finish.*

### COTTAGE STOOL CUTTING LIST

| | | |
|---|---|---|
| Top | 2 off | 381 × 114 × 22mm (15 × 4½ × ⅞in) timber |
| Legs | 2 off | 302 × 171 × 22mm (11⅞ × 6¾ × ⅞in) timber |
| Sides | 2 off | 330 × 127 × 22mm (13 × 5 × ⅞in) timber |

*The underside of the stool showing how the joints fit snugly together.*

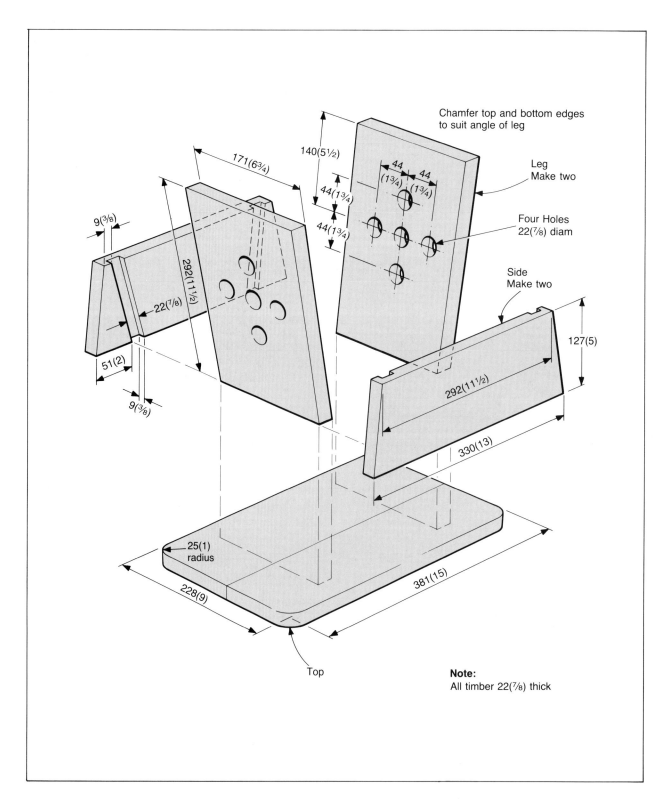

Chamfer top and bottom edges
to suit angle of leg

Leg
Make two

140(5½)

44(1¾)
44(1¾)

44 (1¾)   44 (1¾)

171(6¾)

Four Holes
22(⅞) diam

9(⅜)

292(11½)

Side
Make two

22(⅞)

127(5)

51(2)

9(⅜)

292(11½)

330(13)

25(1)
radius

381(15)

228(9)

Top

**Note:**
All timber 22(⅞) thick

# Coffee grinder

Before embarking on this project, you must acquire the machinery to grind the beans. Coffee grinding mechanisms are available in a range of sizes and different patterns in most good craft shops that specialize in products for the wood turner. Try to find one that grinds the beans *quietly!*

The only joint used in this project is a simple lap carcase joint. The other skills required are in cutting mitre joints carefully either with a tenon saw or electric mitre saw, and in the ability to joint the pieces together accurately. The timber used here is Nordic redwood, as this will match the table, chairs and Welsh dresser in "the set".

## The mill body

Begin by selecting a straight-grained piece of timber – without knots. All the jointing for both the mill body and the drawer unit are formed by a lap joint.

The simplest and certainly the quickest method is to cut to length a piece of timber (leaving a little for waste at the ends). This will form three sides of the body of the mill. It is always easier to hold and work on larger pieces of timber than small pieces cut to their finished size.

Fix one of the pieces of timber to the bench and, using a rebate plane or a router, cut the rebate on both sides. (**1** and **2**) The width of the rebate must equal the thickness of the pieces of timber to be joined.

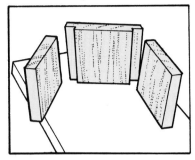

**1** *Three sides of the body of the mill, with two rebates cut in the piece that will form the back.*

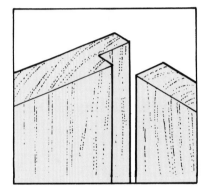

**2** *A close-up of the rebate.*

Now glue the sides to the back. When doing this, it is vital to avoid any "tapering in" at the front edge. If this should happen, the drawer will not fit properly into the mill body.

Bore and countersink holes in the base, and then attach the base to the assembled mill body. (**3**)

The top of the mill body has a large hole bored in it to take the ground coffee into the drawer. Large holes are best bored out with a flat bit. The flat bit was designed for use in high speed electric drills and is relatively inexpensive. To achieve the cleanest hole, drill only part of the way through from one side, then turn the wood over and drill from the other side. (**4**) Turning the wood in this way means that you avoid "break out" on the underside of the timber – nothing looks worse than a ragged hole!

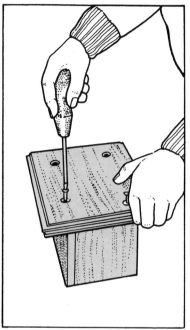

**3** *The base is glued and screwed into the mill body.*

**4** *The long spike on the flat bit provides an excellent location point when the wood is turned over to drill from the other side.*

## Mouldings

Mouldings can be bought in a great variety of shapes and sizes. Ideally,

you should look for a moulding that is of the same thickness as the timber used for the project.

There are two methods of cutting a moulding:

### a) with a mitre and tenon saw

The tenon saw blade fits into the slots and guides the blade as you cut. The better boxes have small brass lugs at the tops of each slot which prevent wear in the sides of the mitre box slots. The moulding being cut is placed in the box and the saw is used to cut the desired angle. In practice, it is a little more difficult than it sounds to achieve perfect 45° mitre cuts.

### b) with an electric mitre saw

Many electric powered saws have a table that can be rotated through 180°. The wood to be cut is held securely in place by a small cramp. The table is rotated to 45°, then the saw is started and pulled down onto the table, giving a perfect mitre cut. (**5**) With this type of saw, it is best to release the trigger, turning the machine off before allowing the blade to return to its starting-place. If you do not do this, small pieces of cut timber can be picked up, or flicked by the blade – possibly damaging both the operator and the wood. The mitre saw is fitted with an electric brake, so it stops almost instantly. This machine is very accurate in operation, and produces perfect cuts with the absolute minimum of skill.

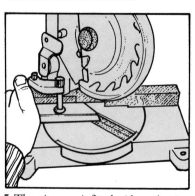

**5** *The mitre saw is fitted with an electric brake, so it stops almost instantly.*

When the mouldings have been cut, they have to be glued onto the sides of the timber. It is fairly difficult to cramp mouldings in place; it is best to use strips of masking tape. (**6**) The masking tape has sufficient strength to hold the moulding to the wood while the glue cures.

**6** *Use masking tape to hold the moulding to the sides while the glue cures.*

Offer up the mouldings to check for fit before glueing.

### The drawer

The lap joint is used for the jointing of the sides of the drawer. The rebate for the lap is cut in exactly the same way as for the mill body. (**7**)

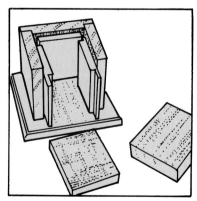

**7** *Offer up the unglued pieces of the drawer to check that they fit in the mill body.*

The bottom of the drawer doubles as a handle. The shaping of the handle can be done with either a coping saw or jigsaw. (**8**) Then work around the edges of the handle with glasspaper for a smooth finish. Now glue the handle straight onto the drawer. The drawer may need some final adjustments before it will fit well. Always remember you can take off a shaving, but you can't stick it back on, so work very carefully at this.

## Attaching the coffee grinder

Different makers will recommend different methods of attaching their grinders. In the one used here, there are two small bolts that go through the top and are secured with nuts on the underside. Unless the holes for the nuts are recessed (countersunk), the drawer back will collide with them. The bolt holes must be drilled and countersunk before the top is glued in place. (**9**)

A nice touch is to glue a piece of green baize on the bottom of the mill. This will prevent it marking the table or dresser top when it is in use.

**8** *Bore a hole in the handle to make it easier to grip.*

**9** *The finished coffee grinder.*

**COFFEE GRINDER CUTTING LIST**

| Mill body | | | |
|---|---|---|---|
| Base | 1 off | 146 × 146 × 16mm (5¾ × 5¾ × ⅝in) timber |
| Sides | 2 off | 109 × 89 × 16mm (4⁵⁄₁₆ × 3½ × ⅝in) timber |
| Back | 1 off | 122 × 109 × 16mm (4¹³⁄₁₆ × 4⁵⁄₁₆ × ⅝in) timber |
| Top | 1 off | 127 × 127 × 16mm (5 × 5 × ⅝in) timber |
| Drawer | | | |
| Base | 1 off | 226 × 89 × 6mm (8⅞ × 3½ × ¼in) timber |
| Sides, front & back | 4 off | 102 × 83 × 12mm (4 × 3¼ × ½in) timber |
| Decorative moulding | make from | 900 × 16mm (36 × ⅝in) moulding |

*This project demonstrates the use of mouldings to set off a basic square wooden box.*

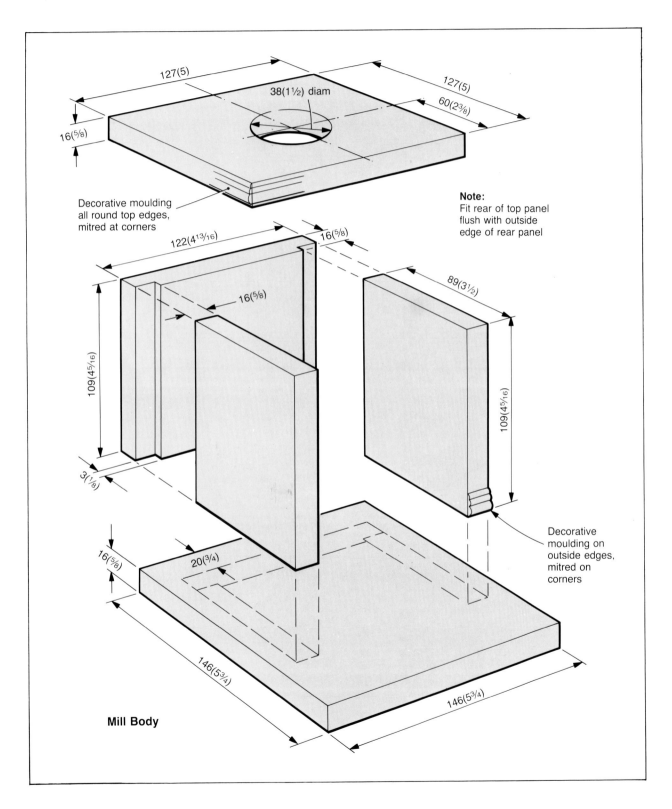

127(5)

127(5)

38(1½) diam

60(2⅜)

16(⅝)

Decorative moulding
all round top edges,
mitred at corners

**Note:**
Fit rear of top panel
flush with outside
edge of rear panel

122(4¹³/₁₆)

16(⅝)

16(⅝)

89(3½)

109(4⁵/₁₆)

109(4⁵/₁₆)

3(⅛)

Decorative
moulding on
outside edges,
mitred on
corners

16(⅝)

20(¾)

146(5¾)

146(5¾)

**Mill Body**

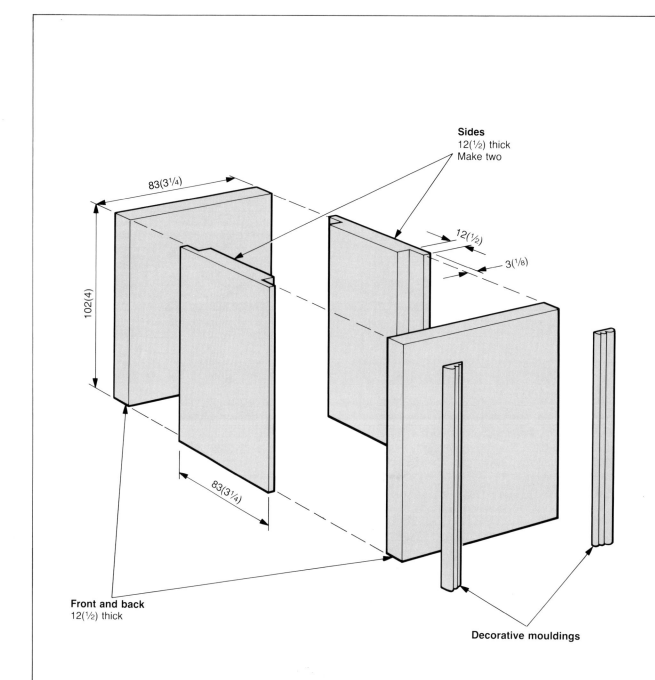

83(3¼)

Sides
12(½) thick
Make two

102(4)

12(½)

3(⅛)

83(3¼)

**Front and back**
12(½) thick

**Decorative mouldings**

**Note:**
Before making the parts on this page,
check dimensions shown with the size of
the opening in the body assembly and
adjust to give a snug sliding fit

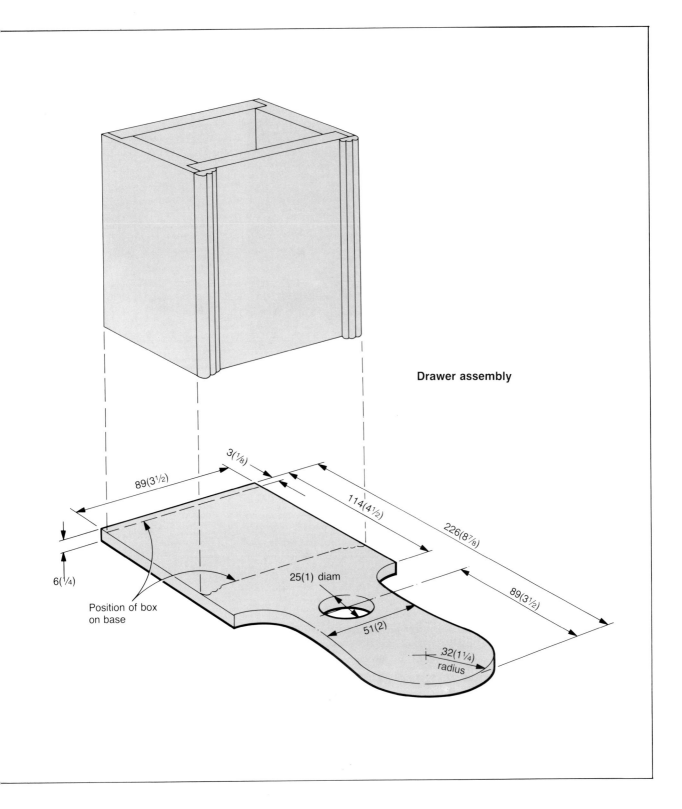

**Drawer assembly**

89(3½)

3(⅛)

114(4½)

226(8⅞)

6(¼)

89(3½)

25(1) diam

51(2)

32(1¼)
radius

Position of box
on base

# *Dining chair*

*Essential tools*
Sliding bevel gauge
Tenon saw
Electric router with fine beading
    cutter
Belt sander

This redwood chair is an ideal companion to the gate leg table. Chairs are always difficult to make because of the number of angles usually used. The only angle in this project is the stretcher rail on the legs. To ensure that you are able to "set out" the legs and rails accurately, it is necessary to make a full-size drawing of the side elevation.

The seat is made with two pieces of timber glued together, and held to the framework by wooden buttons. To make the chair comfortable, it is important that some angle or curvature is given to the top two-thirds of the back of the chair. To avoid the complication of steaming the back legs to shape, I have offset the back by cutting and planing an angle on the inside of the legs.

## Marking out

Draw the side elevation full-size on a sheet of plywood or card. (**1**) Then carefully select the legs and rails, choosing timber that is free from knots and in which the grain runs

straight. If you do not take care at this stage, a leg may fracture when the chair is in use.

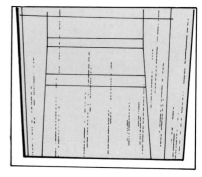

**1** *Make a start by drawing the side elevation full-size on a spare sheet of plywood.*

Mark out in pencil the positions of all the rails and legs. The face side edge markings are essential not only for accuracy, but also to keep the legs and rails in the correct order, so when the time comes, the mortice holes will line up.

Cramp all the legs together when marking out. The shoulder lines for the sides of the chairs have to be taken from the full-size drawing. Place the rails on the drawing and take the angle of the shoulder lines from this. Set a sliding bevel gauge to this angle and use it to mark in all the other rails.

### The joints

Except for the side rails, all the joints are haunched mitre and tenon joints. The haunch has a great advantage in this particular project because it reduces the quantity of waste wood cut out of the mortice, thus leaving a stronger structure.

Before any shaping is done, chop out all the mortices. Then carefully mark in pencil the angles on the legs that have to be cut and planed. The angles have to be planed very carefully, particularly where the side rails fit the mortices in the leg. Plane down to the pencilled gauge line; do not go below, or the shoulder lines on the rails will not meet the legs. It is essential to be accurate at this stage.

When all the mortices are finished, cut the tenons. Ideally, if you set up all the marking gauge lines correctly, the tenons and mortices will fit together without the necessity of paring the tenons. The saw marks the tenon saw leaves make an ideal key when the tenon is glued into the mortice.

To cut a tenon, set the timber in a vice at 45° to the bench top. Make the first cut, then turn the wood around, again set at 45° to the bench top. Mark the second cut. (2)

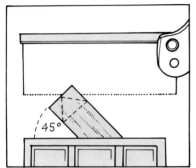

**2** *The timber must be set accurately at 45° to the vice-bench top when making both the first and second cuts of the tenon.*

The third cut is made with the wood at 90° to the bench top. (3)

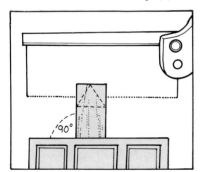

**3** *Alter the angle to 90° for the third cut.*

Now place the wood on the bench block and cut off the cheek on one side, (**4**) before turning the timber over and cutting off the cheek on the other.

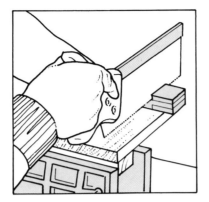

When the tenons have been cut and the cheeks removed, the tenons have to be cut down to form the haunches (*see box below*).

**4** *Use a tenon saw and a bench block when cutting off the cheek.*

## The haunches

**a** *Cut down one side of the tenon, two-thirds of its length.*

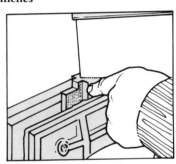

**b** *Make a 90° cut across to remove the waste wood.*

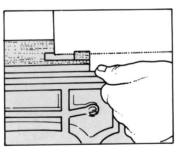

**c** *Now form a slot at the top of the leg to receive the haunch. Cut the sides with a tenon saw.*

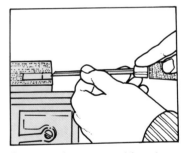

**d** *Remove the waste wood from the leg with a sharp chisel.*

**e** *The mortice and tenon should now fit snugly together.*

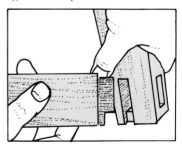

## Shaping and assembling

Shape the top two thirds of the back legs with a plane and fit the back rest slats. Use a router fitted with a fine beading cutter to mould the top edges of each rail. There are a great variety of cutters available, but a small moulding looks best for this chair.

Cut mortice slots in the top rails to take the wooden buttons later. Then assemble the side frames of the chair dry (without glue), cramp up and check very carefully that the shoulder lines "pull up" tightly. Do not attempt to glue up the whole chair in one operation. Glue the side frames together first. Then glue the other rails in place. (**5**)

## The seat

The seat is made from two lengths of timber. It is necessary to glue planks together to acquire enough width. Check that the end grains do not go in the same direction. The opposite directions of the grains will counteract any tendency for the wood to move.

Shape the seat with a plane. Use a belt sander to achieve a flat surface. Then use the same cutter in the router as for the top edges of the rails to "turn" a small bead around the edge of the whole seat.

The seat is fixed to the chair frame by eight wooden buttons. The buttons have the great advantage of allowing the seat to "move". Mark out and cut the buttons from a long length of batten. (**6**) Then fix (button) the seat onto the chair frame. (**7**) Do this by screwing through each button into the base of the seat.

## Finishing off

Rub the chair over with fine glasspaper, before treating the wood with matt gloss varnish and wax polish to match your gate leg table (*see page 117*). (**8**)

**5** *After glueing the side frames, allow the glue to cure (dry) before glueing the other pieces in place.*

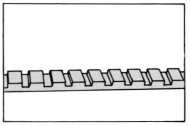

**6** *The eight wooden buttons can be cut out of a long length of batten.*

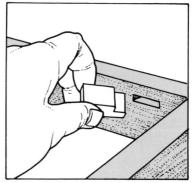

**7** *Fit the wooden buttons into the mortice slots cut in the rails.*

**8** *The finished dining chair.*

| DINING CHAIR CUTTING LIST | | |
|---|---|---|
| Rear leg | 2 off | $870 \times 51 \times 25$mm ($34\frac{1}{2} \times 2 \times 1$in) timber |
| Front leg | 2 off | $438 \times 51 \times 25$mm ($17\frac{1}{4} \times 2 \times 1$in) timber |
| Seat front support rail | 1 off | $444 \times 51 \times 25$mm ($17\frac{1}{2} \times 2 \times 1$in) timber |
| Seat rear support rail | 1 off | $444 \times 51 \times 25$mm ($17\frac{1}{2} \times 2 \times 1$in) timber |
| Seat side support rails | 2 off | $368 \times 51 \times 25$mm ($14\frac{1}{2} \times 2 \times 1$in) timber |
| Leg side rails | 2 off | $397 \times 32 \times 25$mm ($15\frac{5}{8} \times 1\frac{1}{4} \times 1$in) timber |
| Back rest slats | 2 off | $444 \times 72 \times 25$mm ($17\frac{1}{2} \times 2\frac{7}{8} \times 1$in) timber |
| Seat | 2 off | $444 \times 229 \times 22$mm ($17\frac{1}{2} \times 9 \times \frac{7}{8}$in) timber |
| Buttons | 8 off make from | $305 \times 22 \times 18$mm ($12 \times \frac{7}{8} \times \frac{11}{16}$in) timber |
| Jointing boards | make from | $1,000 \times 12$mm ($36 \times \frac{1}{2}$in) diam dowel |

**Above** *The back of the chair showing the clean lines of the back rest.*

**Right** *This view clearly shows the taper of the chair leg.*

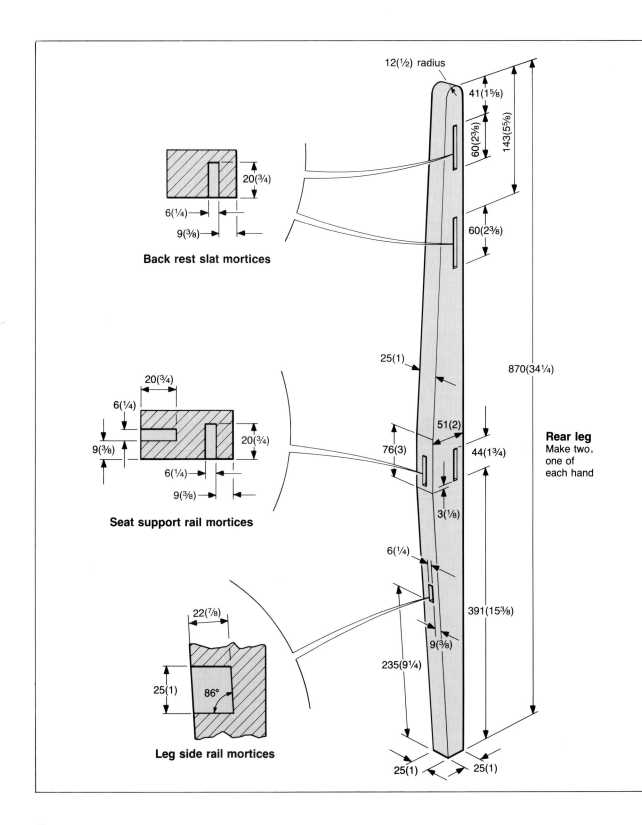

12(½) radius

41(1⁵⁄₈)

143(5⁵⁄₈)

60(2³⁄₈)

60(2³⁄₈)

20(¾)

6(¼)

9(³⁄₈)

**Back rest slat mortices**

20(¾)

6(¼)

20(¾)

9(³⁄₈)

6(¼)

9(³⁄₈)

**Seat support rail mortices**

25(1)

870(34¼)

51(2)

76(3)

44(1³⁄₄)

3(⅛)

**Rear leg**
Make two,
one of
each hand

6(¼)

9(³⁄₈)

391(15³⁄₈)

22(⁷⁄₈)

25(1)   86°

235(9¼)

**Leg side rail mortices**

25(1)   25(1)

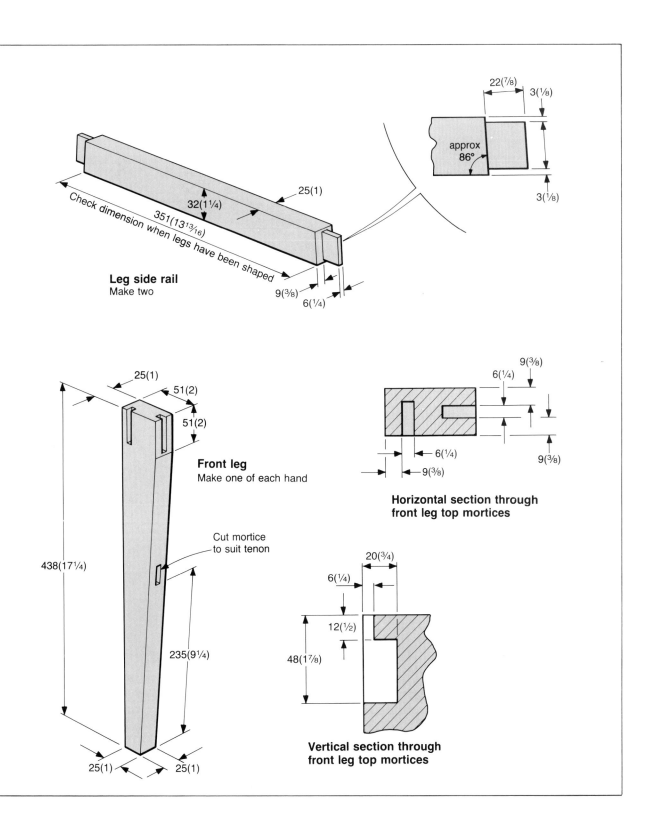

22(⁷/₈)

3(¹/₈)

approx 86°

3(¹/₈)

25(1)

32(1¹/₄)

351(13¹³/₁₆)

Check dimension when legs have been shaped

9(³/₈)

6(¹/₄)

**Leg side rail**
Make two

25(1)

51(2)

51(2)

**Front leg**
Make one of each hand

9(³/₈)

6(¹/₄)

9(³/₈)

6(¹/₄)

9(³/₈)

**Horizontal section through front leg top mortices**

Cut mortice to suit tenon

438(17¹/₄)

235(9¹/₄)

25(1)

25(1)

20(³/₄)

6(¹/₄)

12(¹/₂)

48(1⁷/₈)

**Vertical section through front leg top mortices**

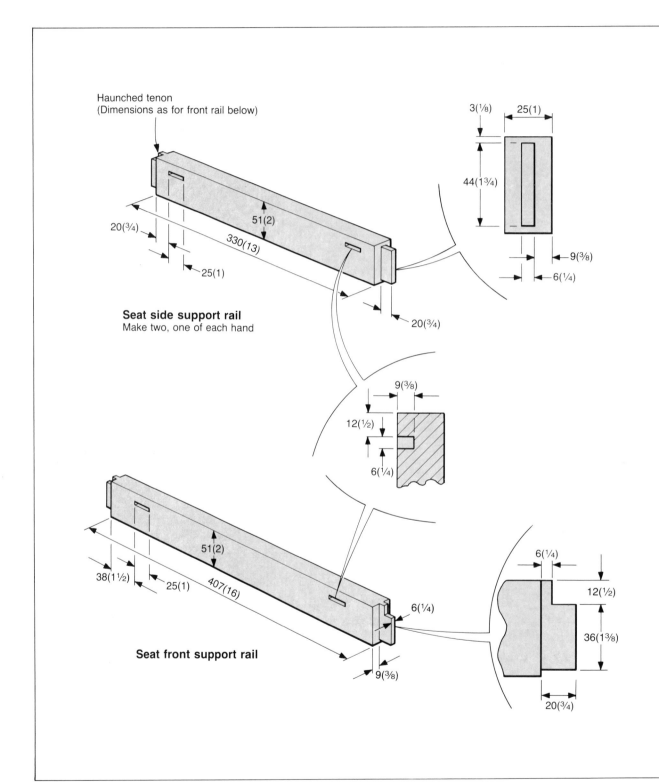

Haunched tenon
(Dimensions as for front rail below)

3(1/8)    25(1)

44(13/4)

9(3/8)

6(1/4)

20(3/4)

51(2)

330(13)

20(3/4)

25(1)

**Seat side support rail**
Make two, one of each hand

9(3/8)

12(1/2)

6(1/4)

51(2)

38(11/2)

25(1)

407(16)

6(1/4)

**Seat front support rail**

9(3/8)

6(1/4)

12(1/2)

36(13/8)

20(3/4)

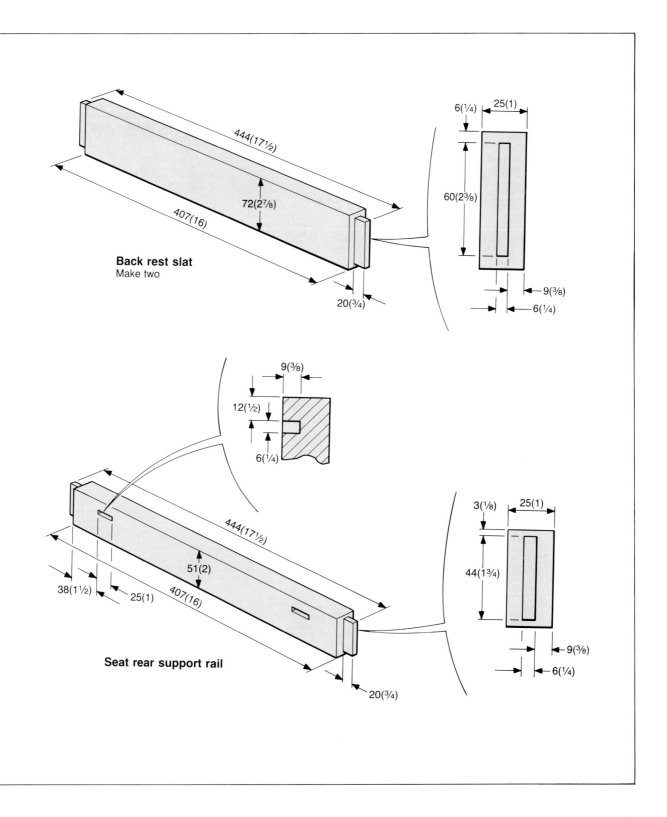

**Back rest slat**
Make two

444(17½)
407(16)
72(2⅞)
20(¾)
6(¼)
25(1)
60(2⅜)
9(⅜)
6(¼)

9(⅜)
12(½)
6(¼)

**Seat rear support rail**

444(17½)
51(2)
38(1½)
25(1)
407(16)
20(¾)
3(⅛)
25(1)
44(1¾)
9(⅜)
6(¼)

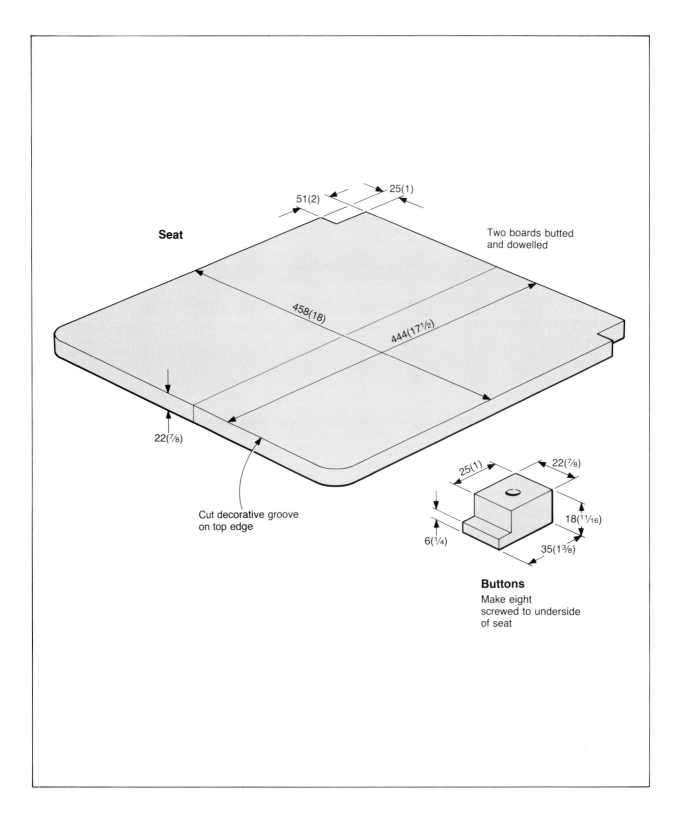

51(2)

25(1)

**Seat**

Two boards butted
and dowelled

458(18)

444(17½)

22(⁷⁄₈)

Cut decorative groove
on top edge

25(1)

22(⁷⁄₈)

18(¹¹⁄₁₆)

6(¼)

35(1⅜)

**Buttons**
Make eight
screwed to underside
of seat

# Corner cabinet

*Featured techniques*
**Mortice and tenon
"Bird's eye" mouth**

*Essential tools*
Shoulder plane
Bench saw or hand held circular
 saw
Rebate plane, plough plane or
 electric router
Marking gauge
Bandsaw or jigsaw
Mitre box
Panel pin punch

These much sought after cabinets make a welcome and attractive addition to any room. Traditionally, they have been made in two sections. The construction of the two halves is basically the same. However, the doors of the top half are glazed, and this requires careful and accurate work.

## The base

In this design I have used traditional methods, but introduced plywood in the construction of the side panels and interior shelves. I have covered its edges or rebated the timber to disguise the rather ugly plywood "sandwich" construction.

The most difficult problem with the corner cabinet is the jointing of the framework. The joints at the two front corners and the back can be very awkward to make.

Begin by drawing out a full-size plan or template of the base on a sheet of hardboard or old plywood. (**1**) This plan will help you to check angles and the position of the upright pieces of the corner unit.

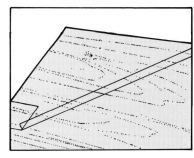

**1** *Draw the cabinet base full-size on spare plywood before embarking on the project. Note the position of the corner post.*

Now plane to size the three corner posts and pencil in on their ends the "bird's eye" mouth that has to be cut out (*see box*). It is essential to use either a bench saw or a hand held circular saw for this operation. In either case, practise on a piece of waste wood before cutting the "bird's eye" mouth. The setting of blade depth, angle and fence are all critical factors, and a little "tweaking" will be necessary to get the correct adjustments.

### Cutting a "bird's eye" mouth

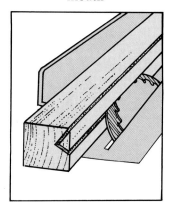

**a** Bench saw – this is the quickest and simplest method of sawing the rebate. The blade is canted over to 45° and the fence positioned to line up with the pencil marks on the leg. Adjust the depth before passing the complete length of the leg over the saw. Do this for both legs. Now reset the fence and complete the cut. A small triangular piece of wood should "drop out" at the end of this cut.

**b** Hand held circular saw – this cutting operation is straightforward as long as you plan the work from the start. Set the blade at 45° to its base, then set the fence and adjust the depth.

Now, cut a rebate to accommodate the plywood on the outer edges of the front legs. (**2**) There are a whole range of tools capable of cutting a rebate (rebate plane, plough plane, electric router, circular saw).

You need to cut rebates on two faces on the back leg of the cabinet. (**3**) All the rebates must be cut to the depth of the thickness of the ply.

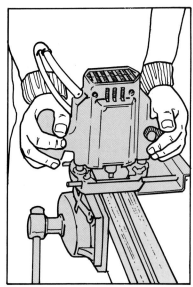

*2 An electric router can be used to cut rebates on the back leg of the cabinet.*

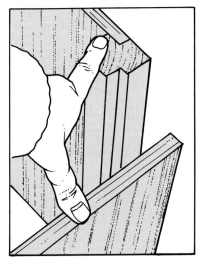

*3 The back leg should have two rebates cut into two faces.*

Once all the rebates have been cut, check with a steel square that the cut is at 90°. If it is not, trim it with a shoulder plane. There are many planes in a woodworker's tool chest, but the shoulder plane has a specific function – to trim the shoulder lines of fences and to trim a rebate where necessary. The blade of the cutter is flush with the side of the steel body. If the blade is set accurately, the 90° corner of the plane body will ensure that the rebate is squared.

### The front frame
Using the full-size plan, set out the shoulder lines for the front frame. The mortices are cut on the vertical rails and the tenons on the horizontal rails. The vertical rails do not run the full length of the legs. This will allow for a plinth to be glued into the rebate at the bottom later.

Once the mortices are marked out, the joints are cut and the framework glued together.

### The plywood
The plywood for the cabinet needs to be cut to length and width. Everyone who has tried to cut plywood knows that one of its big drawbacks is that it shatters, and that large, ugly splinters are a familiar sight. There are several ways in which you can minimise this:
**a** Use a fine-toothed saw.
**b** Jigsaws can be fitted with metal cutting blades which will file away the wood rather than saw it.
**c** Use masking tape on the face side of the ply.
**d** A hand held electric circular saw can be fitted with a tungsten carbide blade.
**e** Experiment on an offcut of plywood to find which method gives the best result.

When the plywood has been cut to size, glue it to the rebates in the legs. (**4**) It is easier to do this in stages. Glue the back leg to one of the ply panels first and allow the glue to cure. Now

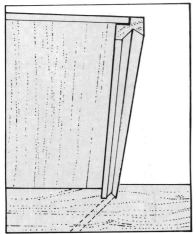

**4** *The plywood panel is glued into the front leg.*

glue the other panel to the back leg. Then glue the front legs to the panels. Assemble the unit on the full-size template as a guide. (**5**) Use both cramps and adhesive tape to hold the pieces together while the glue dries.

**5** *Both plywood panels are glued to front and back legs, standing on the template, which is used as a guide.*

When both pieces of plywood are glued onto the three legs, the cabinet is held together by the framework that is now glued onto the "bird's eye" in the front legs. (**6**) Make sure the frame is glued flush with the top of the cabinet, leaving a section at the bottom to which to fix a plinth.

## The shelves

The shelves are made from pine-faced plywood and are supported in the framework by battens of timber that

**6** *The front frame is glued into the "bird's eye" mouth of the frame.*

are glued onto the plywood sides. (**7**) The middle shelf is supported by a batten that has a rebate cut in it to hide the plywood edge. (**8**)

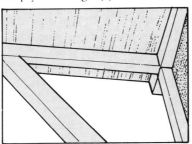

**7** *Glue the plywood batten shelf supports into the sides of the plywood one by one.*

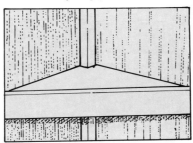

**8** *The sandwich effect of the plywood will be hidden once the batten is in the rebate, leaving a clean line.*

The shelves are not difficult to make but you will find it helpful to cut a full-size plan to shape first. Place a

stiff piece of cardboard onto the top of the unit and from underneath mark round the legs with a pencil. Remove the template, cut it out and offer it up to the cabinet to check the fit. (**9**) If the fit is right, transfer the shape onto the plywood shelf and cut it out. Cut on the waste side – you can always cut a little more off, but you cannot stick any back on!

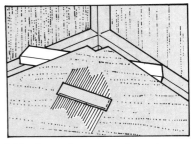

**9** *Needle templates are an alternative to cutting your own and help to get into difficult corners and give an accurate reading of the angle.*

## The doors

The width of the front dictates twin doors rather than a single larger door. Prepare the rails (crosspieces) and stiles (uprights) to width and thickness, leaving a little extra length – about 1.5mm ($^1$/$_{16}$in) – to be trimmed off afterwards. Make sure that the timber you select is straight and the grain clean and, if possible, completely free of knots. Place the four stiles upright in the frame. The distance between the stiles and the other side of the frame will give you the required shoulder line lengths of the rails. Again, add a little to this measurement to allow for trimming.

Make all the mortice and tenons for the doors and cut them out. The doors are designed to take tongued and grooved panelling. You need to make a rebate all around the inside edge of the frame which will take the panels. Traditionally, this was done before the door was glued up, but in this case, glue up first. (**10**) Then use an electric router to cut the rebate.

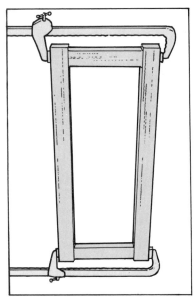

**10** *Glue the doors together before cutting the rebate with an electric router.*

The tongued and grooved panelling is now fitted. Use a full width panel in the middle section and cut the outer edges off the other panels. Now glue the panels onto the doors. (**11**) Offer up the doors to be hung on the frame, and use a smoothing plane to remove shavings until the fit is exact.

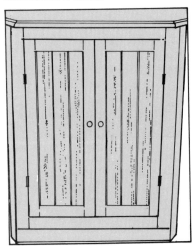

**11** *Cut the outer edges off all the other panels before glueing the panels onto the doors.*

## Hinge fixing

A door properly fitted should close flush with its frame. The stile of the door should be tight against the frame. This is only possible if the hinge used is recessed into either the door, the frame, or both. Here, the brass hinges are recessed into the door only. If the doors do not fit properly, the hinge is not recessed properly or the screw heads are not fully fitting their countersinks in the hinge.

Position the hinge on the door stile and lightly mark the length with a pencil. With a marking gauge, set the fence and the spur point to the thickness of the hinge. Gauge the thickness of the hinge onto the face side of the stile. Now do exactly the same for the depth of the flap, making sure the knuckle of the hinge is proud of the door.

Work over the depth and width of the hinge with a Stanley knife, scribing in the lines carefully. With extreme care, use a chisel to remove the waste wood. Great patience is needed – if you slip, you spoil the door. Carry out this operation on both doors.

Screw the hinges into the doors. Open each hinge fully, position the unattached flap onto the frame and check that the door is positioned correctly. Put only two screws in at this stage, one in the top hinge and one in the bottom. Then close the door, and if you need to make further adjustments there are only two screws to remove. Once the second door has been hinged, you will need to plane a few shavings off the two stiles where the doors close.

One door is fixed at the bottom with a small brass bolt. The other is held in place by two small brass spring ball catches fitted into the door – a hole is drilled in both the bottom and top of the door stile and they are glued in using epoxy resin glue.

The steel balls fit into small brass keeper plates in the top and bottom of the door frame. (**12**) The brass plates have to be outlined with a pencil and then "let in" in the same way as the hinges. Finally, fit the doors with good brass knobs.

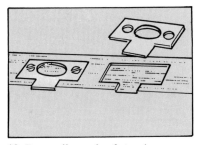

**12** *Brass roller catches fit into keeper plates that are cut into the doors.*

## Assembling

A small plinth is now cut for the bottom of the unit. Use a small moulding cutter in the router to cut the moulding at the top edge. Shape the bottom with a bandsaw or jigsaw. Use a piece of glasspaper wrapped around a dowel rod to remove the saw marks from the curve. Now glue the plinth to the frame. (**13**)

Form the top from three pieces of timber glued together. After the glue has cured, it will be necessary to plane it flat. However careful you are when glueing the pieces of timber together, one edge will rise above the other. Now place the top on the unit and use the sides of the cabinet as a guide to

**13** *The plinth is glued in place at the base of the unit.*

pencil in the pieces that have to be cut off. (**14**)

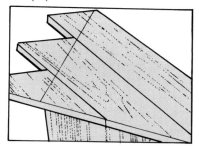

**14** *Glue three pieces of wood together to form the top of the unit, then mark in the triangular shape of the top before cutting off the waste.*

The top is secured to the frame by screws that pass up through battens attached to the plywood sides. (**15**) Use the same moulding cutter as for the plinth to cut a moulding into the front edge.

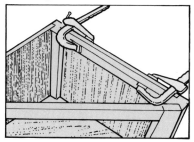

**15** *Battens are glued onto the inside edges of the cabinet, before putting screws up through the underside to hold the top in place.*

**The display cabinet**

Repeat the construction methods for the bottom half of the cabinet until the carcass is complete, mounted and ready for the doors. (**16**) Cut a rebate to take the glass before the door is glued up if you are using the traditional rebate plane. It is an advantage to leave the cheeks on the tenons while the rebates are being cut, as these help to steady the rebate plane as it works. The modern method is to glue the door first and then use an electric router to cut the rebate. (**17**)

**16** *Mount the frame of the top unit onto the base.*

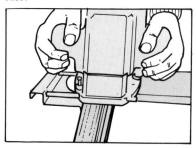

**17** *With the fence set on the router and the cutter adjusted to the right depth, it is a simple job to cut the rebate.*

Use a fairly heavy gauge glass and small moulding to hold the glass in place. Buy the glass and moulding before cutting the rebate, this being the only sure method of getting the correct rebate depth.

The traditional method of mounting glass requires great skill. The cabinet maker never used putty, but a very fine moulding that was mitred and fitted behind the glass. The moulding was held in place by small panel pins. To prevent the glass "chattering" in the door when it was being opened or closed, thin strips of finely skived leather were cut and placed between the glass and the front of the rebate, as well as at the back between the glass and the moulding. Today, it is not so easy to find a finely skived leather, so I have substituted black insulation tape.

On a *clean* dust-free board, unwind a strip of tape the full length of the door rebate. Now, take a Stanley knife with a new blade and a piece of wood to guide the tool, and cut off a thin strip of tape. Fit this into the rebate. (**18**) It is vital that the tape is cut uniformly throughout its length, or when the glass is fitted, the refraction of light in the glass will show up the uneven edges. Fit the glass and then another layer of tape onto the glass.

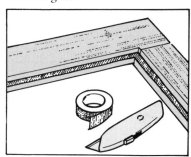

**18** *Fit the insulation tape into the rebate in the door.*

The small beadings are now cut and fitted. It is necessary to cut mitres on the ends, first marking the 45° angle very carefully. (**19**) A small fine-toothed tenon saw is ideal for this work. If you need to practise cutting mitres, use a small piece of waste beading. A mitre box not only holds the saw at the correct angle, but helps to steady the moulding as it is cut.

The beadings are held in place with small brass panel pins. A false move at this point will not only break the glass, but it can also put you back several stages. The point of the panel pin may just nick the glass as it passes into the frame. A panel pin punch is needed to drive the panel pin below the surface of the beading. "Stop" the holes with either beeswax or Brummer stopping. Be sure to stop all holes.

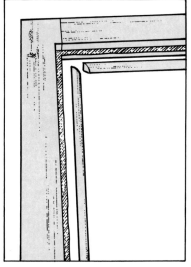

**19** *Mitre the ends of the beading to fit snugly into the corners of the door.*

## Finishing off

Either base or top unit will stand on their own as two separate units. They look equally as good together. (**20**) If they are to be used as one unit, it is best to drill holes to take dowel rods in the base of the top unit. The dowels will locate in holes drilled in the top of the base unit. Unless this method of fixing is adopted there is a tendency for the top unit to slide on the unit beneath, when the doors are being opened or closed. As a final touch, a cornice may be shaped and cut, before being glued on top of the cabinet.

To finish off, use polyurethane varnish, rubbed in with a lint-free cloth. Allow 24 hours for the varnish to "cure". Lightly rub down with a fine glasspaper, and repeat the whole process. Then apply a final coat of wax.

**20** *The finished corner cabinet.*

## CORNER CABINET CUTTING LIST

### Base unit

| | | |
|---|---|---|
| Top | 3 off | 826 × 165 × 16mm (32½ × 6½ × ⅝in) timber |
| | 1 off | 1,000 × 6mm (39 × ¼in) diam dowel |
| Front leg | 2 off | 912 × 44 × 44mm (35⅞ × 1¾ × 1¾in) timber |
| Back leg | 1 off | 912 × 44 × 44mm (35⅞ × 1¾ × 1¾in) timber |
| Side panel | 2 off | 912 × 528 × 9mm (35⅞ × 20¾ × ⅜in) plywood |
| Shelf support | 6 off | 495 × 35 × 20mm (19½ × 1⅜ × ¾in) timber |
| Middle shelf front support | 1 off | 718 × 44 × 22mm (28¼ × 1¾ × ⅞in) timber |
| Bottom shelf front support | 1 off | 718 × 35 × 20mm (28¼ × 1⅜ × ¾in) timber |
| Front frame | 2 off | 864 × 51 × 22mm (34 × 2 × ⅞in) timber |
| | 2 off | 724 × 51 × 22mm (28½ × 2 × ⅞in) timber |
| Plinth | 1 off | 762 × 47 × 28mm (30 × 1⅞ × 1⅛in) timber |
| Shelf | make from | 584 × 584 × 9mm (23 × 23 × ⅜in) plywood |
| Door frame | 4 off | 762 × 51 × 22mm (30 × 2 × ⅞in) timber |
| | 4 off | 292 × 51 × 22mm (11½ × 2 × ⅞in) timber |
| Door panelling | 6 off | 686 × 89 × 16mm (27 × 3½ × ⅝in) tongued and grooved boards |
| | | |
| Ancillaries | 4 off | 51mm (2 in) brass hinges |
| | 3 off | brass spring ball catches and keepers |
| | 1 off | brass bolt |
| | 2 off | brass knobs |

### Top unit

| | | |
|---|---|---|
| Top | 3 off | 762 × 165 × 20mm (30 × 6½ × ¾in) timber |
| Cornice | make from | 864 × 67 × 25mm (34 × 2⅝ × 1in) timber |
| | 1 off | 1,000 × 6mm (39 × ¼in) diam dowel |
| Front leg | 2 off | 912 × 41 × 32mm (35⅞ × 1⅝ × 1¼in) timber |
| Back leg | 1 off | 912 × 41 × 41mm (35⅞ × 1⅝ × 1⅝in) timber |
| Side panel | 2 off | 912 × 498 × 9mm (35⅞ × 19⅝ × ⅜in) plywood |
| Shelf support | 6 off | 467 × 32 × 20mm (18⅜ × 1¼ × ¾in) timber |

| | | |
|---|---|---|
| Middle shelf front support | 1 off | $658 \times 44 \times 22$mm ($25\frac{7}{8} \times 1\frac{3}{4} \times \frac{7}{8}$in) timber |
| Bottom shelf front support | 1 off | $658 \times 32 \times 20$mm ($25\frac{7}{8} \times 1\frac{1}{4} \times \frac{3}{4}$in) timber |
| Front frame | 2 off | $864 \times 51 \times 22$mm ($34 \times 2 \times \frac{7}{8}$in) timber |
| | 2 off | $660 \times 51 \times 22$mm ($26 \times 2 \times \frac{7}{8}$in) timber |
| Plinth | 1 off | $698 \times 47 \times 28$mm ($27\frac{1}{2} \times 1\frac{7}{8} \times 1\frac{1}{8}$in) timber |
| Shelf | make from | $533 \times 533 \times 9$mm ($21 \times 21 \times \frac{3}{8}$in) plywood |
| Door frame | 4 off | $762 \times 51 \times 22$mm ($30 \times 2 \times \frac{7}{8}$in) timber |
| | 4 off | $260 \times 51 \times 22$mm ($10\frac{1}{4} \times 2 \times \frac{7}{8}$in) timber |
| Glass beading | make from | $4,000 \times 9 \times 9$mm ($150 \times \frac{3}{8} \times \frac{3}{8}$in) segment moulding |
| | | |
| Ancillaries | 4 off | 51mm (2in) brass hinges |
| | 3 off | brass spring ball catches and keepers |
| | 1 off | brass bolt |
| | 2 off | $686 \times 222$mm ($27 \times 8\frac{3}{4}$in) $\times$ 3mm ($\frac{1}{8}$in) glass |
| | 1 off | roll black insulation tape |
| | 2 off | brass knobs |

*The final assembly of the front, the side and the top cornice of the base unit.*

*The framework of the base unit holds the whole structure together.*

*A view of the inside of the top unit, with the shelves in position.*

*The base of the top unit, showing how the "bird's eye" joint fits into side pillars.*

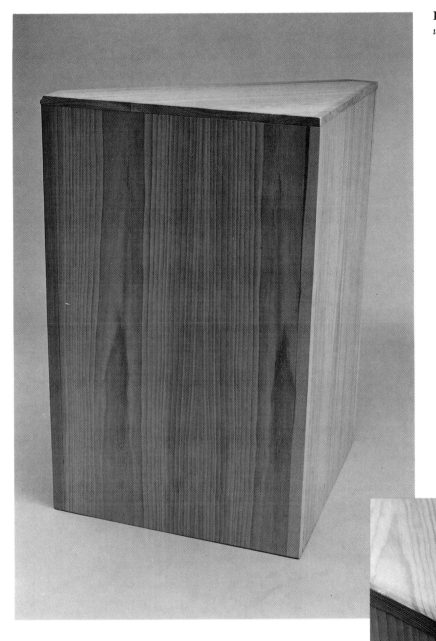

**Left** *The smooth, clean lines of the base unit.*

**Right** *The moulding that runs round the top of the top unit.*

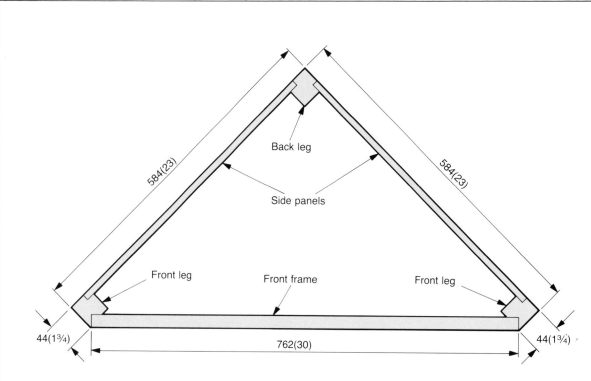

584(23)

584(23)

Back leg

Side panels

Front leg          Front frame          Front leg

44(1¾)          762(30)          44(1¾)

**Base unit plan**

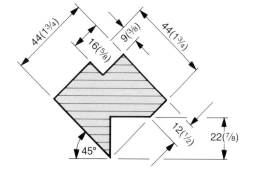

44(1¾)

16(⅝)

9(⅜)

44(1¾)

45°          12(½)          22(⅞)

**Section through front legs**

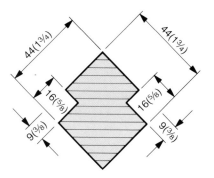

44(1¾)

44(1¾)

16(⅝)

9(⅜)

16(⅝)

9(⅜)

**Section through back leg**

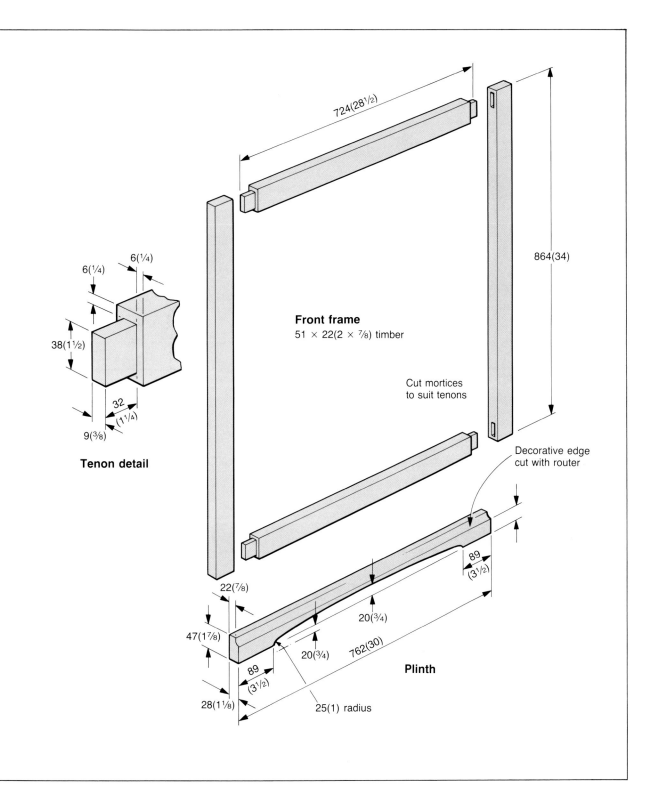

6(¼)  6(¼)

38(1½)

32
(1¼)

9(⅜)

**Tenon detail**

724(28½)

864(34)

**Front frame**
51 × 22(2 × ⅞) timber

Cut mortices
to suit tenons

Decorative edge
cut with router

89
(3½)

20(¾)

762(30)

**Plinth**

22(⅞)

47(1⅞)

20(¾)

89
(3½)

28(1⅛)

25(1) radius

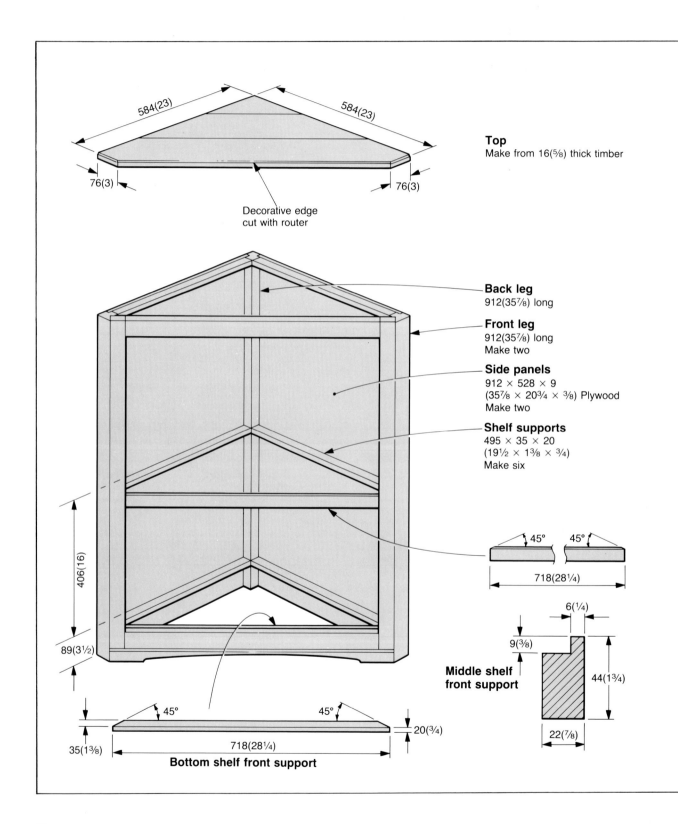

**Top**
Make from 16(⅝) thick timber

584(23)

584(23)

76(3)

76(3)

Decorative edge
cut with router

**Back leg**
912(35⅞) long

**Front leg**
912(35⅞) long
Make two

**Side panels**
912 × 528 × 9
(35⅞ × 20¾ × ⅜) Plywood
Make two

**Shelf supports**
495 × 35 × 20
(19½ × 1⅜ × ¾)
Make six

406(16)

89(3½)

45°     45°

718(28¼)

6(¼)

9(⅜)

44(1¾)

**Middle shelf
front support**

22(⅞)

45°          45°

20(¾)

35(1⅜)          718(28¼)

**Bottom shelf front support**

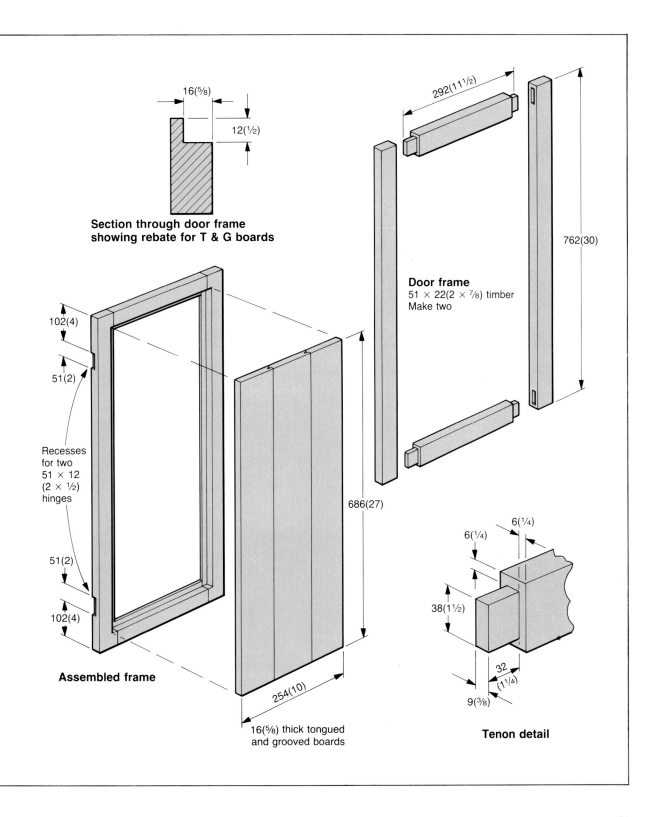

16(⅝)

12(½)

**Section through door frame
showing rebate for T & G boards**

292(11½)

762(30)

**Door frame**
51 × 22(2 × ⅞) timber
Make two

102(4)

51(2)

Recesses
for two
51 × 12
(2 × ½)
hinges

51(2)

102(4)

686(27)

**Assembled frame**

254(10)

16(⅝) thick tongued
and grooved boards

6(¼)

6(¼)

38(1½)

32
(1¼)

9(⅜)

**Tenon detail**

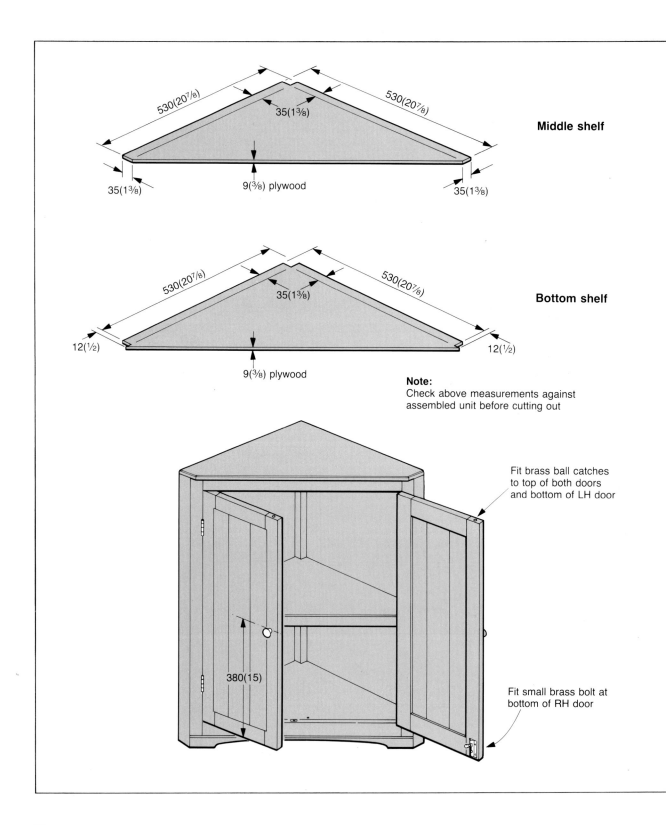

**Middle shelf**

530(20⅞)

35(1⅜)

35(1⅜)

9(⅜) plywood

35(1⅜)

**Bottom shelf**

530(20⅞)

530(20⅞)

35(1⅜)

12(½)

12(½)

9(⅜) plywood

**Note:**
Check above measurements against
assembled unit before cutting out

Fit brass ball catches
to top of both doors
and bottom of LH door

380(15)

Fit small brass bolt at
bottom of RH door

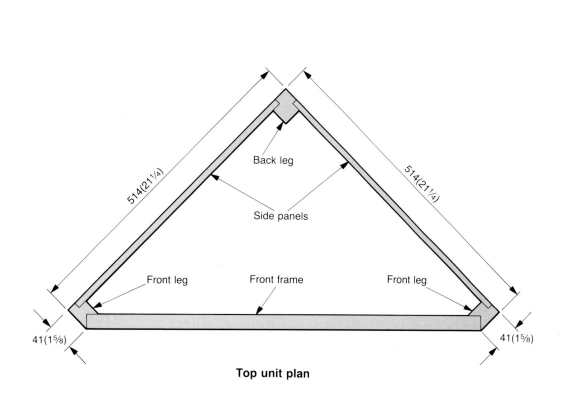

**Top unit plan**

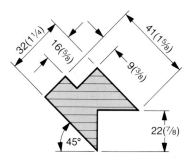

**Section through front legs**

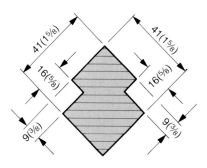

**Section through back leg**

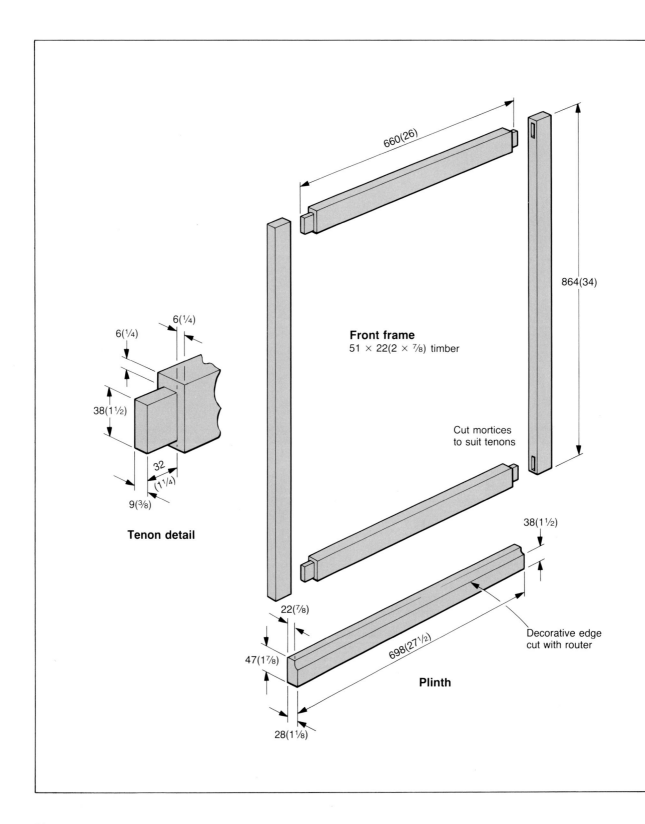

660(26)

864(34)

**Front frame**
51 × 22(2 × ⁷⁄₈) timber

Cut mortices
to suit tenons

6(¼)

6(¼)

38(1½)

32
(1¼)

9(⅜)

**Tenon detail**

38(1½)

22(⁷⁄₈)

Decorative edge
cut with router

698(27½)

47(1⁷⁄₈)

**Plinth**

28(1⅛)

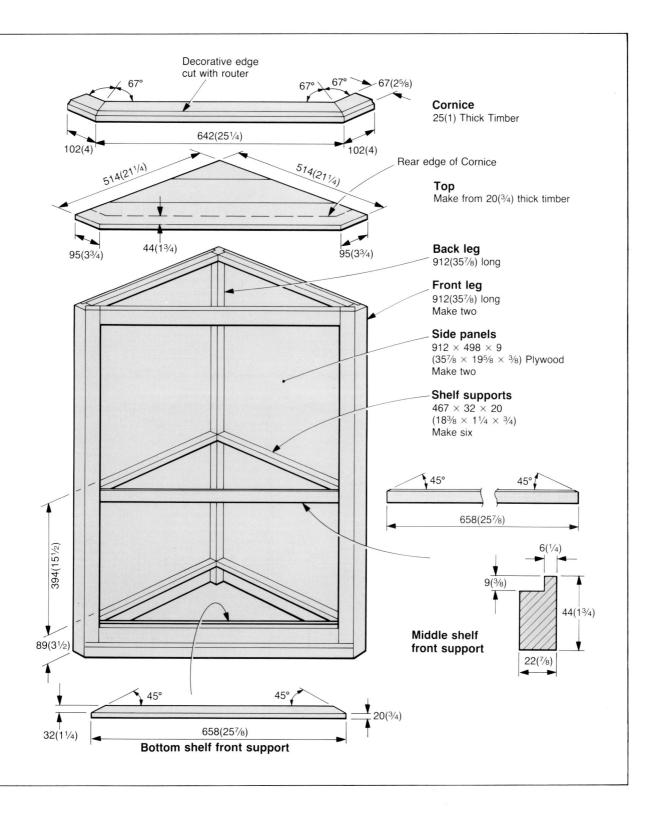

Decorative edge cut with router

67° 67° 67° 67(2⅝)

**Cornice**
25(1) Thick Timber

642(25¼)

102(4) 102(4)

514(21¼) 514(21¼)

Rear edge of Cornice

**Top**
Make from 20(¾) thick timber

95(3¾) 44(1¾) 95(3¾)

**Back leg**
912(35⅞) long

**Front leg**
912(35⅞) long
Make two

**Side panels**
912 × 498 × 9
(35⅞ × 19⅝ × ⅜) Plywood
Make two

**Shelf supports**
467 × 32 × 20
(18⅜ × 1¼ × ¾)
Make six

45° 45°

658(25⅞)

6(¼)

9(⅜)

44(1¾)

**Middle shelf front support**

22(⅞)

394(15½)

89(3½)

45° 45°

20(¾)

32(1¼) 658(25⅞)

**Bottom shelf front support**

55

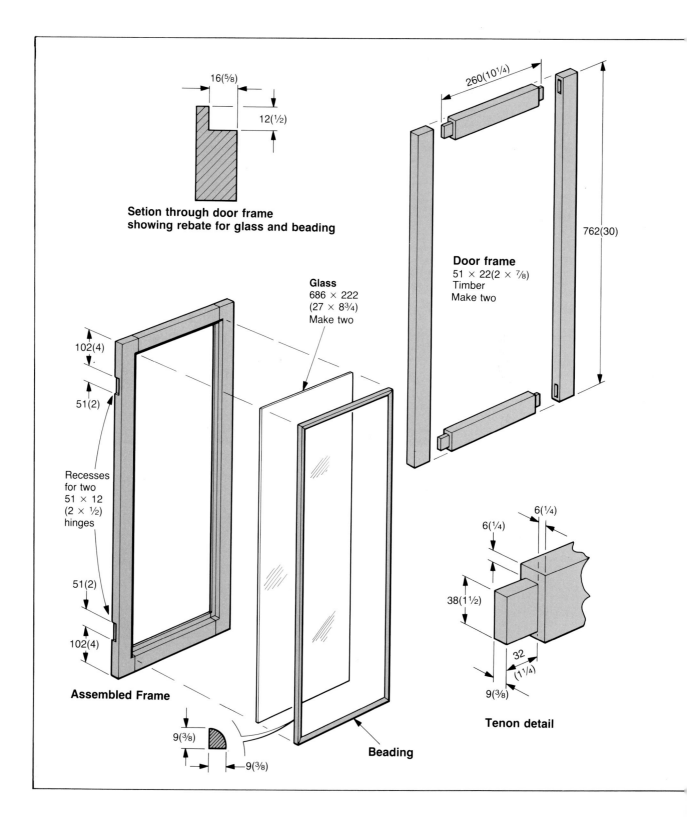

16(⅝)

12(½)

**Setion through door frame
showing rebate for glass and beading**

260(10¼)

762(30)

**Door frame**
51 × 22(2 × ⅞)
Timber
Make two

**Glass**
686 × 222
(27 × 8¾)
Make two

102(4)

51(2)

Recesses
for two
51 × 12
(2 × ½)
hinges

51(2)

102(4)

**Assembled Frame**

6(¼)

6(¼)

38(1½)

32
(1¼)

9(⅜)

**Tenon detail**

9(⅜)

9(⅜)

**Beading**

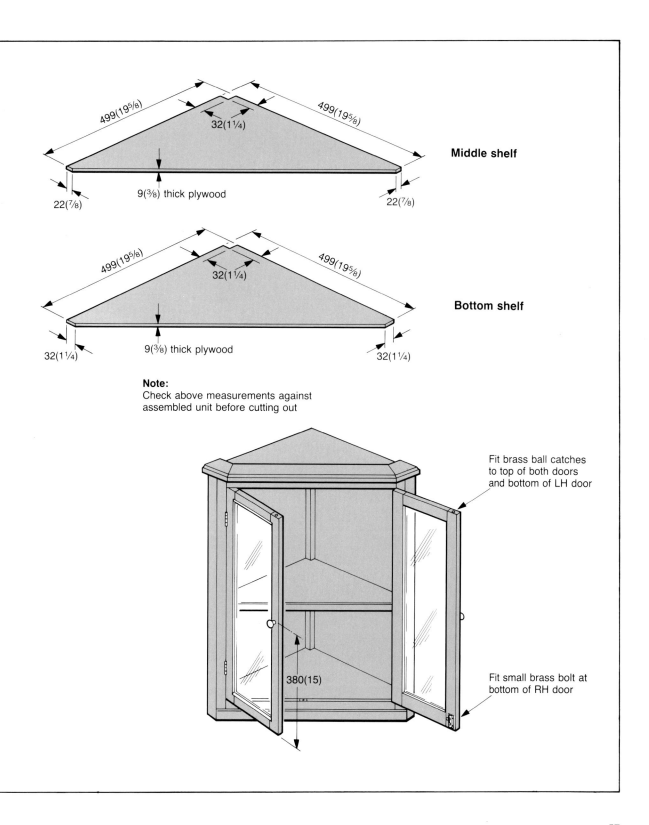

499(19⅝)    499(19⅝)

32(1¼)

**Middle shelf**

9(⅜) thick plywood

22(⅞)    22(⅞)

499(19⅝)    499(19⅝)

32(1¼)

**Bottom shelf**

9(⅜) thick plywood

32(1¼)    32(1¼)

**Note:**
Check above measurements against
assembled unit before cutting out

Fit brass ball catches
to top of both doors
and bottom of LH door

380(15)

Fit small brass bolt at
bottom of RH door

# Welsh dresser

*Essential tools*
Tenon saw
Plough plane or rebate plane
Coping saw
Dovetail gauge
Bevel edged or firmer chisel
Spokeshave
Smoothing plane .

The Welsh dresser is a classical and much sought-after piece of furniture. There are many variations on the basic design and the way in which it is constructed.

This one is made in Nordic redwood and all the in-fill panels are in tongued and grooved wall panelling. The drawers are made with dovetails and pieces of timber are glued together to form the top.

**The framework**

The two end frames are made with halving joints. This is not traditional but it makes the construction simpler. Half the thickness of the two pieces of timber must be removed so that they slot together snugly. Mark out the gauge lines, then cut down the vertical lines with a tenon saw. With a large bevel edged or firmer chisel, chop out the wood from the middle of the joint. Then glue the end frames together.(**1**)

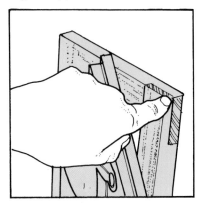

**1** *Before glueing the two pieces of wood together, clean up the wood with a smoothing plane.*

The end frames are held together at the top and bottom by stretcher rails that form the basic framework. The joint used for this is a single stub mortice and tenon.(2)

**2** *The two end frameworks are held together by a single stub mortice and tenon.*

Before the frameworks are jointed, the end panels have to be rebated to take the T&G boards. Use a router for the rebates which are cut on the inside edges of the frame.(3)

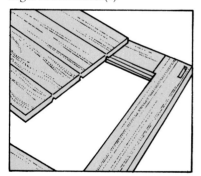

**3** *It is vital that the T&G boards line up flush with the inside edge, because if they stand "proud" it will not be possible to fit the drawers.*

The rails and frameworks supporting the drawers and centre shelf have twin stub mortice and tenons. The twin stubs are stopped – they do not go right through the framework sides. The twin stubs make it possible to have a fairly wide

rail, and the stub going into the mortice hole ensures that the rail will not twist.

Mark out all the stub mortice and tenon holes (there are a lot of them). Pencil in the pieces to be cut off or chopped out. For the tenons, cut down all the vertical lines.(4) Then remove the waste from the middle of the twin stub tenons with a coping saw.(5)

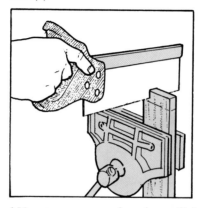

**4** *Use a tenon saw to cut down the pencilled in vertical lines.*

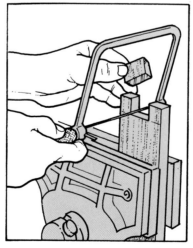

**5** *Note the angle of the blade in the coping saw when it is used to cut horizontally.*

Now cut off the stub tenon cheeks, and then the stub tenon ends. (**6** and **7**) Place the rail on a flat board and use a very sharp chisel to trim off the waste wood left by the coping saw.(**8**)

**6** *Cut off the stub tenon cheeks with a tenon saw.*

**7** *Cut off the stub tenon ends before cleaning up the wood.*

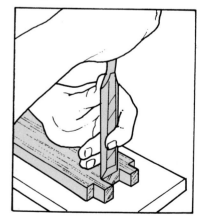

**8** *Note the angle and the way the chisel is held.*

All the stub mortice and tenon joints have to be cut using this method. The mortice holes are then chopped to take the tenons.(9)

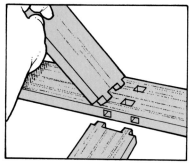

**9** *The stub mortice and tenons "lined up" to form the drawer framework.*

When all the stub mortice holes and tenons have been cut, the drawer framework should be glued together. (**10**) Then glue the framework and all the lower rails into the side panels. (**11**)

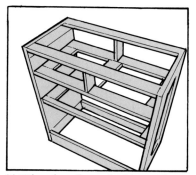

**11** *When the rails are glued in position, check again for squareness.*

## The doors

The doors are made by jointing the corners with halving joints. Always offer up to the opening the timbers you are using, and mark onto them exact measurements. When marking out, make both doors a fraction oversize. This will allow you to plane off the edges to achieve a perfect fit.

When the halvings have been marked out, place the timber in a vice and saw down to the bottom edge with a tenon saw. (**12**) Then reverse the wood in the vice and repeat the procedure. Finally place the wood at 90° in the vice and saw down to the bottom edge. (**13**) The two 45° cuts will guide the blade as it travels.

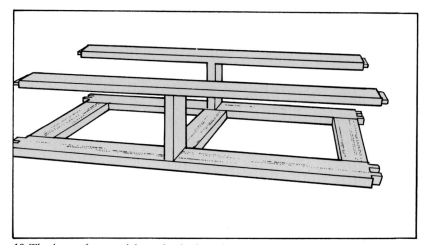

**10** *The drawer framework has to be glued together carefully, checking to make sure that everything is square.*

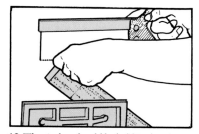

**12** *The timber should be held in the vice at a 45° angle.*

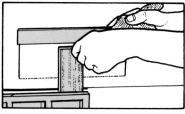

**13** *The two 45° cuts will guide the blade of the tenon saw as it cuts.*

Now use a bench hook to hold the timber securely and remove the cheek of the halving joint. (**14**)

**14** *The position of the hands are important when you are cutting off the cheek.*

The door frames are now glued up and there will be some tidying up of the corners to be done with the smoothing plane.

Next rebate the doors on the inside edges to take the panels. (**15**) When the panels have been fitted into the door frame, hinge the doors to the framework. (**16**) I prefer brass hinges because I think they look so much better than steel.

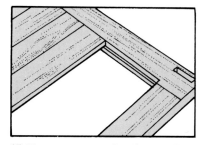

**15** *Use a router to cut the rebates on the inside edges of the doors.*

**16** *Brass hinges are the best for this job.*

## The drawers

Traditional drawers require a great deal of work. Even so, dovetail drawers with their inbuilt strength and proper drawer slips at the bottom (no ploughed grooved sides), do the job so well that it is worth the effort needed to make them.

Before marking out the fronts and backs of the drawers, place the prepared timbers up against the finished framework and take your measurements directly off the frame.

With a dovetail gauge set out the tails, and do not forget that you must allow for the drawer slip at the bottom. Cut down the sides of the pins, (**17**) then remove the waste in the middle. (**18** and **19**)

**17** *Cut down the pins with a back saw.*

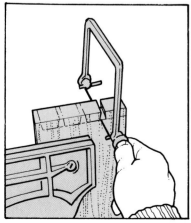

**18** *Use a coping saw to remove the waste at the bottom.*

**19** *A bevel edged chisel is used to clean down to the gauge line.*

Now position the side of the drawer onto the front, and mark through the tails the place where the pins need to be cut out. (**20**) Support the drawer front with a piece of waste wood and remove the waste from the back of the joint very carefully. (**21**)

**20** *A finished set of tails should be used to mark out the pins onto the side.*

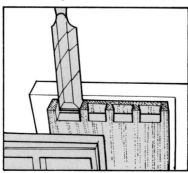

**21** *Work carefully with the chisel to avoid splitting the wood.*

This procedure has to be repeated for a further 7 drawer corners, so you should be good at it by the end! (**22**)

**22** *A finished joint.*

The front of the drawers are now ploughed out to take the drawer bottoms. (**23**) Now drawer slips should be ploughed out and fitted. Making the ploughed slips can be rather fiddly – the big problem is how to hold them while they are being worked on. The best technique is to plough out the groove on the board before cutting the slip to size.

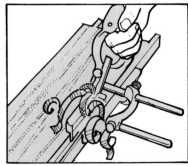

**23** *The groove can be cut with a router, but a plough plane is ideal for the job.*

Now fit the drawer into the carcase. (**24**) If the fitting is too tight, do not force the drawer. Pull it out, hold it up to the light, and where it is sticking will show up as a shiny spot or line. Work very carefully with the drawers – it is easy to take off a shaving, but you cannot stick one back on! (**25**)

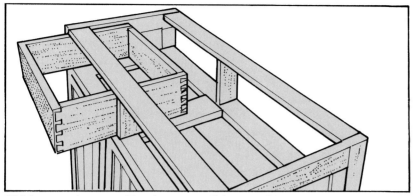

**24** *Use a very sharp smoothing plane to trim off the joints of the drawers.*

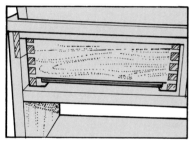

**25** *The back of the drawer in the carcase. Note the dovetails and drawer slips at the bottom of the drawer.*

## The back

The framework of the back is morticed and tenoned together. The rebate to take the panelling is cut with a router. The back panel is screwed straight onto the framework,(**26**) and the screw holes are plugged to hide them.

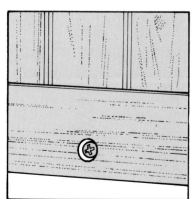

**26** *The screw holes of the framed and panelled back are plugged.*

A plinth is needed for the bottom of the unit. As with the drawer slips it is far easier to cut the shaping before it is cut off the main plank. The plinth is joined at the corners by a neatly cut mitre joint. The mitre joint can be cut in a mitre box, or with an electric mitre saw (*see page 204*). When the plinths have been cut, they are glued to the carcase.(**27**)

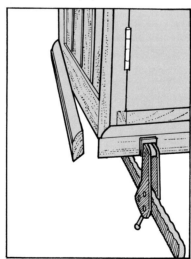

**27** *Use cramps when glueing the plinths to the carcase.*

## The top

Cut and prepare all the shelves, sides and top pieces of timber. The sides are placed together in order to mark out the stopped housing joints. Stopped housing joints prevent the joint

showing from the front edge and therefore look better. It is important at the marking out stage to get the housing joints pencilled in correctly, or there will be a lop-sided shelf unit.

The rebates at the back of the uprights that will take the back panel have to be marked in and cut out next.(**28**) The shelf width will also have to be reduced to allow for the back panel to be placed correctly.

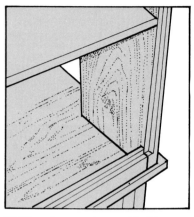

**28** *The rebates can be cut with either a rebate plane or a router.*

The top front rail is shaped next and joints cut on the ends with a jigsaw or coping saw.

Now the whole unit is glued together.(**29**)

The back panel is made up from

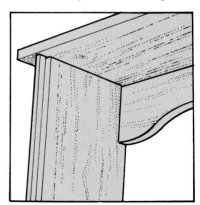

**29** *The fine rebated line which is a feature of this unit is cut after the unit is glued together.*

T&G wall boards. These fit into the rebate at the bottom of the unit. The boards are held in place firmly by screws that are fitted with cup washers.(**30**) A batten is glued to the top inside edge to secure the boards at the top.

Now glue small wooden beads along the front edges of the shelves to prevent plates falling off the shelves.

The framework can be secured to the base unit with brass plates fitted at the back. Alternatively dowel rods can be fitted into the top of the dresser to locate in holes that are drilled in the ends of the shelf unit.

**Finishing off**

Use water-based acrylic varnish – this is easy to use, does not smell unpleasant and washes off the brush. (**31**)

**31** *The finished dresser.*

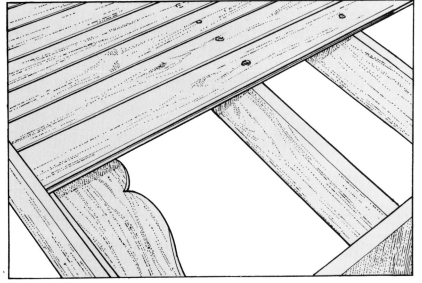

**30** *The T&G wall boards being fitted.*

*A nice finishing touch is the addition of brass handles.*

## WELSH DRESSER CUTTING LIST

### Base unit

| | | |
|---|---|---|
| Side frames | 4 off | 882 × 64 × 22mm (34¾ × 2½ × ⁷/₈in) timber |
| | 4 off | 457 × 64 × 22mm (18 × 2½ × ⁷/₈in) timber |
| | 8 off** | 766 × 121 × 16mm (30¼ × 4¾ × ⁵/₈in) T&G board |
| Top | 1 off | 952 × 502* × 22mm (37½ × 19¾* × ⁷/₈in) timber |
| Top stretcher rail | 2 off | 894 × 64 × 22mm (35¼ × 2½ × ⁷/₈in) timber |
| Drawer support frame | 2 off | 894 × 64 × 22mm (35¼ × 2½ × ⁷/₈in) timber |
| | 1 off | 354 × 76 × 22mm (14 × 3 × ⁷/₈in) timber |
| | 2 off | 354 × 64 × 22mm (14 × 2½ × ⁷/₈in) timber |
| | 2 off | 178 × 64 × 22mm (7 × 2½ × ⁷/₈in) timber |
| | 1 off | 330 × 32 × 22mm (13 × 1¼ × ⁷/₈in) timber |
| Centre shelf | 1 off | 870 × 432* × 20mm (34¼ × 17* × ¾in) timber |
| Centre shelf support frame | 2 off | 894 × 64 × 22mm (35¼ × 2½ × ⁷/₈in) timber |
| | 2 off | 354 × 64 × 22mm (14 × 2½ × ⁷/₈in) timber |
| Bottom shelf | 1 off | 870 × 412* × 20mm (34¼ × 16¼* × ¾in) timber |
| Bottom stretcher rail | 2 off | 894 × 64 × 22mm (35¼ × 2½ × ⁷/₈in) timber |
| Bottom shelf support battens | 2 off | 412 × 38 × 22mm (16¼ × 1½ × ⁷/₈in) timber |
| | 2 off | 203 × 38 × 22mm (8 × 1½ × ⁷/₈in) timber |
| Plinth | 1 off | 953 × 44 × 20mm (37½ × 1¾ × ¾in) timber |
| | 2 off | 477 × 44 × 20mm (18¾ × 1¾ × ¾in) timber |
| Door frame | 2 off | 622 × 64 × 22mm (24½ × 2½ × ⁷/₈in) timber |
| | 2 off | 622 × 44 × 22mm (24½ × 1¾ × ⁷/₈in) timber |
| | 4 off | 444 × 44 × 22mm (17¼ × 1¾ × ⁷/₈in) timber |
| | 8 off** | 546 × 121 × 16mm (21½ × 4¾ × ⁵/₈in) T&G board |

### Drawer assembly

| | | |
|---|---|---|
| Front | 2 off | 425 × 152 × 22mm (16¾ × 6 × ⁷/₈in) timber |
| Sides | 4 off | 422 × 152 × 22mm (16⅝ × 6 × ⁷/₈in) timber |
| Back | 2 off | 425 × 121 × 22mm (16¾ × 4¾ × ⁷/₈in) timber |
| Bottom | 2 off | 415 × 369 × 9mm (16⅜ × 14½ × ³/₈in) plywood |
| Beading | 4 off | 384 × 12 × 6mm (15⅛ × ½ × ¼in) segment |
| Drawer slip | 4 off | 406 × 25 × 16mm (16 × 1 × ⁵/₈in) timber |

### Back assembly

| | | |
|---|---|---|
| Horizontal rails | 2 off | 914 × 64 × 22mm (36 × 2½ × ⁷/₈in) timber |
| Vertical rails | 3 off | 819 × 64 × 22mm (32¼ × 2½ × ⁷/₈in) timber |
| | 8 off** | 703 × 121 × 16mm (27¾ × 4¾ × ⁵/₈in) T&G board |

### Top unit

| | | |
|---|---|---|
| Sides | 2 off | 914 × 219 × 22mm (36 × 8⅝ × ⁷/₈in) timber |
| Shelves | 2 off | 883 × 191 × 22mm (34¾ × 7½ × ⁷/₈in) timber |
| Top | 1 off | 1,003 × 244 × 22mm (39½ × 9⅝ × ⁷/₈in) timber |
| Top front rail | 1 off | 883 × 102 × 22mm (34¾ × 4 × ⁷/₈in) timber |
| Concealing batten | 2 off | 865 × 20 × 12mm (34 × ¾ × ½in) timber |
| Shelf lip | 2 off | 865 × 9 × 3mm (34 × ³/₈ × ¹/₈in) timber |
| | 8 off** | 914 × 121 × 16mm (36 × 4¾ × ⁵/₈in) T&G board |

\* Accumulative dimensions for jointed boards
\*\* Will vary according to width of boarding used

*An inside view of the base unit.*

*The back of the base unit.*

*The back of the top unit.*

*A detail of the drawer, showing the dovetails.*

**Above** *A clear view of the shelf and the framework of the drawers.*

**Right** *The underside of the top of the base unit showing the screw fixing and halving joint.*

**Left and below** *Two views of the plinth glued onto the outer edges of the base unit.*

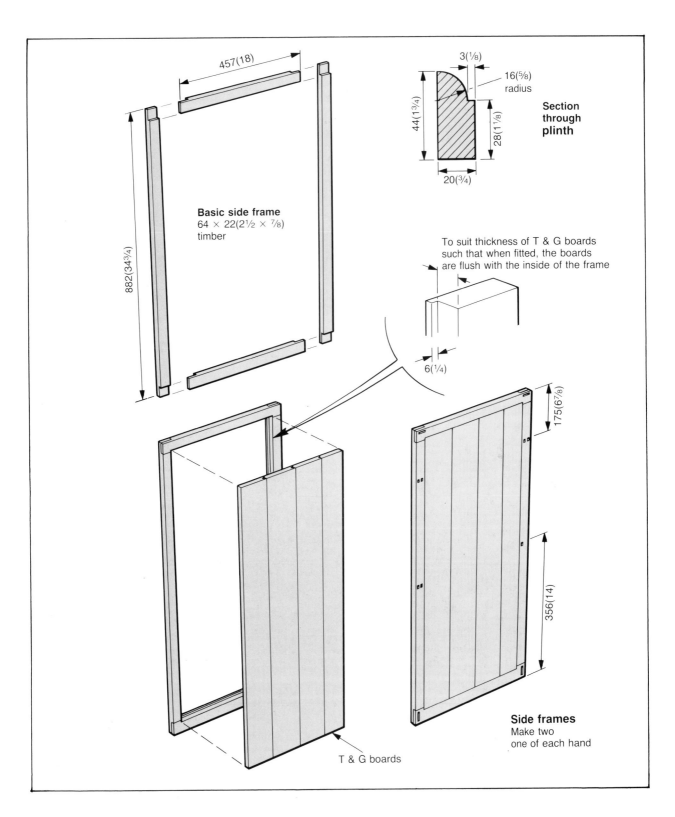

457(18)

3(⅛)

16(⅝) radius

44(1¾)

28(1⅛)

**Section through plinth**

20(¾)

**Basic side frame**
64 × 22(2½ × ⅞) timber

882(34¾)

To suit thickness of T & G boards such that when fitted, the boards are flush with the inside of the frame

6(¼)

175(6⅞)

356(14)

T & G boards

**Side frames**
Make two
one of each hand

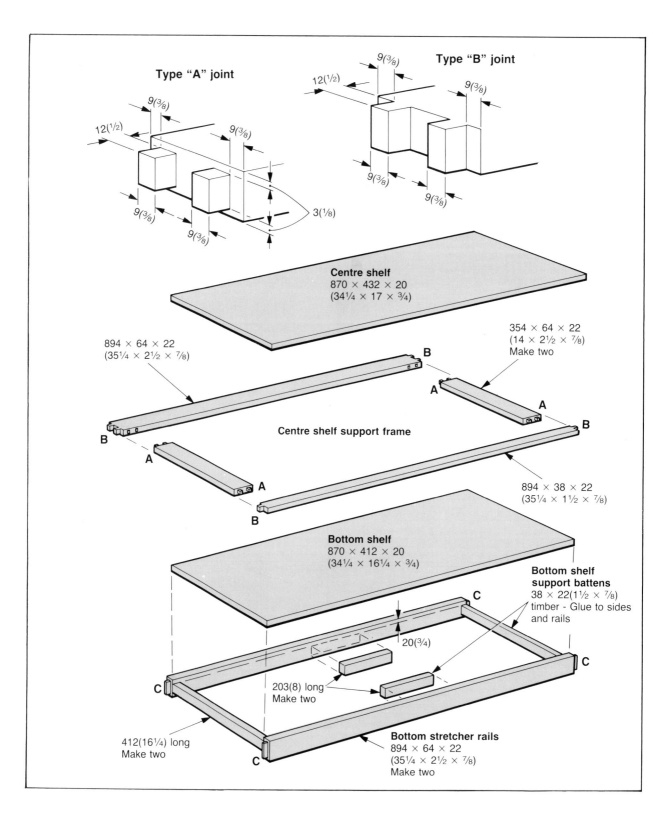

Type "A" joint

Type "B" joint

Centre shelf
870 × 432 × 20
(34¼ × 17 × ¾)

894 × 64 × 22
(35¼ × 2½ × ⅞)

354 × 64 × 22
(14 × 2½ × ⅞)
Make two

Centre shelf support frame

894 × 38 × 22
(35¼ × 1½ × ⅞)

Bottom shelf
870 × 412 × 20
(34¼ × 16¼ × ¾)

Bottom shelf
support battens
38 × 22(1½ × ⅞)
timber - Glue to sides
and rails

20(¾)

203(8) long
Make two

412(16¼) long
Make two

Bottom stretcher rails
894 × 64 × 22
(35¼ × 2½ × ⅞)
Make two

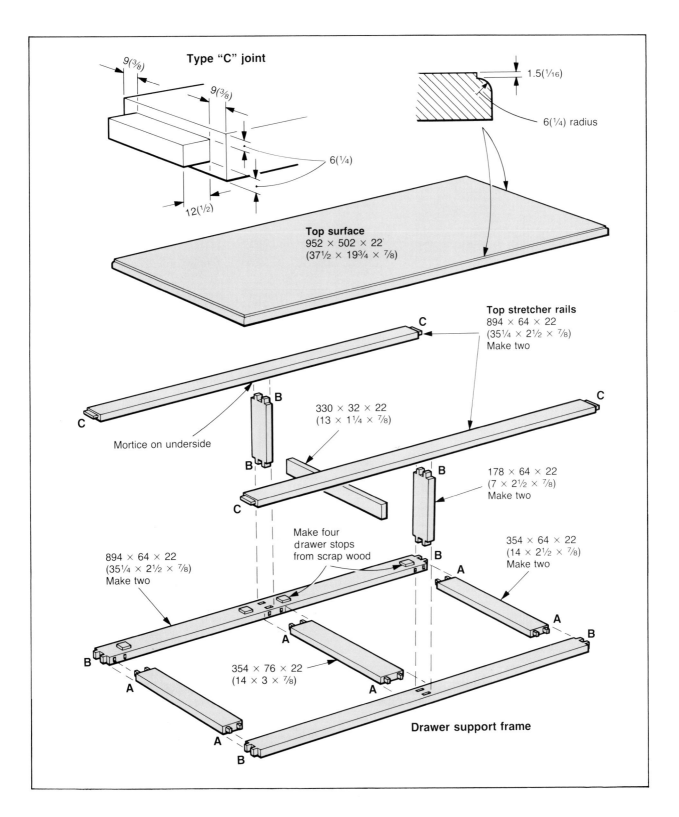

Type "C" joint

9(3/8)

9(3/8)

6(1/4)

12(1/2)

1.5(1/16)

6(1/4) radius

**Top surface**
952 × 502 × 22
(37½ × 19¾ × 7/8)

**Top stretcher rails**
894 × 64 × 22
(35¼ × 2½ × 7/8)
Make two

Mortice on underside

330 × 32 × 22
(13 × 1¼ × 7/8)

178 × 64 × 22
(7 × 2½ × 7/8)
Make two

Make four
drawer stops
from scrap wood

354 × 64 × 22
(14 × 2½ × 7/8)
Make two

894 × 64 × 22
(35¼ × 2½ × 7/8)
Make two

354 × 76 × 22
(14 × 3 × 7/8)

**Drawer support frame**

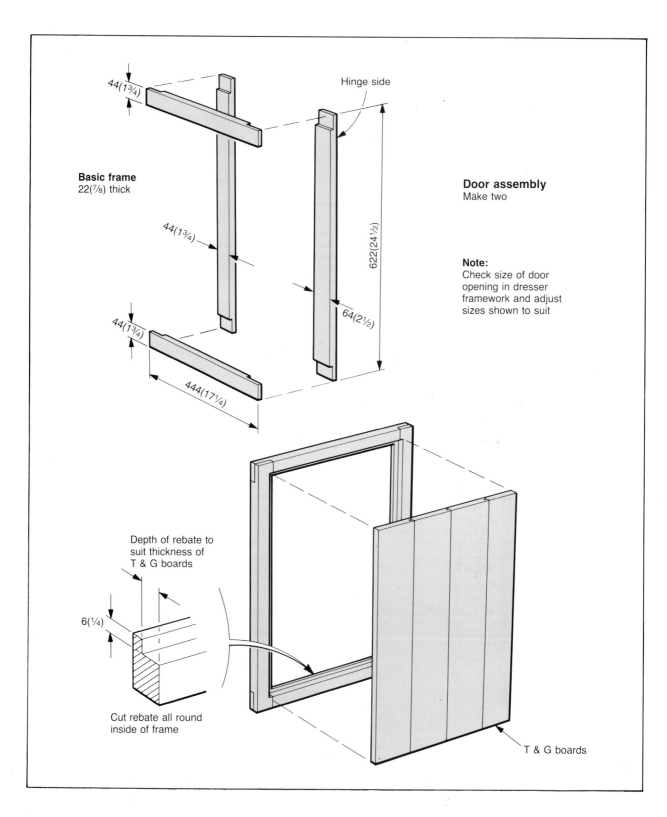

44(1¾)

Hinge side

**Basic frame**
22(⅞) thick

44(1¾)

622(24½)

**Door assembly**
Make two

**Note:**
Check size of door
opening in dresser
framework and adjust
sizes shown to suit

64(2½)

44(1¾)

444(17¼)

Depth of rebate to
suit thickness of
T & G boards

6(¼)

Cut rebate all round
inside of frame

T & G boards

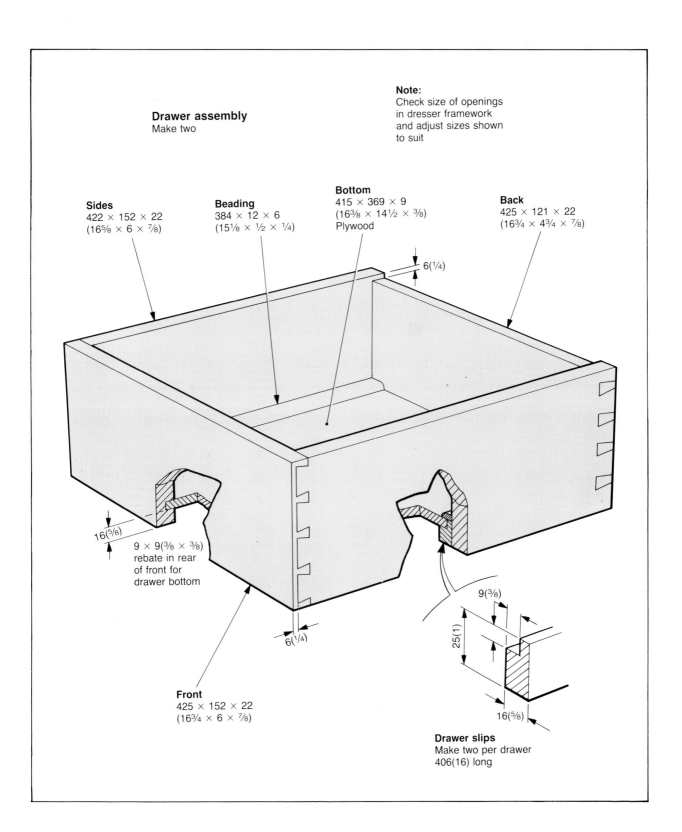

**Drawer assembly**
Make two

**Note:**
Check size of openings
in dresser framework
and adjust sizes shown
to suit

**Sides**
422 × 152 × 22
(16⅝ × 6 × ⅞)

**Beading**
384 × 12 × 6
(15⅛ × ½ × ¼)

**Bottom**
415 × 369 × 9
(16⅜ × 14½ × ⅜)
Plywood

**Back**
425 × 121 × 22
(16¾ × 4¾ × ⅞)

6(¼)

16(⅝)

9 × 9(⅜ × ⅜)
rebate in rear
of front for
drawer bottom

6(¼)

**Front**
425 × 152 × 22
(16¾ × 6 × ⅞)

9(⅜)

25(1)

16(⅝)

**Drawer slips**
Make two per drawer
406(16) long

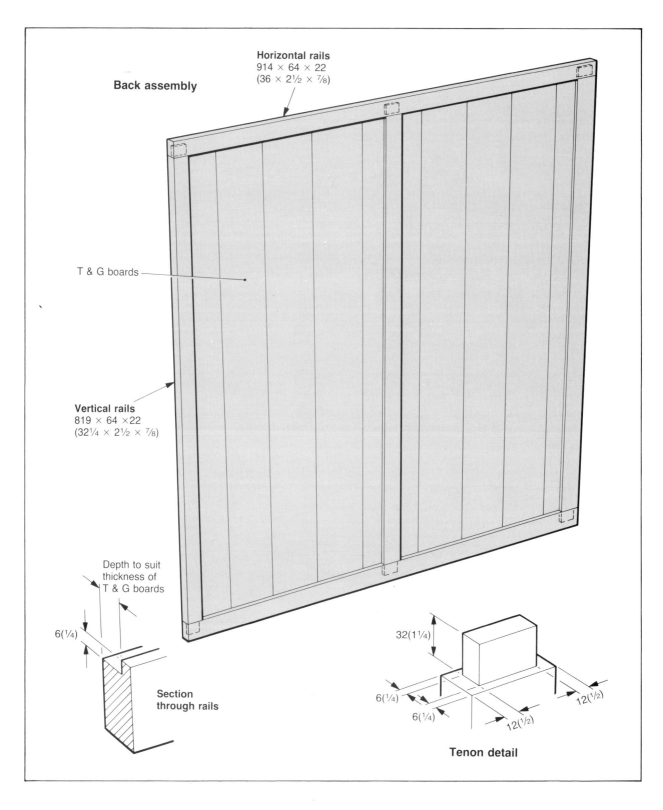

**Back assembly**

Horizontal rails
914 × 64 × 22
(36 × 2½ × ⅞)

T & G boards

Vertical rails
819 × 64 ×22
(32¼ × 2½ × ⅞)

Depth to suit
thickness of
T & G boards

6(¼)

**Section
through rails**

32(1¼)

6(¼)

6(¼)

12(½)

12(½)

**Tenon detail**

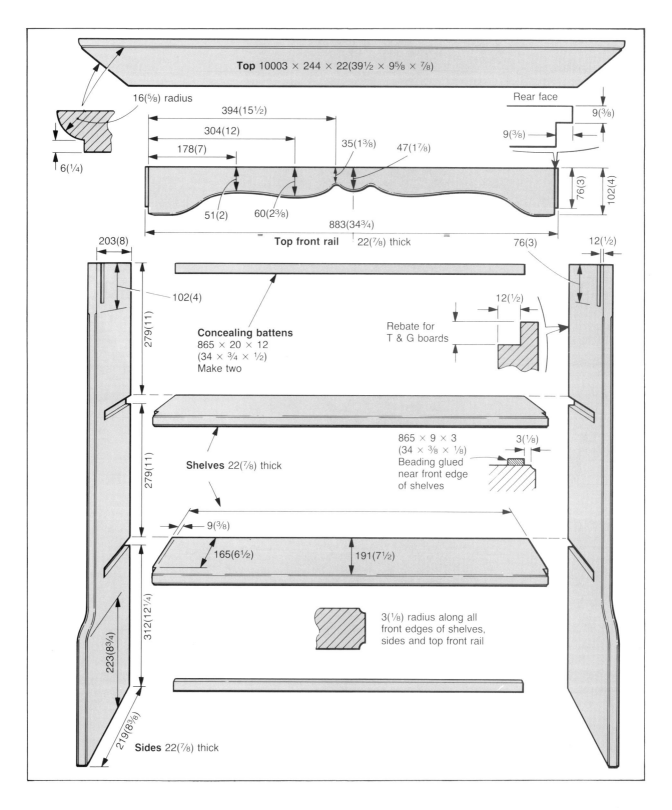

**Top** 10003 × 244 × 22(39½ × 9⅝ × ⅞)

16(⅝) radius

Rear face

9(⅜)

9(⅜)

6(¼)

394(15½)

304(12)

178(7)

35(1⅜)

47(1⅞)

76(3)

102(4)

51(2)

60(2⅜)

883(34¾)

**Top front rail** 22(⅞) thick

76(3)

203(8)

12(½)

102(4)

279(11)

**Concealing battens**
865 × 20 × 12
(34 × ¾ × ½)
Make two

Rebate for
T & G boards

12(½)

279(11)

**Shelves** 22(⅞) thick

865 × 9 × 3
(34 × ⅜ × ⅛)
Beading glued
near front edge
of shelves

3(⅛)

9(⅜)

165(6½)

191(7½)

312(12¼)

3(⅛) radius along all
front edges of shelves,
sides and top front rail

223(8¾)

219(8⅜)

**Sides** 22(⅞) thick

# *Fire surround*

**Essential tools**
Electric router or moulding plane
Sash cramps
Electric screwdriver
Mitre box
Electric drill

Fire surrounds have become increasingly popular in recent years. However, the expense of buying a ready-made unit has made home owners look at the alternative – that is, to make your own. I have always thought that any piece of furniture with mouldings looks more difficult to make than it really is. This type of project looks daunting, but in reality it is not difficult.

If you do not have a router, or moulding planes, then buy ready-made mouldings at a local superstore. One "wood processing" company have actually produced a kit of moulded parts. The details are a matter of personal choice. Tudor roses or Grecian urns can be carved, if you wish, to place on the centre piece. However, you may prefer to glue on a length of simple moulding. There is a real temptation to overdecorate so it is best to make the basic framework, place the mouldings in position and stand back to look before glueing them.

This particular fire surround was constructed in Nordic redwood, which is easily available from builders

merchants and most D.I.Y. stores. Redwoods will take a wood stain particularly well. All the main cross battens, both horizontal and vertical, are fixed by counterboring and glueing the battens in place. This means that a hole is bored in the timber to take the complete screw head below the surface of the wood. You can buy drills and counterboring tools all in one, so the job of boring a pilot hole for the screw and counterboring a hole for the screw's head can be done in one operation.

Traditional mouldings were cut with moulding planes. The sole and the cutter of the moulding plane "mirrored" that of the moulding being formed. Today, the electric router has taken over from many of the traditional tools. There are quite literally dozens of router cutter shapes available. However, in this design I have used just two cutters, both of which have a U-shaped cutting end which produces a very clean line ideal for the job. If you have not used a router before, you will grasp all its possibilities after only a very short acquaintance. It is one of the most versatile pieces of machinery.

### The framework
You need to create a framework or box section onto which all mouldings and the mantel shelf can be attached. First cut to length the side uprights and the main cross pieces. Attach the cross pieces to the side uprights using two battens.(**1**)

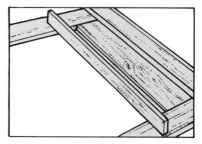

**1** *Place the cross piece uprights and battens in position.*

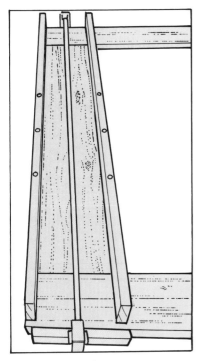

**2** *Use a sash cramp to pull the pieces tightly together before screwing the battens into place.*

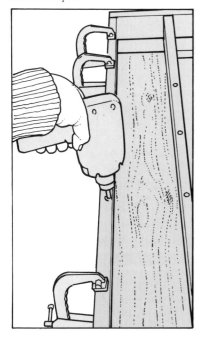

**3** *An electric screwdriver will easily drive screws into the counterbore holes.*

The battens are attached to the main pieces by counterboring the screws. Remember to measure the length of screw, and adjust the depth of the hole (counterbore) to prevent the point of the screw piercing the face of the timber.

Now glue the top horizontal board to the side pieces. Butt the pieces before glueing.(**2**) Drive in counter-sunk screws to hold the pieces together.

Secure battens down the length of each side upright using counterbored screws as before.(**3**) Cut small blocks of timber and glue these into place at the bottom of the side uprights. (**4**)

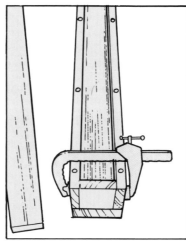

**4** *Use a small clamp to hold the pieces together while the glue cures.*

Now the framework has been constructed, the interesting work of making mouldings can begin.(**5**)

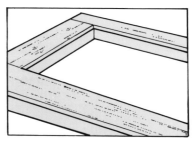

**5** *The framework is now ready to take the mouldings.*

**The mouldings**
When routing the mouldings, make sure that the timber to be cut is held securely. Wherever possible, keep the timber in its largest and widest sections while routing is done, as it is easier to handle. When routing, screw small pieces of wood in place at either end and at one side of the timber.(**6**)

**6** *A small section fixed securely ready for routing. Note how it hangs over the side of the bench.*

These will prevent the timber from moving while the router is cutting. The fence of the router will run along the timber edge, so it is important to fix the timber over the edge of the bench to prevent the fence "fouling" the bench beneath.

When you need to route the ends or edges of the timber, the base of the router needs a wider section of timber to work off than that provided by the thickness of one board. In this case, clamp a piece of waste wood along the side or end of the timber.(**7**)

Under no circumstances should you resort to fixing the router in the vice and passing timber along the cutting edge. This is extremely dangerous and could result in the loss of part of a finger! If possible, cut mouldings on wide planks, and when the moulding is complete cut the moulded section off. This is the safest method of working.

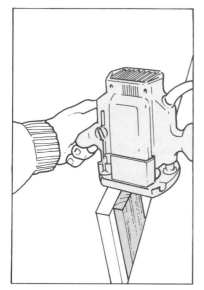

7 *The piece of waste wood will give both the router and the operator a wider base from which to work.*

When the routing is completed, tidy up. If you use high-speed steel cutters in the router, you will get a very clean cut. However, if you use the more expensive tungsten carbide (T.C.T.) cutter, you will need to touch up the grooves with a very fine glasspaper.(**8**)

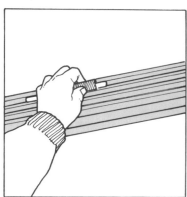

8 *Use a small-diameter dowel rod wrapped in fine glasspaper to finish off the grooves.*

All the mouldings are glued straight onto the framework. Glue the small oblong pieces into place at the bottom of the two side uprights. Above these, the two fine moulded columns are glued in position.(**9**)

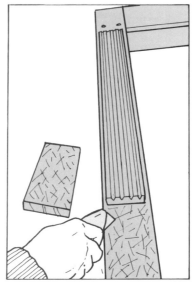

9 *Use a Stanley knife to create a "key" on the faces that are to be glued together. This allows the glue to get a better hold.*

Now glue the central piece of wood to the middle of the horizontal section of the framework, and glue the reeded sections to either side, adding the end pieces last.(**10**)

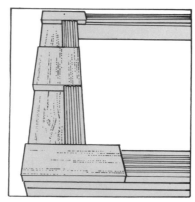

10 *When all the mouldings are attached, the framework is ready to take the mantle shelf and its mouldings.*

**The mantle shelf**

This is made up from three different sections. The first shelf is screwed straight onto the framework. Before it is attached, the edge has to be moulded using a cutter that has a ball bearing on the bottom. The great advantage of this type of arrangement is that there is no need to use a fence to guide the router. It does not matter if you stop while halfway along the board either, as the ball bearing will prevent the pilot nose of the cutter burning the timber.

Now screw the shelf onto the framework.(**11**)

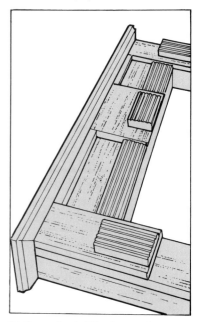

11 *Screw the shelf firmly onto the horizontal section of the framework.*

On top of this shelf a further section should be moulded and glued in place. This is not a shelf, but a moulded length of timber that has its corners mitred. After routing the moulding on the timber, carefully mark in pencil on the timber where the mitre joints have to be cut. With a marking knife, knife over the pencil lines; this will ensure that when the pieces are sawn the edges are clean.

A mitre box – which has pre-cut grooves set at 45° and 90° – is used to cut the 45° angles.(**12**) The timber is then glued onto the top of the shelf.(**13**) Finally, make the top shelf, using a router once again to mould the edges. Glue a decorative moulding along the front and side edges. Mitre the joints to give a neat finish. (**14**)

**Finishing off**
There are a variety of acrylic wood stains available, so you can choose a colour to match your home decor.

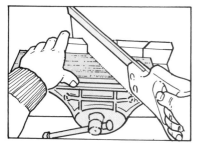

**12** *The wood is held carefully in the mitre box for cutting.*

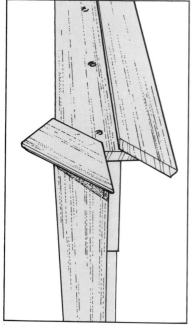

**13** *Hold the timber onto the shelf with "G" cramps until it has cured.*

**14** *The finished fire surround.*

**FIRE SURROUND CUTTING LIST**

| | | |
|---|---|---|
| Side uprights | 2 off | 1,092 × 102 × 20mm (43 × 4 × ¾in) timber |
| Cross piece | 1 off | 915 × 178 × 20mm (36 × 7 × ¾in) timber |
| Cross battens | 2 off | 1,079 × 64 × 20mm (42½ × 2½ × ¾in) timber |
| Side battens | 2 off | 1,092 × 64 × 20mm (43 × 2½ × ¾in) timber |
| | 2 off | 914 × 64 × 20mm (36 × 2½ × ¾in) timber |
| Blocks | 2 off | 64 × 64 × 20mm (2½ × 2½ × ¾in) timber |
| Moulding blocks | 1 off | 305 × 178 × 20mm (12 × 7 × ¾in) timber |
| | 2 off | 305 × 20 × 20mm (12 × ¾ × ¾in) timber |
| | 2 off | 235 × 102 × 20mm (9¼ × 4 × ¾in) timber |
| | 2 off | 188 × 102 × 20mm (7⅜ × 4 × ¾in) timber |
| Moulding strips | make from | 2,440 × 64 × 20mm (96 × 2½ × ¾in) timber |
| First shelf | 1 off | 1,194 × 137 × 20mm (47 × 5⅜ × ¾in) timber |
| Centre piece | make from | 1,676 × 70 × 20mm (66 × 2¾ × ¾in) timber |
| Top shelf | 1 off | 1,397 × 187 × 20mm (55 × 7⅜ × ¾in) timber |
| Decorative moulding | make from | 1,825 × 20 × 12mm (72 × ¾ × ½in) timber |

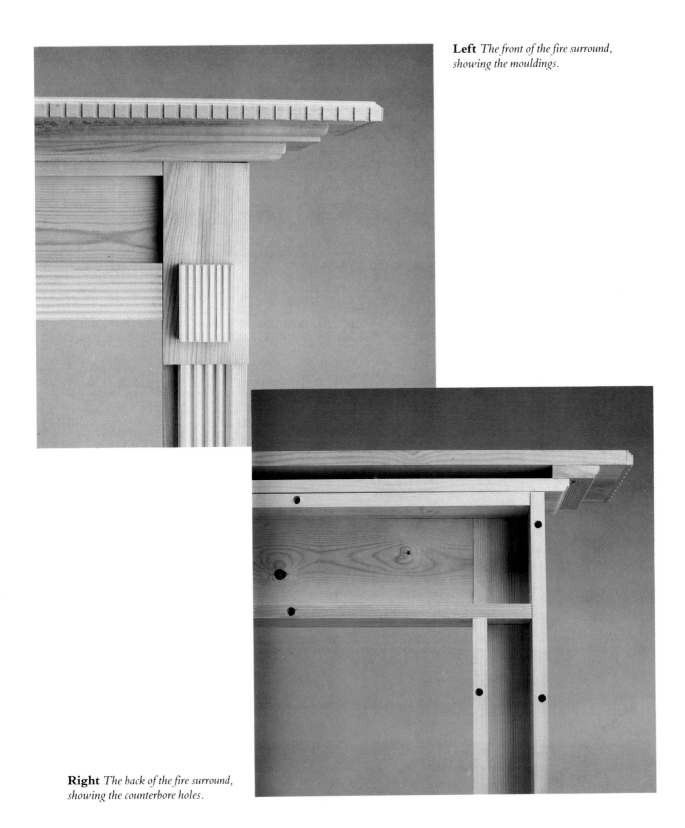

**Left** *The front of the fire surround, showing the mouldings.*

**Right** *The back of the fire surround, showing the counterbore holes.*

*A view of the back of the completed fireplace.*

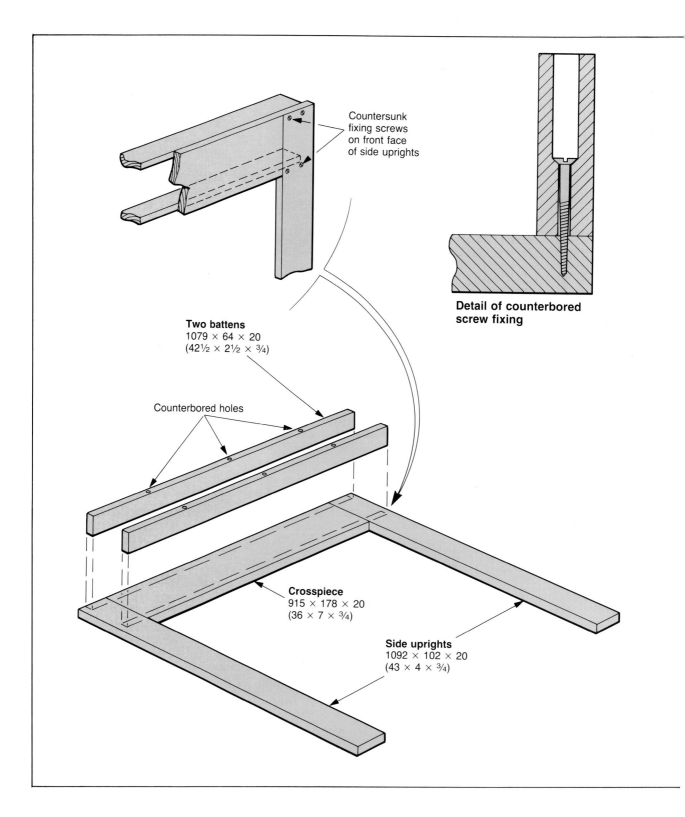

Countersunk
fixing screws
on front face
of side uprights

**Detail of counterbored
screw fixing**

**Two battens**
1079 × 64 × 20
(42½ × 2½ × ¾)

Counterbored holes

**Crosspiece**
915 × 178 × 20
(36 × 7 × ¾)

**Side uprights**
1092 × 102 × 20
(43 × 4 × ¾)

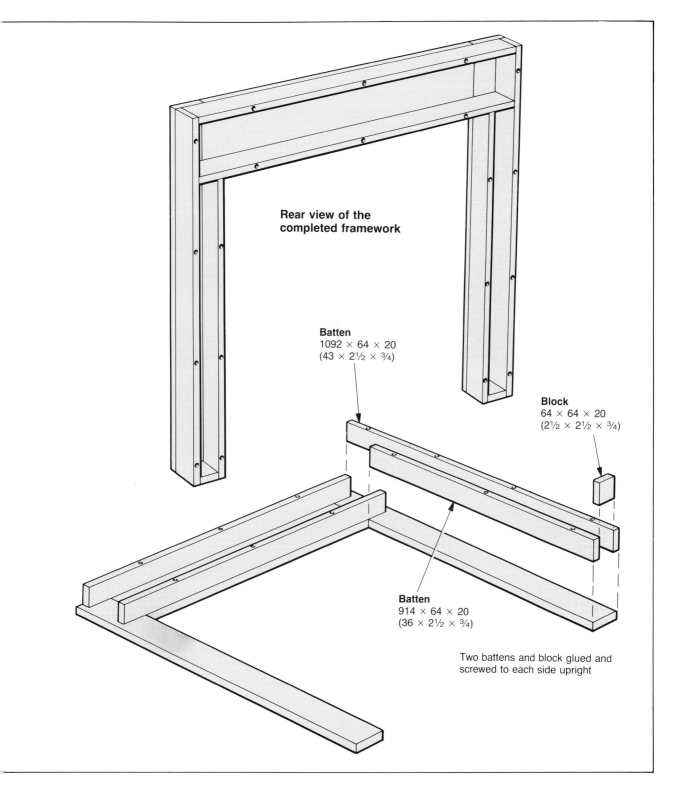

**Rear view of the completed framework**

**Batten**
1092 × 64 × 20
(43 × 2½ × ¾)

**Block**
64 × 64 × 20
(2½ × 2½ × ¾)

**Batten**
914 × 64 × 20
(36 × 2½ × ¾)

Two battens and block glued and
screwed to each side upright

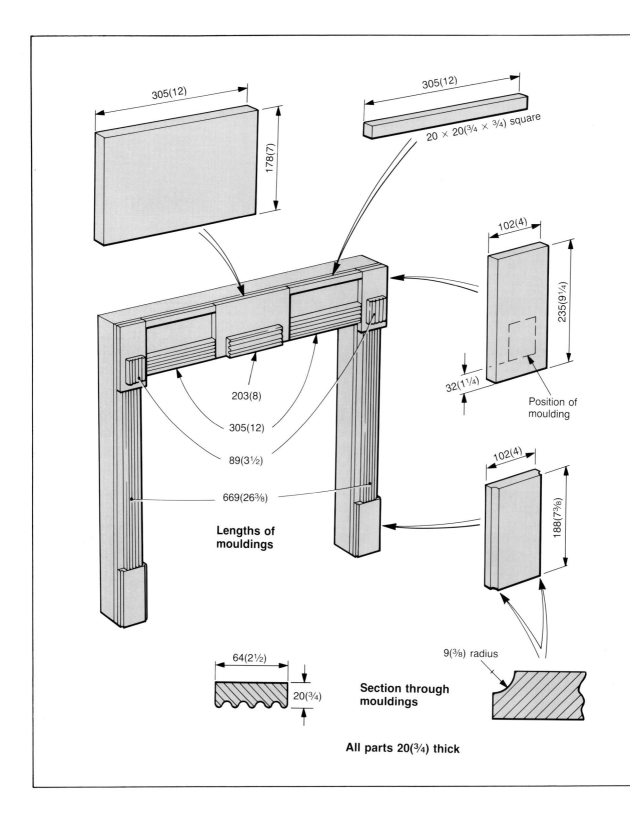

305(12)

178(7)

305(12)

20 × 20(¾ × ¾) square

102(4)

235(9¼)

32(1¼)

Position of
moulding

203(8)

305(12)

89(3½)

669(26⅜)

**Lengths of
mouldings**

102(4)

188(7⅞)

9(⅜) radius

64(2½)

20(¾)

**Section through
mouldings**

**All parts 20(¾) thick**

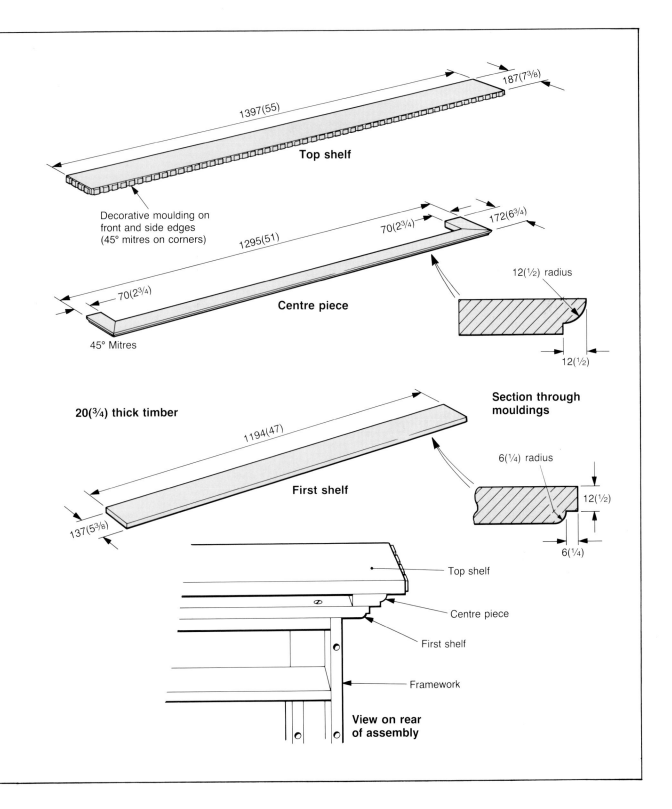

1397(55)

187(7³/₈)

**Top shelf**

Decorative moulding on
front and side edges
(45° mitres on corners)

1295(51)

70(2³/₄)

172(6³/₄)

70(2³/₄)

**Centre piece**

45° Mitres

12(½) radius

12(½)

20(¾) thick timber

1194(47)

**First shelf**

137(5³/₈)

**Section through
mouldings**

6(¼) radius

12(½)

6(¼)

Top shelf

Centre piece

First shelf

Framework

**View on rear
of assembly**

# Nest of tables

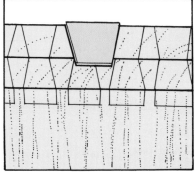

**1** *Mark out dovetail pins with a dovetail template.*

Essential tools
Dovetail saw, backsaw or tenon
  saw
Coping saw
Bevel edged chisel

The first woodworkers soon discovered that large, flat pieces of timber are prone to movement throughout their lifetime, so craftsmen developed the framed panel construction for making furniture. However, they also developed the dovetail joint and a great many variations are used in woodworking for both practical and decorative purposes.

The dovetail is very strong when you wish to joint two pieces of wood. In this particular design, it is used not only to hold the pieces of wood together, but to stabalise the movement of the pieces of timber being used.

In this design I have built four tables. You can, if you wish, make larger or even smaller ones as an addition to the nest. The dovetail used is a through dovetail, chosen to show the decorative effect of the "tails and pins" at the edges of the wood. At the ends I have used a mitre joint, as it really does look better.

## Cutting through dovetails

As the name suggests, on one piece of the wood to be jointed there is a "tail" and on the other a "pin". Careful marking out of the pins or tails across the timber is important, as each pin and tail need to be equally spaced. However, before marking out, you need to make a dovetail template.(**1**) This can be made from hardwood or use a small metal template made from an off-cut of brass.

The old "rule of thumb" governing the dovetail slope is 1 in 8 for hardwoods and 1 in 6 for softwoods. Most cabinet makers have two dovetail templates in their tool boxes. Marking out the wrong slope will mean that you get weak corners, and too shallow a slope will result in the joint pulling apart.

In cabinet making there has always been an argument as to which part of the joint you cut first. Those who cut the tails first are known as "tail men" and those who cut the pins as the "pin men". It is really a matter of personal choice. However, it is important that both pins and tails are marked out very carefully.

Mark out and cut the pins first. Mark out the pins across the plank, leaving a space for the mitred corner at the edge of each piece. As this is a through dovetail, it is necessary to mark the full thickness of the timber onto both pieces.

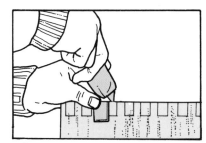

**2** *Work over the pencil lines with a marking knife.*

Once the pins have been pencilled in, work over them with a marking knife.(**2** and **3**)

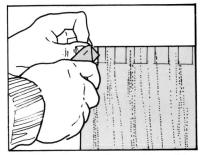

**3** *Mark in the gauge lines with a marking knife.*

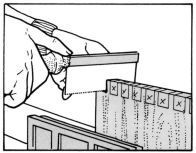

**4** *You can cut down the pins with a backsaw, dovetail or tenon saw.*

A backsaw is now used to cut down the vertical lines on the pins.(**4**) Traditionally a dovetail saw, which is really a smaller version of the tenon saw, was used. However, the real difference is that the smaller teeth – 18 to 22 points per 24mm (1in) – make it ideal for this fine work. I always cut

**5** *Remove the waste with a coping saw.*

on the gauge lines, and then use a coping saw to remove the waste wood in the middle.(**5** and **6**) Now, using a sharp chisel, pare away the waste right down to the gauge line.(**7** and **8**) The mitres at each end require very careful paring. The secret is always to use a razor sharp chisel.

**6** *The waste wood coming away.*

**7** *Pare away the waste wood. Note how the chisel is held between the fingers.*

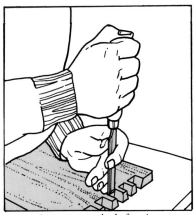

**8** *An alternative method of paring away the waste. The backing board helps to prevent the wood being "broken out" on the back edge. Note how the chisel is held.*

Once the pins have been cut, place the table side onto the table top. Line the pins up with the gauge line on the top and make sure that the timber is flush at both ends. With a very sharp pencil, mark from the pins onto the table top.(**9**) Remove the side and go over the pencil lines firmly with a marking knife.

**9** *The pins are placed onto the top of the table. Mark out the tails with a pencil.*

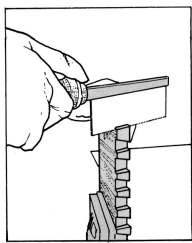

**10** *The leg is turned onto its side and the backsaw is used to cut the mitre.*

Now cut out the tails. Once again use the dovetail saw to cut down the verticals of the tails.(**10**) Obviously, the saw has to be angled to the angle of the tail as you cut. Use the coping saw to cut out the waste.

Today, woodworkers seem to be unaware of the true importance or indeed of the true worth of the bevel edged chisel.(**11**) It was really for fine dovetail work that this chisel was made. If a firmer chisel was used, then its square edge would damage the side of the dovetail.

The bevel on the side of the chisel corresponds with the side of the dovetail sufficiently to prevent the tail being spoilt. Today's bevel edged chisels tend to be just a little thicker in section than the originals.(**12**)

Once all the waste has been removed and the mitre pared on the two ends, the moment of truth has arrived – will it fit? If you have marked it all out properly, then it will. However, the tendency is for woodworkers to work well on the waste side of their gauge lines and the joint then needs some "easing off" before the pins and tails will go together properly.

**11** *With a bevel edged chisel, pare away the waste. The position of the hands on the chisel is important.*

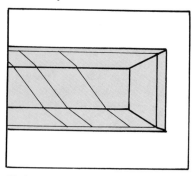

**12** *A cross-section through a chisel.*

## Final assembly

To achieve a fit, place the table end in a vice and place the top onto the pins. Using a waste piece of wood, gently tap the tails onto the pins with a hammer – don't force it! Remove the top and looking carefully you will see

**13** *Fitting the tails into the pins.*

shiny spots where the pins and tails are binding. Continue with this method until the joint fits.(**13**)

With four tables to make, practice will make perfect and by the end you will certainly get pins and tails to fit straight from "saw and chisel"!

*Accurate marking out is essential to ensure a snug fit.*

**NEST OF TABLES CUTTING LIST** 20 (¾) thick timber

|  | Top<br>1 off | Sides<br>2 off | Rail<br>1 off |
|---|---|---|---|
| 1 largest | 595 × 267mm (23⅜ × 10½in) | 374 × 267mm (14¾ × 10½in) | 583 × 32mm (22⅞ × 1¼in) |
| 2 | 550 × 248mm (21⅝ × 9¾in) | 349 × 248mm (13¾ × 9¾in) | 538 × 32mm (21⅛ × 1¼in) |
| 3 | 505 × 229mm (19⅞ × 9in) | 323 × 229mm (12¾ × 9in) | 493 × 32mm (19⅜ 1¼in) |
| 4 smallest | 460 × 210mm (18½ × 8¼in) | 298 × 210mm (11¾ × 8¼in) | 448 × 32mm (17⅝ × 1¼in) |

*The back rail gives stability to the legs.*

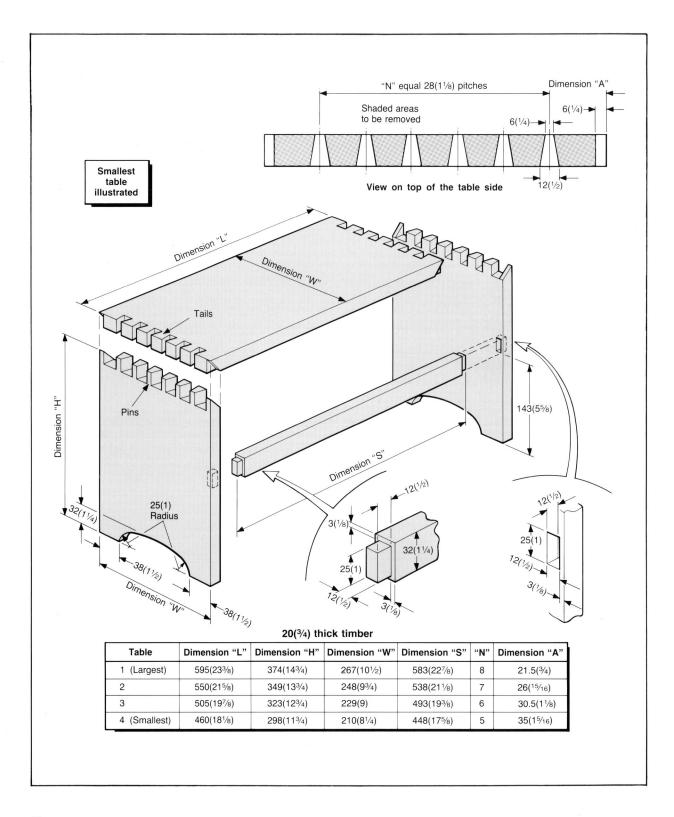

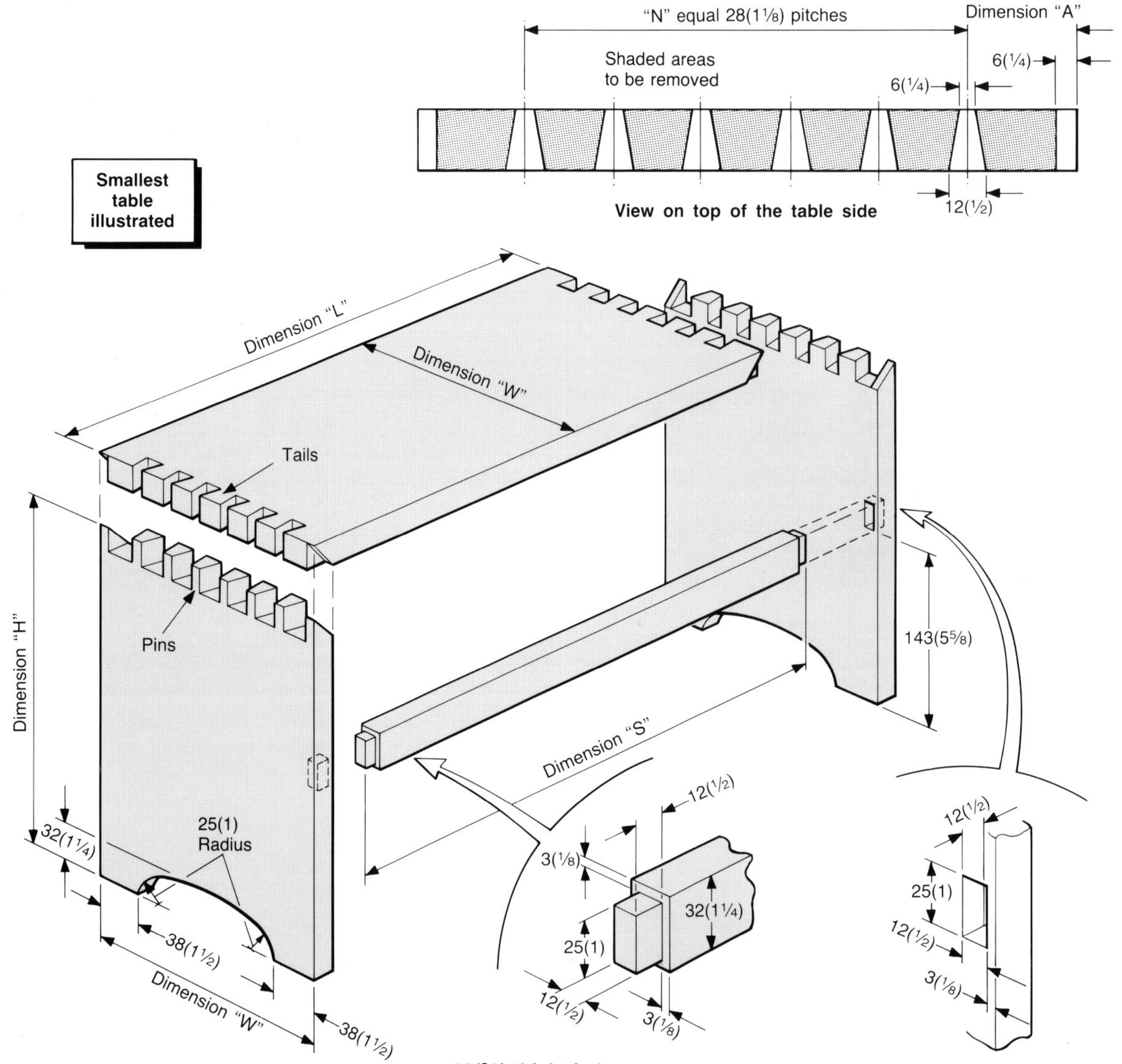
"N" equal 28(1⅛) pitches
Dimension "A"
Shaded areas to be removed
6(¼)
6(¼)
12(½)
View on top of the table side
Smallest table illustrated
Dimension "L"
Dimension "W"
Tails
Pins
Dimension "H"
143(5⅝)
Dimension "S"
32(1¼)
25(1) Radius
38(1½)
Dimension "W"
38(1½)
12(½)
3(⅛)
32(1¼)
25(1)
12(½)
3(⅛)
12(½)
25(1)
12(½)
3(⅛)

**20(¾) thick timber**

| Table | Dimension "L" | Dimension "H" | Dimension "W" | Dimension "S" | "N" | Dimension "A" |
|---|---|---|---|---|---|---|
| 1 (Largest) | 595(23⅜) | 374(14¾) | 267(10½) | 583(22⅞) | 8 | 21.5(¾) |
| 2 | 550(21⅝) | 349(13¾) | 248(9¾) | 538(21⅛) | 7 | 26(15/16) |
| 3 | 505(19⅞) | 323(12¾) | 229(9) | 493(19⅜) | 6 | 30.5(1⅛) |
| 4 (Smallest) | 460(18⅛) | 298(11¾) | 210(8¼) | 448(17⅝) | 5 | 35(1 5/16) |

# Country style bookcase

**Essential tools**
Electric router
Tenon saw
Coping saw or jigsaw
Counterbore drill
Plug cutter

## Fixing the shelves

The shelves are now fixed together with the top and bottom rails. Once again, it is vital to be accurate and draw in the shoulder lines clearly. It is also necessary to do a lot of marking out on the shelves – of the twin tenons that go through the shelf ends, of the two sets of shoulder lines, and of the mortice holes that take the wedges.

All the shelf joints are identical. The twin tusk tenons go right through the ends. To prevent the shelf from twisting, the shelf is housed into the ends, and to hold it all together the wedges go through the mortice holes in the tusk tenons. The shape of the wedges naturally puts pressure on to the ends and, once all the wedges are driven home and back fitted, the result is a very stable unit.

Now make a start by cutting the mortices in the ends. Before any cutting out is done, "knife over" – go over the pencil lines you made earlier with a knife – the areas that will be cut out. This severs the wood fibres and will leave a cleaner edge. The twin mortice holes need cutting from both sides, (**1**) while the housing only needs to be cut on the inside face. (**2**) It is always best to check everything twice before you begin cutting – there is nothing more frustrating than a housing cut on the wrong side!

Working from both sides, chop out the mortices. If you attempt to cut right through from one side only you run the risk of splitting the other. Take out an even depth of chips as you go. The housings are all cut on the inside edges with a chisel or an electric router. The electric router has become fairly common in most workshops and it certainly speeds up the cutting of the housings. It is at this stage that you will appreciate all the gauge lines knifed in as this leaves the cut edges from chisel and router very clean.

Now tackle the twin tusk tenons. It is best to cut the mortice wedge holes in these first. (**3** and **4**) With all

Wooden wedges have always been very important in most woodworking projects. Some joints have actually been devised with the wedge as the sole "fixing" method, and most effective they are. Today, because of the modern glues that are available, wedges are usually used as a decorative feature rather than for their strength in fixing and holding the

timber together. In this bookcase, the wedge is a fixing device for the timber; it also gives the bookcase a rustic look.

The dimensions of the bookcase can be varied according to need, and the design holds good for a longer or shorter unit. Most softwoods would be suitable for this project.

First fix both shelf ends together with "G" cramps or tape, and pencil in where the shelves will go. It is essential to make face, side and edge markings. Take the "G" cramps off and continue the pencil lines all round the ends. Accuracy at this stage is vital for a tidy job.

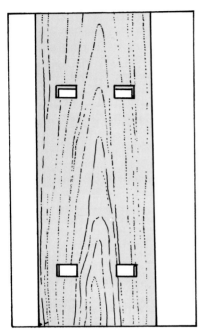

**1** *Mark out with a pencil where the shelves are to go. Then knife over the pencil marks of the areas to be cut out. Now, cut out twin mortice holes in the ends.*

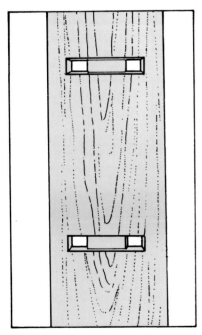

**2** *With a chisel, a router or a drill, cut out the housing between the twin mortice holes on the* inside *edge of each end only.*

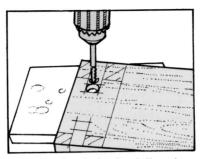

**3** *Working from both sides, drill out the centres of the mortice wedge holes.*

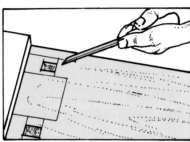

**4** *Use a very sharp chisel to square up the edges of the wedge holes.*

existing timber "in place" there is far less chance of a split. Cut the twin tusks with a tenon saw. The waste between the two tenons is removed with a coping saw or a jigsaw. Once this has been done, use a very sharp chisel to "tidy up" along the shoulder line. (**5**) This operation has to be done on all the shelves.

**5** *Now cut the twin tusk tenons with a tenon saw. Remove the waste between them with a coping saw. Use the chisel to tidy up along the shoulder line.*

## Glueing up

The top and the plinth at the bottom are simply fitted into mortice holes. The plinth at the bottom gives the bottom shelf support, while at its top back edge it holds the tongued and grooved back in a rebate.

Before attempting to glue up the shelves, fit everything together to check that all the joints marry up. (**6** and **7**)

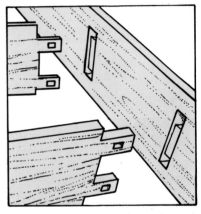

**6** *Fit the tusk tenons into the mortices and check that all the joints marry up.*

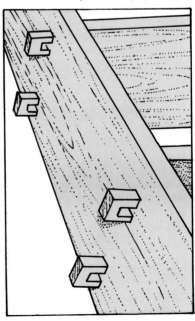

**7** *When the tusk tenons are in place they should look like this.*

Next, cut and shape the wedges. It is advisable to make a few spares. I cut some fractionally larger than others, so if I find that one set of joints requires just a little more pressure I have the slightly larger wedges available.

The ends are cut to shape using a jigsaw. (**8**)

*8 Shape the ends with a jigsaw.*

When you are sure that everything fits together well, clean up before glueing – it saves a great deal of time. I always use my hand plane to work over all the shelves, ends etc. It is surprising how dirty pine gets while the joints are being cut, and the clean up means that all the pencil marks can be completely removed.

Glueing up is best done with an assistant as this is quite a large piece of work to handle. It is best to lay it flat on the floor. Apply a little glue to the joints, and with the wedges that should be sufficient to fix the shelves and ends tightly together. However, sometimes you need to use a set of sash cramps to give the shelves an extra "twank" just to pull everything together.

A spot of glue on the sides of each wedge is a good idea. Don't drive the wedges in too hard. There is a point at which you will be able to feel that it is tight, and at that point stop driving it in. (**9**) It is a good idea to protect the

end of the wedge with a piece of waste wood, or the end of the wedge gets rather chewed up.

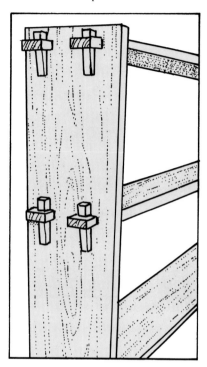

*9 Now put the cut and shaped wedges through the tenons.*

## Shelf dividers

Shelf dividers are very useful to keep books tidy. The traditional method of fixing them is to cut housing joints in the shelves and slot the dividers into the housings. However, I would opt for a much simpler method of fixing the shelf units. Cut dividers to length, push fit them between the shelves, and then screw them on from either side of the shelf. (**10**) Screws would look ugly on the surface of the shelves, so use a 12mm (½in) counterbore drill to sink the screws and then a plug cutter to fashion 12mm plugs from waste wood. Glue the plugs into the counterbore holes. You can buy a counterbore drill and a plug cutter as a set, and will discover, once you have them, just how useful they are.

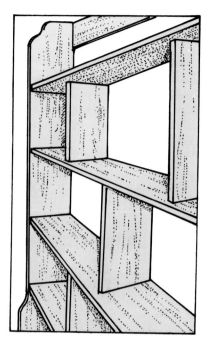

*10 Push fit the shelf dividers if you are using them. Then sink the screws with a counterbore drill, disguising the holes with 12mm (½in) plugs made from waste wood.*

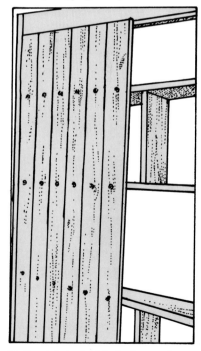

*11 Panel the back of the bookcase – the easiest part of the job.*

### Fixing the back

The back is the easiest part of the job, and is made from tongued and grooved panels. These boards are readily available as wall panelling in most builders merchants and all the large D.I.Y. stores.

Cut the panels to length and simply screw them into place. (11) If you wish to save waste with the shorter lengths this can be done, but it is advisable after two short pieces have been used to fit a full length piece next. Once the tongues and grooves are locked together a good strong back is formed. You will have to cut and fit in the last panel rather carefully as it is most unlikely that the panels will fit exactly.

The appearance of the unit is greatly enhanced if you use a router with a small beading cutter on the shelf fronts and sides. This small chamfered line removes any tendency for the unit to become square in appearance.

Now everything is in place, use fine glasspaper to work over the whole unit before applying the finish of your choice.

*The decorative and functional wood wedges.*

**COUNTRY STYLE BOOKCASE CUTTING LIST**

| | | |
|---|---|---|
| Shelf ends | 2 off | 1,975 × 216 × 32mm (77¾ × 8½ × 1¼in) timber |
| Narrow shelves | 4 off | 1,791 × 168 × 20mm (70½ × 6⅝ × ¾in) timber |
| Wide shelves | 2 off | 1,791 × 200 × 20mm (70½ × 7⅞ × ¾in) timber |
| Wedges | make from | 965 × 54 × 12mm (38 × 2⅛ × ½in) timber |
| Dividers | 1 off | 238 × 146 × 20mm (9⅜ × 5¾ × ¾in) timber |
| | 2 off | 359 × 146 × 20mm (14⅛ × 5¾ × ¾in) timber |
| | 4 off | 308 × 146 × 20mm (12⅛ × 5¾ × ¾in) timber |
| | 2 off | 257 × 146 × 20mm (10⅛ × 5¾ × ¾in) timber |
| Top rail | 1 off | 1,676 × 102 × 22mm (66 × 4 × ⅞in) timber |
| Plinth | 1 off | 1,676 × 83 × 22mm (66 × 3¼ × ⅞in) timber |
| Back | 12 off | 1,803 × 121 × 16mm (71 × 4¾ × ⅝in) tongue and grooved board |

*The chamferred edge takes off the squareness of the shelves.*

*Alternatively staggered shelf supports.*

*The woodplugs that are used to hide the counterbore holes.*

*The back fits neatly into rebates cut at the side and base.*

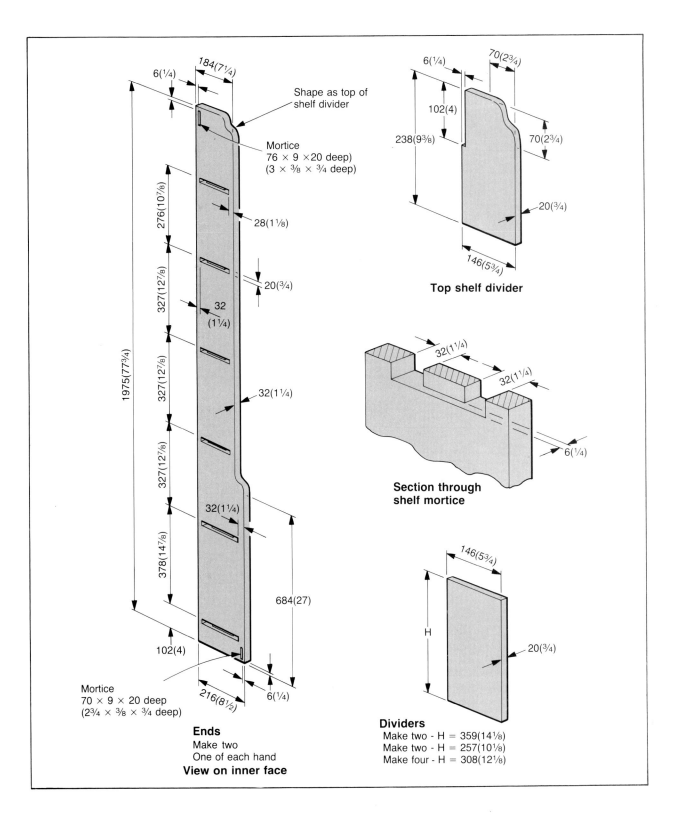

**Top shelf divider**

**Section through shelf mortice**

Shape as top of shelf divider

Mortice
76 × 9 ×20 deep)
(3 × ³⁄₈ × ³⁄₄ deep)

Mortice
70 × 9 × 20 deep
(2³⁄₄ × ³⁄₈ × ³⁄₄ deep)

**Ends**
Make two
One of each hand
**View on inner face**

**Dividers**
Make two - H = 359(14¹⁄₈)
Make two - H = 257(10¹⁄₈)
Make four - H = 308(12¹⁄₈)

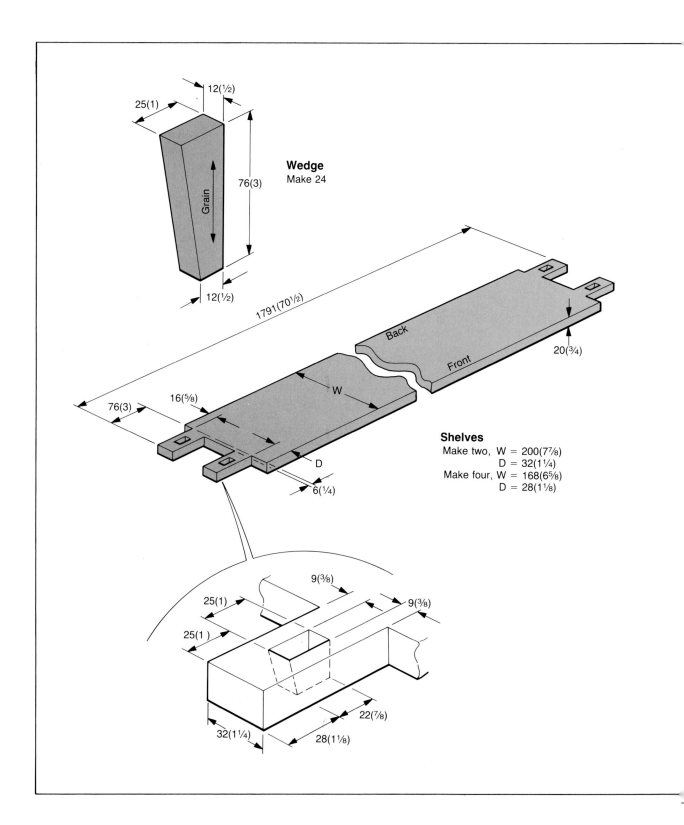

**Wedge**
Make 24

25(1)
12(½)
Grain
76(3)
12(½)

1791(70½)

Back
Front
20(¾)

76(3)
16(⅝)
W
D
6(¼)

**Shelves**
Make two, W = 200(7⅞)
D = 32(1¼)
Make four, W = 168(6⅝)
D = 28(1⅛)

25(1)
9(⅜)
9(⅜)
25(1)
22(⅞)
32(1¼)
28(1⅛)

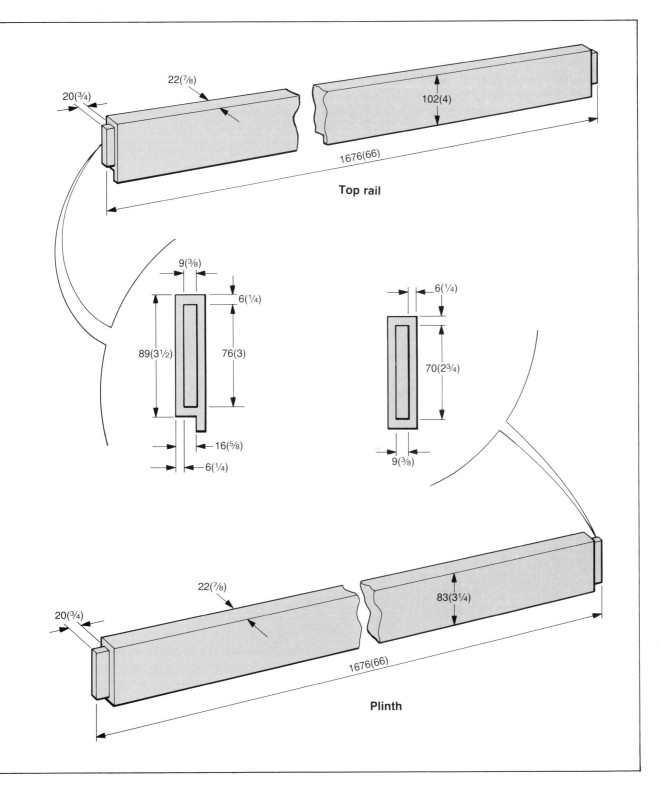

22(⁷⁄₈)

20(³⁄₄)

102(4)

1676(66)

**Top rail**

9(³⁄₈)

6(¹⁄₄)

89(3¹⁄₂)

76(3)

16(⁵⁄₈)

6(¹⁄₄)

6(¹⁄₄)

70(2³⁄₄)

9(³⁄₈)

22(⁷⁄₈)

20(³⁄₄)

83(3¹⁄₄)

1676(66)

**Plinth**

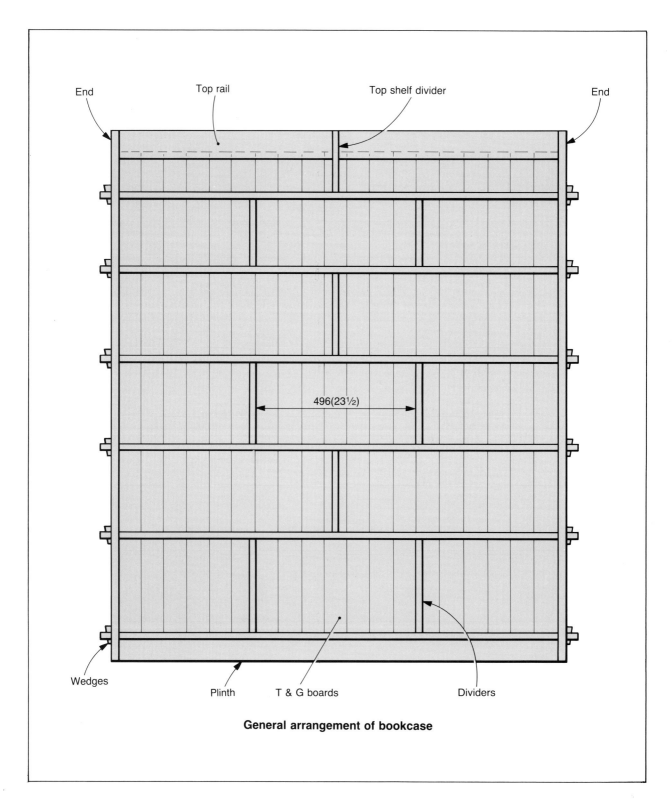

**General arrangement of bookcase**

# Gate leg table

The great advantage of the gate leg table is that it saves so much space because the leaves of the top can be folded down when not in use.

The centre section of the table needs to be fairly solid to give the leaves and folding gate legs support. The centre section can be used for drawers to hold napkins, tablecloths or cutlery. This particular table has two drawers. Special attention has been paid to the design of the folding gates which fold away neatly behind the main four legs of the centre section.

## Main centre section

Make a start by marking out the four main legs of the centre section. To accommodate the drawers the side rails need to be very deep. If the legs had mortices cut out in them to the full width of the rails then the top of the legs would be weakened, so it is necessary to adapt a different jointing technique – a twin tenon. This has the great advantage of two smaller mortices in the tops of the legs and correspondingly smaller tenons to fit. To prevent the rail twisting at either end and in the middle, haunches are cut on the tenons.

Using a mortice gauge, mark the mortices in the legs and the tenons on

**1** *Follow the pencil lines carefully with the tenon saw.*

101

the rails. Then cut down the tenons with a brass-backed tenon saw. Make sure that you do not cut below the gauge line.(**1**)

Now remove the waste between the tenons with a coping saw. With the blade set at a 90° angle to the back of the coping saw, feed the blade down the left side of the section to be removed.(**2** and **3**) The haunches on

**2** *Sawing gently, work the blade round until it is horizontal.*

**3** *Cut along the bottom of the section. Note the position of the hands.*

the ends are now cut with the tenon saw.(**4**)

Once the tenons are finished on the long side rails, the mortices have to be cut.(**5**) Always remember to fasten the leg firmly to the bench top with a "G" cramp. It is not good practice to chop mortices in the vice. This is because all the hammering with a mallet will loosen the coach bolts that

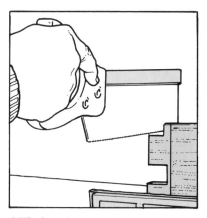

**4** *The haunches are now cut.*

hold the vice to the bench.

I usually draw a pencil line on the back of the chisel to give an indication of when I have chopped to the correct depth. It is always best to take shallow cuts with the mortice chisel, removing an even row of chips. The shape of the chisel is designed to make the chips of wood rise up out of the wood. After cutting along the mortice you will have a row of raised chippings that now need to be cut away. It is a good idea not to go right up against the gauge line, but keep back a little and lever out some of the chips. The technique is to use many cuts – not than just half a dozen.

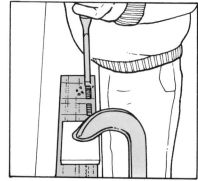

**5** *It is important to stand behind or in line with the mortice being chopped.*

The section between the two mortices is cut out in exactly the same way, only you must remember only a

shallow trench is needed – don't get carried away!

Mark in the depth of the haunch, then use a tenon saw to cut down the gauge lines.(**6** and **7**)

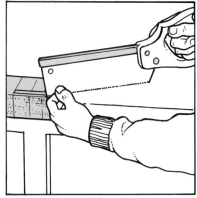

**6** *Cut the haunch at the top. Note the position of the thumb supporting the tenon saw blade.*

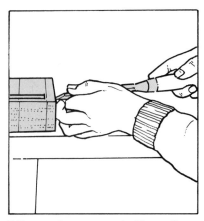

**7** *Remove the waste wood with a mallet and chisel. This is very easy to do as the wood breaks away along the grain.*

It should now be possible to fit both mortice and tenons together – straight from "saw and chisel". However, if you are not in practice, or if this is your first big project, do not be too concerned if you have to do a little bit of trimming with a chisel to get the joint to fit snugly.(**8**)

The rough surface left by the saw on the tenon provides a natural "key" for the glue to bond to when the joints

**8** *With a leg in the vice the tenon is pushed into the mortices.*

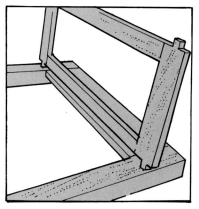

**10** *It is always a good idea to pencil numbers or letters on the joints once they have been fitted – it saves time and patience when you come to glue everything together.*

place. First cut out the tie rail, with twin tenons on each end. Then offer up the rail to the top of the leg.**(12)**

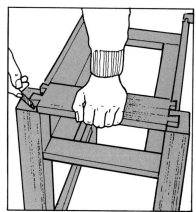

**12** *Pencil in the dovetails.*

are all assembled. Now cut the mortice and tenons for the rails at the bottom of the table legs.

The drawer is supported by two rails and two runners. The runners fit into the rails with single stub (or stopped) mortice and tenon joints.**(9)**

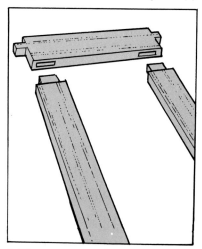

**9** *The runners are stub morticed and tenoned into the rails.*

The rails in turn fit into the legs with the same joints. A twin joint is not possible here because the second stub mortice would "run into" the mortice and tenon joint on the long rails.

Assemble the runners and rails and offer up to the legs to check for fit.**(10)** If the fit is not exact, trim as necessary

using a chisel. Now assemble the pieces of the centre section made so far, but do not glue yet.**(11)**

**11** *Assemble the pieces prepared so far to check for fit.*

A top rail with two dovetails cut in it not only ties the legs together at the top, but also ties the leg and top rail together. The rail also provides a good place for screws to be fixed to hold the table top centre section in

Once the dovetails have been marked in pencil, place the side framework on the bench and chop out the dovetail sockets.**(13)** Before you

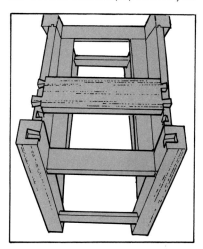

**13** *The complete rail.*

fit the rail in place, drill and countersink holes on the front and back edges (underside) of the rail. These pre-prepared holes are a great help when you need to fix the top.

The short side rails, drawer rails, runners and dovetail rails can now be glued in place. You will find it extremely helpful when glueing not to try and do it all in one go. It is far easier to glue the long rails of both sides together first. This step-by-step assembly prevents the whole job becoming festooned with sash cramps.

Check for squareness of the frame when the sash cramps have been tightened. it is vital that the framework is square, otherwise the drawers will not run true.

**The drawers**

Today, modern technology has established many easy methods for constructing drawers. The traditional drawer has been developed over hundreds of years and, although at first glance you may consider that all the different techniques are the invention of some cabinet maker who was looking for a job, you would be wrong – there is a reason for each part of the construction.

Begin by preparing one front, two sides and one back for both drawers. Plane the front to fit the drawer opening in the table. It is always best to make this a very tight fit. Mark in pencil the bottom of the drawer front L and R so that you will always know which way to position it.(**14**)

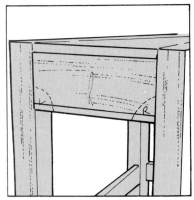

14 *The front must fit snugly – note the L and R pencil marks.*

The joint at the front of the drawer is a lapped dovetail. This is a particularly practical joint for this application as it is hidden from the front edge, but the dovetails prevent the drawer sides separating when the drawer is in use. The contents of a drawer can be quite heavy and the dovetail is especially strong.

Mark the dovetail pins on the end of the drawer front. Then cut down the sides.(**15**)

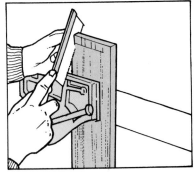

15 *Use a backsaw to cut down the sides.*

A bevel edged chisel is used to chop out the waste. However, before starting, position a piece of timber behind the drawer front, thus giving rigidity while the cutting out is done.(**16**) It is necessary to work

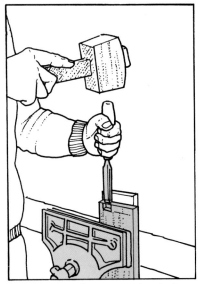

16 *Cutting out the waste needs to be done carefully and it is necessary to chop right back to the gauge line.*

carefully, as the chisel is cutting with the grain and there is a tendency to split the timber. Removing the waste wood is a combination of both cutting techniques.(**17**)

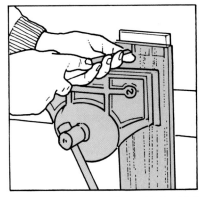

17 *Final tidying up is done with the chisel in both hands. Note exactly how the chisel is held.*

Once the pins on the drawer front have been cut down, mark the tails onto the drawer sides.(**18**) Then cut

18 *Mark the position of the tails with a pencil.*

out the tails.(**19**) Use a coping saw to remove the waste between the tails, then a small bevel edged chisel to trim down to the gauge line. Any other chisel would mark the sides of the tails.

Tidy up the edges of the drawer with a chisel.(**20**) If you have marked out the finished joint carefully, it will

**19** *Use a small dovetail saw to cut out the tails.*

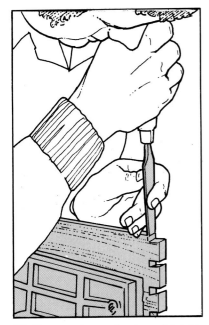

**20** *Always make sure that the work is held securely, otherwise a nasty cut may be the result.*

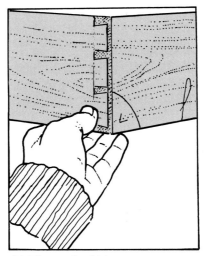

**21** *The completed joint.*

**22** *Use a plough plane or a router to cut the groove.*

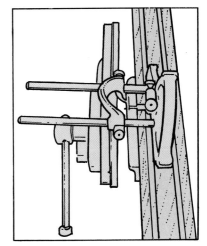

**23** *Take a new piece of wood to cut the moulding.*

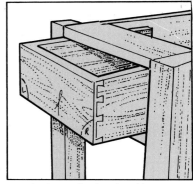

**24** *The drawer fitted in the table.*

go together without unsightly gaps.(**21**) At the back of the drawer, the dovetails are through dovetails and these should now be marked out and cut (*see technique on p.86*)

With all the joints cut, the front of the drawer needs to be "ploughed out" to receive the drawer base.(**22**) Traditionally cabinet makers did not groove out the drawer sides as this tends to weaken them. A moulding

therefore should be cut to take the drawer base. I always start with a wider piece of timber than I need as it makes it possible to hold the timber while the groove is being cut.(**23**)

The drawer is now fitted together and cramped up "dry" (without glue). Once this is done, be particularly careful to check for squareness – this is absolutely vital, otherwise the drawer will not close when fitted. When you are satisfied, remove the cramps, apply glue to the dovetails, and recramp the drawer, again being very careful to check for squareness.

When the glue has dried the

mouldings are glued onto the drawer sides. Make sure that the grooves will take the drawer base and line up all

around the drawer. Trim and fit plywood for the drawer base.(**24**)

### The gate legs

The gate legs are formed by cutting mortice and tenon joints. Once the frameworks are completed, they have to be hinged to the main body of the table. In order to get the legs to fold flat against the main framework the hinges have to be recessed totally into the gate leg frameworks.(**25**)

The leg that supports the table flap is not fitted up tight against the main table legs, but set back just a little.

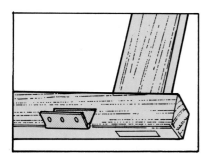

**25** *Fit the hinges into the gate legs, then screw them to the main table framework.*

This helps to give a good handhold on the leg when it has to be folded out from the main framework. Before finally fitting the legs to the main framework, use a router to smooth all the edges.(**26**) These cutters are expensive, but they are well worth the cost and give a superb finish.

**26** *The router cutter is fitted with a ball bearing that prevents the cutter from burning wood as the cutter is worked around the frames.*

### The table top

The table top is made from fairly narrow planks. The reason for using these is to minimise the movement of the timber. It is also important to arrange the grain direction at the end of each plank to counteract that of the one next to it.

The planks are held together with glue and dowel rods. The dowel rods give a greater glueing area and thus increase the strength of the jointed planks. Place the planks side by side and mark across the plank edges using a carpenters' square. The holes to take the dowel rods should be drilled a little oversize to allow for alignment of the parts and for the glue.

After the holes have been drilled, the edges of the planks need to be "trued" using a jointer plane. As the name suggests, this plane is only used when jointing planks. The length of the sole ensures that the plank edge is really flat. Truing up all the planks takes a little time and patience, but the end result is worth the trouble.

To give extra strength to the planks being jointed, use a Stanley knife to cut a key onto the plank edges. You do not have to score deep lines, but a criss-cross pattern allows the glue to get into the wood fibres.

The centre section is glued up in one operation as are the two leaves. It is essential to use sash cramps for this job. Place the cramps on both the top and the underside of the timber being glued. The cramp bars help to keep the planks flat while the glue cures. When the glue has dried, use a plane or belt sander to get the top flat.

Brass back hinges are used to fix the table top flaps to the centre section. The back flap hinges are recessed on the underside of the table. It is advisable to use four hinges per flap.

The table flaps can now be shaped using a jigsaw. Remove the saw cuts with a spokeshave and make sure that the edges are perfectly smoothed.

### Fixing the table top

The centre section of the table is screwed to the top. The screws pass through the top dovetail rail. The

*The finished gate leg table folded ready to stow away.*

positioning of the table top is far easier if the top is placed onto the work bench and the centre framework turned upside down and placed onto the top. Adjust the top so that it is equidistant from all edges, then fix with screws.

To give the leaves extra support and to provide gate leg "stops", a batten of timber is now screwed to the underside of each leaf. Make a paper pattern of the leg shape, transfer this onto the batten and cut out the recess that will accommodate the leg and act as the stop. The battens are now screwed onto the leaves.

Now turn the table the right way up, open the leaves and the gate legs. Check that everything is flush.

The table needs a nice rounded edge. This is easily accomplished with an electric router and cutter.

## Finishing off

You will always find that planks of timber that have been glued together require a good deal of work. A belt sander fitted with a "sanding shoe" is a great help in achieving an even, flat surface. After this treatment, a cabinet scraper will give the very best surface; however, sharpening and using a cabinet scraper needs some practice.

The table legs and frames are now all very carefully "worked out" with fine grade glasspaper. The wood is then treated with gloss varnish. Use a lint-free cloth to apply the varnish as it gives a much better finish than a brush. When the varnish is dry, work over the whole framework and top again with very fine glasspaper.

Repeat this whole process three times. Finally finish off with a good wax polish.

| GATE LEG TABLE CUTTING LIST | | |
|---|---|---|
| Table top | 8 off | 498 × 98 × 22mm (19⅝ × 3⅞ × ⅞in) timber |
| Leaves | 16 off | 473 × 98 × 22mm (18⅝ × 3⅞ × ⅞in) timber |
| Main legs | 4 off | 762 × 67 × 57mm (30 × 2⅝ × 2¼in) timber |
| Side rails | 2 off | 673 × 152 × 22mm (26½ × 6 × ⅞in) timber |
| Lower ties | 2 off | 673 × 57 × 22mm (26½ × 2¼ × ⅞in) timber |
| | 2 off | 381 × 57 × 22mm (15 × 2¼ × ⅞in) timber |
| Top rails | 2 off | 375 × 102 × 22mm (14¾ × 4 × ⅞in) timber |
| Drawer support | 2 off | 381 × 67 × 22mm (15 × 2⅝ × ⅞in) timber |
| | 2 off | 673 × 48 × 22mm (26½ × 1⅞ × ⅞in) timber |
| Gate legs | 2 off | 584 × 38 × 32mm (23 × 1½ × 1¼in) timber |
| | 2 off | 762 × 38 × 32mm (30 × 1½ × 1¼in) timber |
| | 2 off | 286 × 70 × 32mm (11¼ × 2¾ × 1¼in) timber |
| | 2 off | 286 × 57 × 32mm (11¼ × 2¼ × 1¼in) timber |
| Gate leg stops | 2 off | 416 × 83 × 22mm (16⅜ × 3¼ × ⅞in) timber |
| Drawer stops | 4 off | 130 × 22 × 20mm (5⅛ × ⅞ × ¾in) timber |
| Drawer front | 1 off | 318 × 111 × 20mm (12½ × 4⅜ × ¾in) timber |
| Drawer sides | 2 off | 327 × 111 × 16mm (12⅞ × 4⅜ × ⅝in) timber |
| Drawer back | 1 off | 318 × 89 × 16mm (12½ × 3½ × ⅝in) timber |
| Drawer base | 1 off | 321 × 273 × 6mm (12⅝ × 10¾ × ¼in) plywood |
| Base supports | 2 off | 314 × 20 × 12mm (12⅜ × ¾ × ½in) timber |
| Concealing strip | 2 off | 298 × 12 × 6mm (11¾ × ½ × ¼in) timber |
| Ancillaries | 8 off | 25 × 38mm (1 × 1½in) hinges |
| | 2 off | 25 × 76mm (1 × 3in) hinges |
| | 2 off | 20 × 51mm (¾ × 2in) hinges |
| | 2 off | ornate brass handles |

*The cutlery drawer with the concealing strip that holds the bottom in place.*

*The gate leg arrangement.*

*The batten under the table that provides essential support.*

*The bottom of the drawer.*

*The inside of the drawer.*

*A close-up of the back of the drawer showing how the drawer bottom fits neatly into the rebate at the side.*

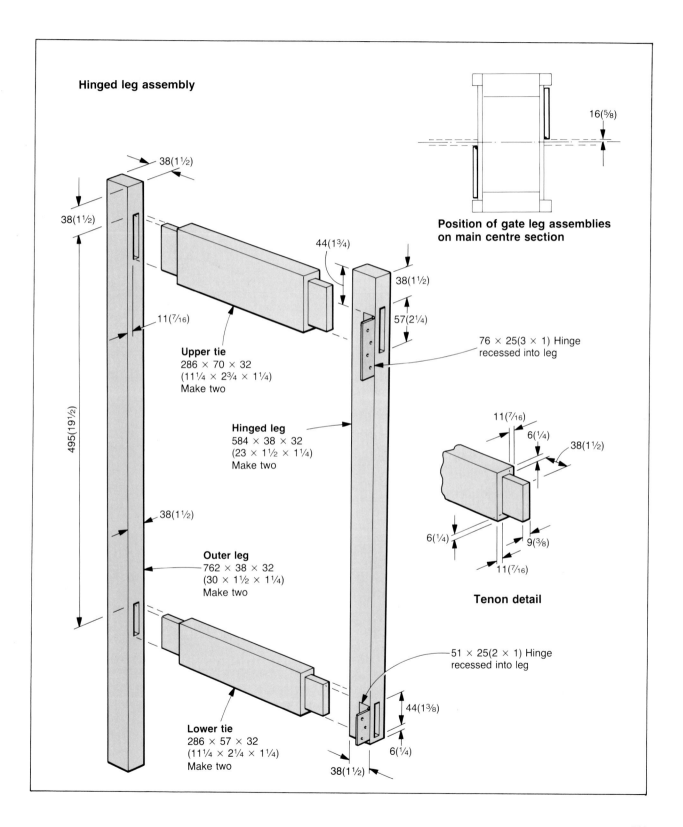

**Hinged leg assembly**

38(1½)

38(1½)

11(⁷⁄₁₆)

**Upper tie**
286 × 70 × 32
(11¼ × 2¾ × 1¼)
Make two

495(19½)

38(1½)

**Outer leg**
762 × 38 × 32
(30 × 1½ × 1¼)
Make two

**Lower tie**
286 × 57 × 32
(11¼ × 2¼ × 1¼)
Make two

44(1¾)

38(1½)

57(2¼)

76 × 25(3 × 1) Hinge
recessed into leg

**Hinged leg**
584 × 38 × 32
(23 × 1½ × 1¼)
Make two

51 × 25(2 × 1) Hinge
recessed into leg

44(1⅜)

6(¼)

38(1½)

16(⅝)

**Position of gate leg assemblies
on main centre section**

11(⁷⁄₁₆)

6(¼)

38(1½)

6(¼)

9(⅜)

11(⁷⁄₁₆)

**Tenon detail**

111

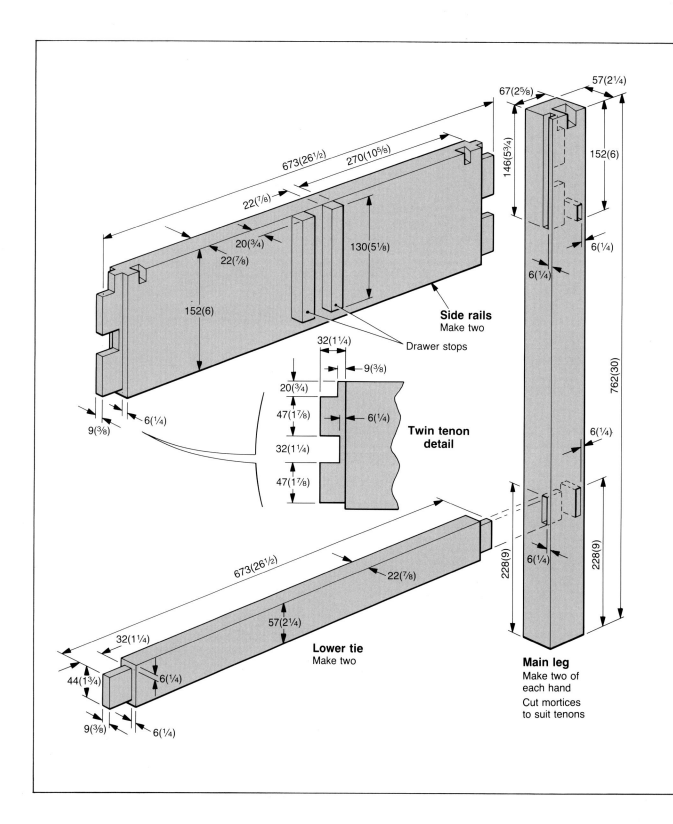

673(26½)    270(10⅝)

22(⅞)

20(¾)

22(⅞)

130(5⅛)

**Side rails**
Make two

Drawer stops

152(6)

9(⅜)    6(¼)

32(1¼)

9(⅜)

20(¾)

47(1⅞)    6(¼)

**Twin tenon detail**

32(1¼)

47(1⅞)

673(26½)

22(⅞)

57(2¼)

**Lower tie**
Make two

32(1¼)

44(1¾)    6(¼)

9(⅜)    6(¼)

67(2⅝)    57(2¼)

146(5¾)    152(6)

6(¼)

6(¼)

762(30)

6(¼)

6(¼)

228(9)    228(9)

**Main leg**
Make two of
each hand
Cut mortices
to suit tenons

*Country style bookcase (see page 91) and corner shelf unit (see page 10).*

*Coffee grinder (see page 21), dining chairs (see page 28) and gate leg table (see page 101).*

*Rocking cradle (see page 142) and cottage stools (see page 16).*

*Corner cabinet (see page 37).*

*Bed settee (see page 126).*

*Welsh dresser (see page 58).*

*Fire surround (see page 76).*

*Pine bed (see page 150).*

*Nest of tables (see page 86).*

*Computer desk (see page 116).*

Gazebo (see page 185), garden table and benches (see page 159)

*Garden shed (see page 169).*

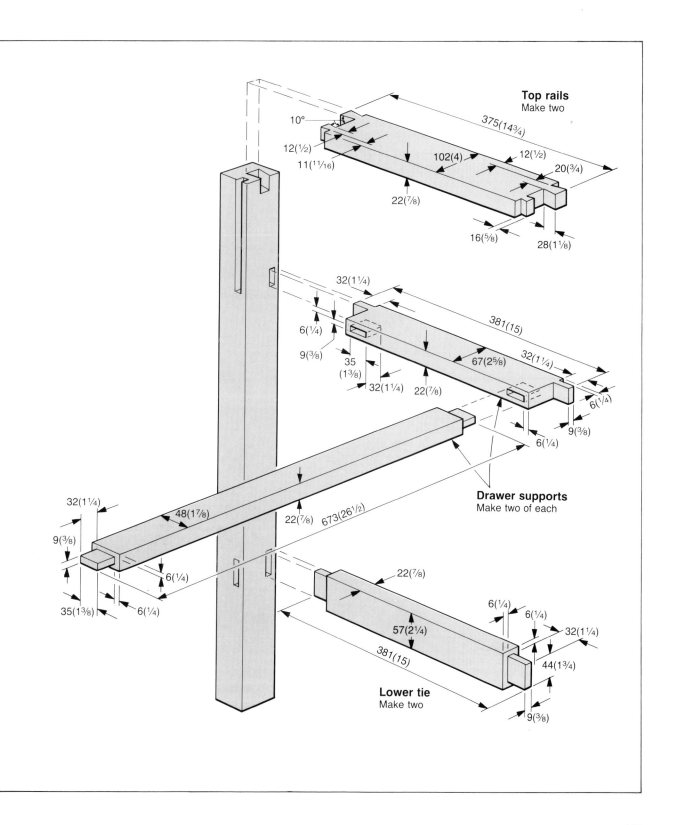

**Top rails**
Make two

375(14¾)

10°

12(½)

11(¹¹⁄₁₆)

102(4)

12(½)

20(¾)

22(⁷⁄₈)

16(⁵⁄₈)

28(1⅛)

32(1¼)

6(¼)

9(⅜)

381(15)

35
(1⅜)

32(1¼)

67(2⅝)

32(1¼)

22(⁷⁄₈)

6(¼)

9(⅜)

6(¼)

**Drawer supports**
Make two of each

32(1¼)

48(1⅞)

22(⁷⁄₈)

673(26½)

9(⅜)

6(¼)

35(1⅜)

6(¼)

22(⁷⁄₈)

6(¼)

6(¼)

32(1¼)

57(2¼)

44(1¾)

381(15)

9(⅜)

**Lower tie**
Make two

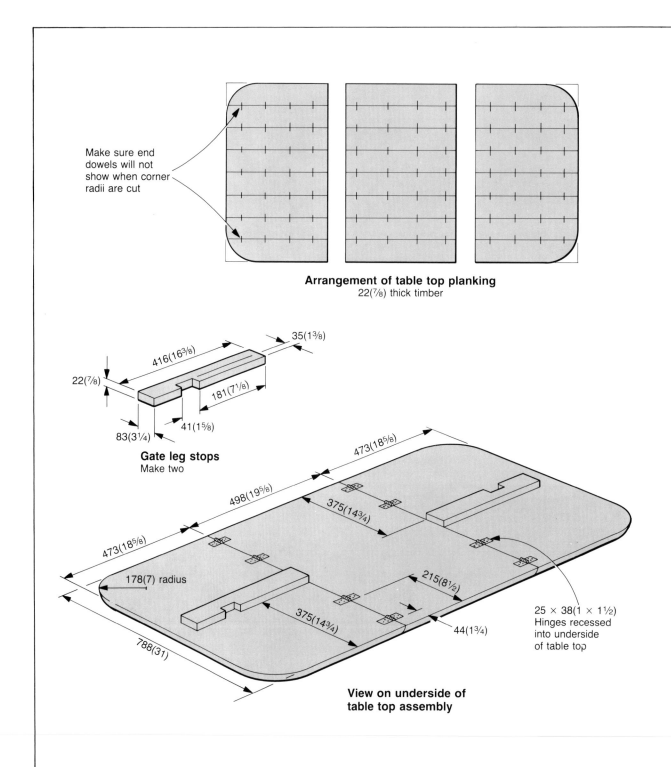

Make sure end dowels will not show when corner radii are cut

**Arrangement of table top planking**
22($^7/_8$) thick timber

35(1$^3/_8$)

416(16$^3/_8$)

22($^7/_8$)

181(7$^1/_8$)

83(3$^1/_4$)

41(1$^5/_8$)

**Gate leg stops**
Make two

473(18$^5/_8$)

498(19$^5/_8$)

375(14$^3/_4$)

473(18$^5/_8$)

178(7) radius

215(8$^1/_2$)

375(14$^3/_4$)

44(1$^3/_4$)

788(31)

25 × 38(1 × 1$^1/_2$)
Hinges recessed into underside of table top

**View on underside of table top assembly**

114

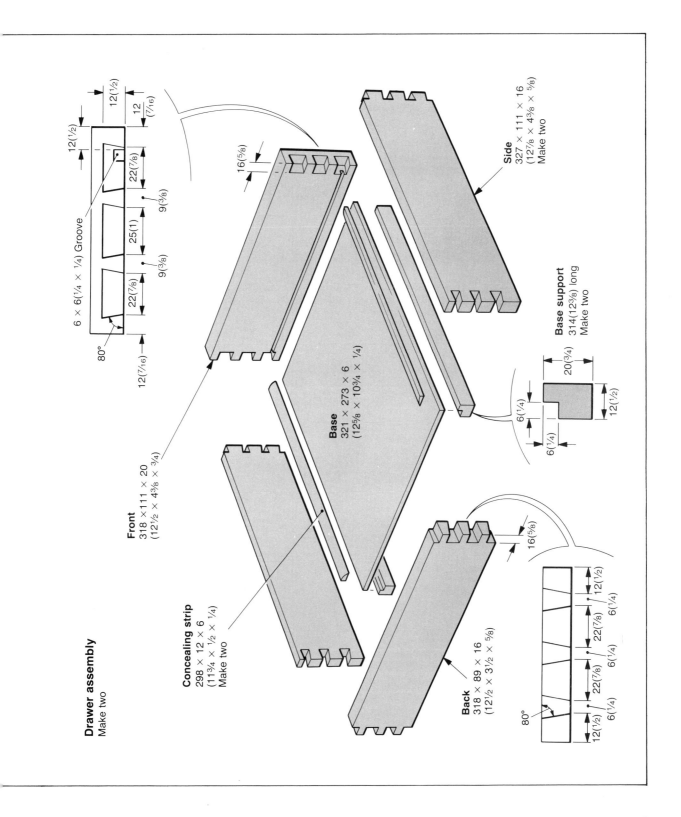

**Drawer assembly**
Make two

6 × 6(¼ × ¼) Groove

12(½)
12(7/16)
12(½)
22(7/8)
9(3/8)
25(1)
9(3/8)
22(7/8)
80°
12(7/16)

16(5/8)

**Front**
318 × 111 × 20
(12½ × 4⅜ × ¾)

**Concealing strip**
298 × 12 × 6
(11¾ × ½ × ¼)
Make two

**Base**
321 × 273 × 6
(12⅝ × 10¾ × ¼)

**Side**
327 × 111 × 16
(12⅞ × 4⅜ × ⅝)
Make two

**Base support**
314(12⅜) long
Make two

20(¾)
6(¼)
6(¼)
12(½)

**Back**
318 × 89 × 16
(12½ × 3½ × ⅝)

16(5/8)
12(½)
6(¼)
22(7/8)
6(¼)
22(7/8)
6(¼)
12(½)
80°

115

# Computer desk

**Essential tools**
Tenon saw
Smoothing plane
Handsaw or electric circular saw
  with tungsten tipped blade
Stanley knife or electric trimmer
Melamine tape

A computer desk is the most efficient way to house home computer equipment. Measure your machinery to see if it will fit in and on this desk, and if not, adjust the basic desk measurements accordingly. The design keeps all the cables in trunking, so that there is a clear working surface. The framework of the desk is constructed by a variety of halving joints, and the work surfaces are in melamine faced chipboard. The recessing techniques to cut melamine without breaking the edges are described in detail.

### The halving joint

The halving joint is one of the most useful joints to master. A halving joint is when two pieces of timber are jointed by removing half the thickness of each and slotting them together. In this particular case, the whole framework of the desk is constructed by different kinds of halving joint.

Technically, where a halving joint comes at the end of two pieces, it is called a "halved angle". If the joint comes in the middle of a rail, it is called a "halved T". And if two pieces of wood cross over each other, it is known as a "cross halving". What all these joints have in common is the marking out and cutting.

### The framework

From the working drawing, mark out the legs, feet and cross rails. Carefully select the face side face edge. With a marking gauge, score all the necessary lines and then shade over the area to be cut out. (**1**)

Using a tenon saw, cut down the vertical gauge lines on either side of the wood to be removed. If you also make a parallel cut between the gauge lines, you will find it easier to take out the waste wood. Be careful not to saw below the horizontal gauge line.

With a 24mm (1in) bevel edged or firmer chisel, start cutting out the wood in the middle of the joint. (**2**)

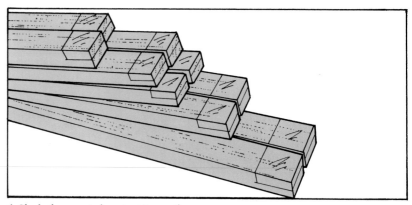

**1** *Shade the areas to be cut out in pencil.*

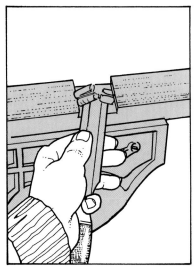

**2** *Angle the chisel upwards and work from both sides of the piece of timber.*

Halfway through, turn the piece of timber around in the vice. (**3**) The apex formed then has to be chiselled away. Check with a steel straight edge that the bottom of the joint is level across its entire length.

Now repeat the cutting and chiselling operation on the other half of the joint.

When both joints are cut they

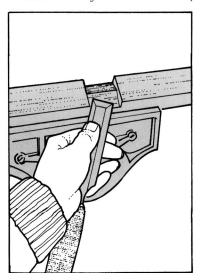

**3** *An apex will form in the centre of the timber.*

should be a very tight fit, allowing for a shaving to be removed by smoothing plane when cleaning up before the glueing stage. (**4**)

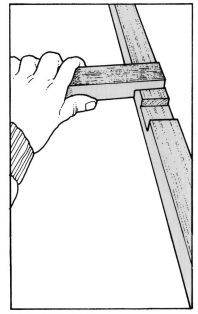

**4** *The finished joint.*

When all the joints have been cut, clean up all the timbers with a sharp smoothing plane. Then glue the two end frames together.

Both end frames are held together at the lower end by two cross rails. At the top, cross rails are fitted to give support to the melamine board. Glue the rails in place. (**5**)

**The work surfaces**

The storage area and desk top are made from melamine board secured at the ends in rebates. The solid pine ends match the legs and desk framework.

The melamine chipboard has to be cut to length. It is quite easy to buy the correct width, but the lengths are more difficult. The problem with this type of board is to cut it cleanly. Like plywood, it is easy to end up with broken edges. However, there are a number of techniques which lead to a good clean cut.

**a) Masking tape**

Masking tape attached to the entire length of the area to be cut will help prevent the edges from "breaking out".

**b) A hand saw**

A very fine-toothed hand saw is ideal for cutting melamine board. However, the saw is very quickly blunted.

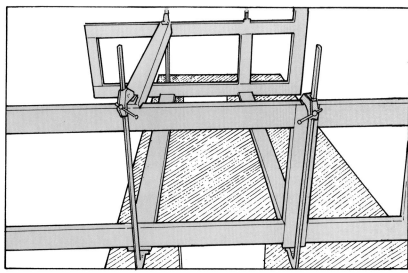

**5** *Hold the cross rails in place with cramps until the glue has cured.*

117

## c) The electric saw

The most successful method is to use an electric saw. The saw needs a blade with tungsten carbide teeth, which are more suitable for cutting man-made boards than the teeth of a hand saw.

It is very important that the board is supported along its entire length and that, when it is cut, one half does not "fall off", or the teeth of the saw will "chip off" the edge. For such wide boards, it is necessary to fix a batten across the board, and to secure it with a clamp at 90° to the edge. This batten acts as a guide as the saw cuts across the board.

It is essential to wear protective goggles when cutting, as wood particles will fly off the saw blade, and may damage your eyes.

Run the machine up to full speed before beginning to cut. Keeping your wrists steady, feed the machine very steadily across the board. (6)

6 *When cutting the melamine with an electric saw, "lock up" your wrists and drive one steady cut without pausing or hesitating.*

Do not hurry the process, and make sure that you make the cut with one clean pass. If you hesitate or slightly rock the machine, the blade will damage the melamine surface. If at all possible experiment on a piece of waste wood first.

The pine ends now have to be rebated to take the board. The depth of each rebate is the thickness of the melamine board. (7)

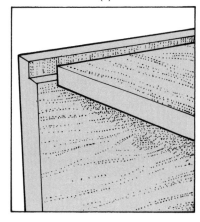

7 *The rebates can be cut with a rebate plane or router.*

When all the ends have been rebated, glue and screw the melamine into the rebate. (8) To give the board support in the middle, glue and screw a central divider into place.

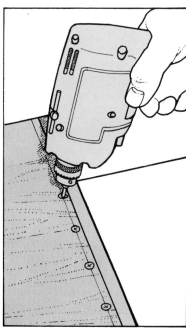

8 *Use superscrews to fix the melamine board to the ends.*

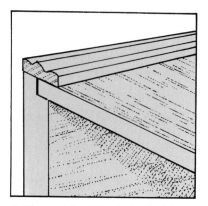

9 *The moulding hides the heads of the screws.*

## Finishing off

When the melamine board is secured, a moulding should be glued on at the ends of the top side of the desk, and down the front edge. (9) The moulding covers up the screw heads and makes an edge to the end of the desk top.

Now fit the desk unit into the framework.

Where ends of melamine board have been cut, a roll of matching, pre-glued melamine tape is available for laminating. This tape is usually glued on using an ordinary domestic iron as a heat source. (10) The tape is fractionally wider than the board, so it is necessary to trim off the excess. This can be done with a Stanley knife or an electric trimmer.

10 *Heat the iron to medium before pressing tape into place.*

**COMPUTER DESK CUTTING LIST**

| | | |
|---|---|---|
| **End frames** | | |
| Legs | 4 off | 1,051 × 51 × 28mm (41⅜ × 2 × 1⅛in) timber |
| Feet | 2 off | 584 × 51 × 28mm (23 × 2 × 1⅛in) timber |
| Cross rails | 4 off | 352 × 51 × 28mm (13⅞ × 2 × 1⅛in) timber |
| Tie members | 3 off | 1,302 × 51 × 28mm (51¼ × 2 × 1⅛in) timber |
| Back | 1 off | 1,302 × 352 × 16mm (51¼ × 13⅞ × ⅝in) melamine faced chipboard |
| **Work surfaces** | | |
| Top & bottom | 2 off | 1,219 × 457 × 16mm (48 × 18 × ⅝in) melamine faced chipboard |
| End blocks | 2 off | 457 × 165 × 32mm (18 × 6½ × 1¼in) timber |
| Centre block | 1 off | 425 × 133 × 32mm (16¾ × 5¼ × 1¼in) timber |
| Capping strip | make from | 1,270 × 32 × 3mm (50 × 1¼ × ⅛in) moulding |
| Raised platforms | make from | 622 × 416 × 16mm (24½ × 16⅜ × ⅝in) melamine faced chipboard |
| **Cable trunking** | | |
| Front | 1 off | 660 × 57 × 16mm (26 × 2¼ × ⅝in) melamine faced chipboard |
| Top | 1 off | 660 × 51 × 16mm (26 × 2 × ⅝in) melamine faced chipboard |

*The desk from underneath, showing the cable aperture.*

*The cup screws fix the sides to the main framework.*

*The side elevation showing the angled VDU supports.*

*The crossbar supporting the front underside of the desk.*

*The shaped leg from underneath.*

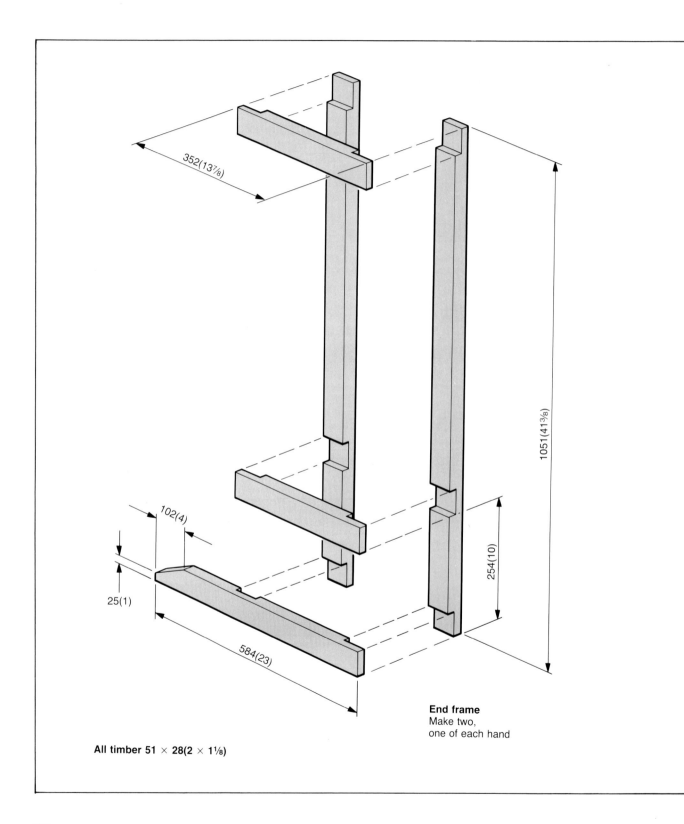

352(13⅞)

1051(41⅜)

102(4)

254(10)

25(1)

584(23)

**End frame**
Make two,
one of each hand

**All timber 51 × 28(2 × 1⅛)**

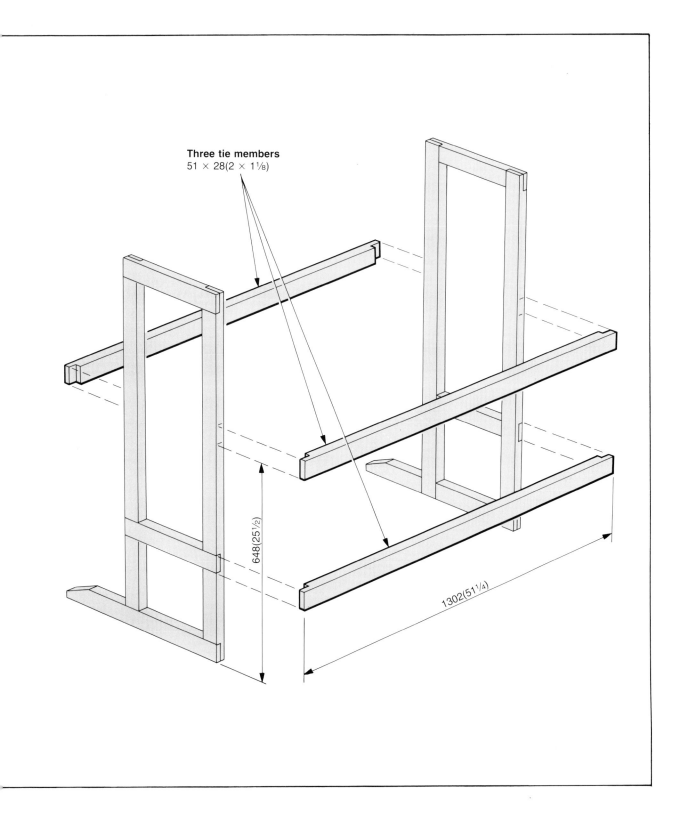

Three tie members
51 × 28(2 × 1⅛)

648(25½)

1302(51¼)

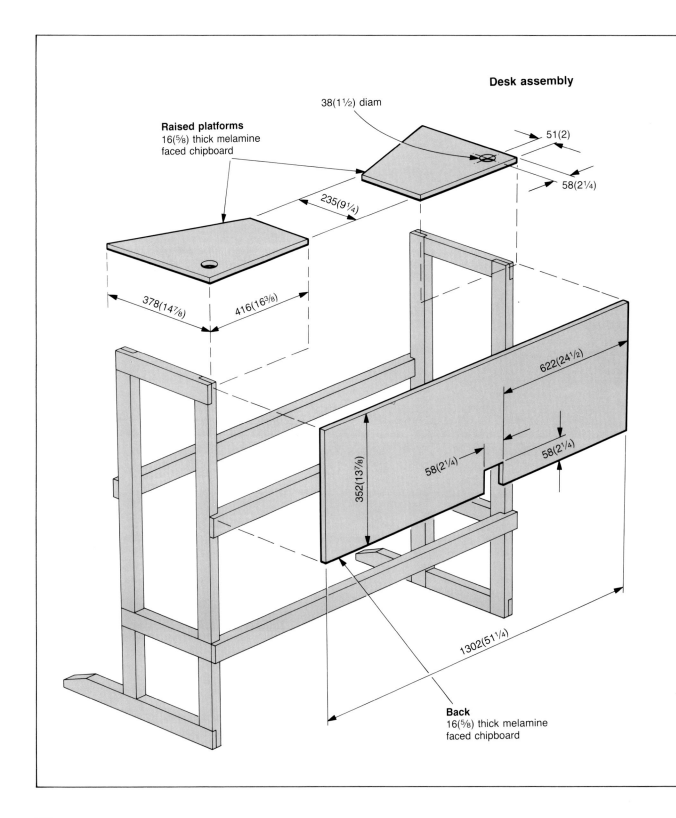

**Desk assembly**

38(1½) diam

51(2)

58(2¼)

**Raised platforms**
16(⅝) thick melamine
faced chipboard

235(9¼)

378(14⅞)    416(16⅜)

622(24½)

352(13⅞)

58(2¼)    58(2¼)

1302(51¼)

**Back**
16(⅝) thick melamine
faced chipboard

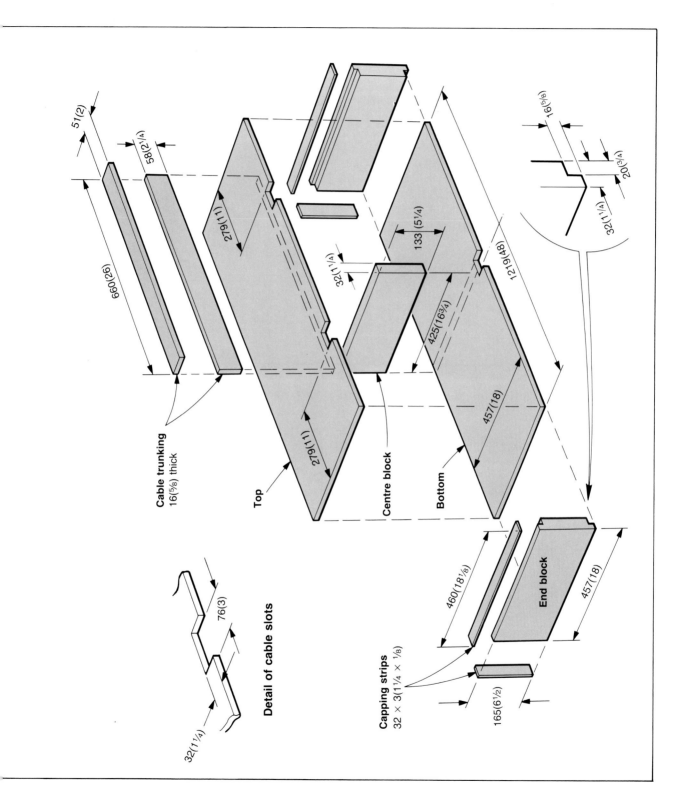

51(2)

58(2¼)

16(⅝)

20(¾)

32(1¼)

660(26)

279(11)

133 (5¼)

32(1¼)

1219(48)

425(16¾)

279(11)

457(18)

**Cable trunking**
16(⅝) thick

**Top**

**Centre block**

**Bottom**

**End block**

460(18⅛)

457(18)

76(3)

**Detail of cable slots**

32(1¼)

32(1¼)

**Capping strips**
32 × 3(1¼ × ⅛)

165(6½)

# Bed settee

**Essential tools**
Mortice gauge
Tenon saw
Electric router and guide fence
Candle wax
Plug cutter
Bevel edged chisel
Smoothing plane
Candle wax

Convertible bed settees are particularly useful for the overnight visitor. The techniques in this project are fairly easy to master, but the sections and panels are heavy to handle so you will need a second pair of hands to lift the bed during final assembly.

I have designed the head of the bed to be the back of the settee, with the pillows supported by slats. This will prevent the pillows falling off the end. However, a compromise has to be made in the depth of the seating. For this design, there have to be some very deep cushions along the back to

give the users back support when the bed is used as a settee.

For this project, I used Nordic redwood, but similar woods are available at good timber merchants. The cushions and mattresses can be made by the householder. However, I had mine made by a specialist chair company. As this piece of furniture is large and bulky, I have made it so that it can easily be dismantled if it needs to be moved.

There are three main frameworks into which a series of sliding slats fits. The joint holding the frameworks together is a combed joint – a strong joint that allows a large glueing area. For this project too, it is worth mastering the use of the smoothing plane because it produces a far better surface than glasspaper. A smoothing plane with a well-sharpened blade is a real joy. Those who are used to working with tools need only close their eyes to know from the sound of the blade if it is sharp or blunt. A

well-sharpened blade produces a fine shaving "whistling" as it works, and a little candle wax rubbed onto the sole of the plane will make it work more smoothly.

**The frameworks**
Make a start by placing all the rails for the side frames together and marking in the shoulder lines. Separate the rails and, following the side-edge marks, transfer these all around the rails. With a mortice gauge, mark out one-third of the width. (**1**)

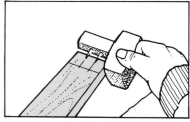

**1** *Make sure that the side of the mortice gauge always works from the face side of the rails.*

Now pencil in the parts of the joint to be cut off. (2)

**2** *Mark in the joints on the rails – it is always frustrating to cut out the wrong bits by mistake!*

Place the wood vertically in a vice and cut down the vertical lines of the joint with a tenon saw. Then turn the rail horizontally in the vice and cut off the side pieces. (**3**) This part of the joint is the peg section and the next step is to cut out the socket into which the peg fits.

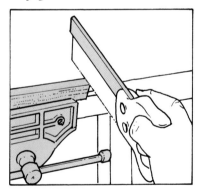

**3** *Hold the wood firmly in a vice when cutting out the side pieces of the joint with a tenon saw.*

With the tenon saw again, cut down the vertical lines to the gauge lines at the bottom. Then take a coping saw with the blade rotated to be at right angles to the framework and carefully cut off the section in the middle. (**4**)

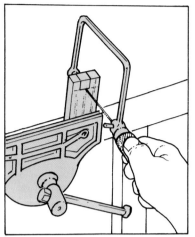

**4** *Change the direction of the teeth in the coping saw to cut round the section in the middle of the socket.*

Use a chisel to ensure that the bottom of the joint is flat, then fit the joint together. (**5**)

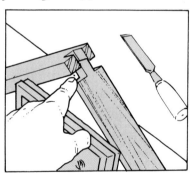

**5** *If you have cut and chiselled along the gauge lines, the joints should fit together snugly and easily.*

The two side frames, the back frame and the front frame – which holds all the slats – are constructed in this way.

**Glueing**
When the frameworks have been made they are glued and cramped together. Once the glue has cured, plane off the joint. It is important, when using a smoothing plane, to work from the edge towards the middle of the rail. (**6**) This prevents

splitting and ensures that the end grain of the middle joint will be nicely blended into the other parts of the joint.

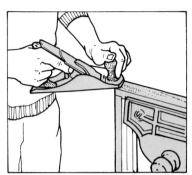

**6** *Always plane the rail from the outer edge towards the middle. If you plane in the other direction the grain will split.*

When all the frameworks are made, battens of timber must be glued along the inside of the top and the bottom rails. (**7**)

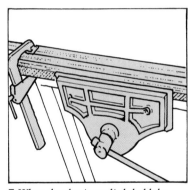

**7** *When the glue is applied, hold the battens in position with cramps.*

**The slats**
Slats should now be planed up and fitted into the frames. It is important that the ends are cut squarely, or they will look very untidy and ragged when fitted into the framework. (**8**) Glue the slats in place, and when the glue has cured, work over the framework with a smoothing plane. This is always necessary, however accurately you make the frame and fit the slats. (**9**)

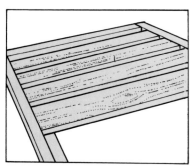

**8** *The slats should be spaced evenly in the framework.*

**9** *Where the slats meet the side frame there will be a slight raised edge, and it is this that has to be planed flush.*

A smooth finished surface is necessary for the next stage. The slats make the framework look very square and "boxy". To combat this, use a router to cut a chamfer on all the inside edges. The router needs a guide fence to keep it running straight, or a cutter with a ball bearing on the bottom which will automatically follow an edge. (**10**)

**10** *The cutter will give the framework a well-rounded and smooth edge.*

## The back and sides

Now place all three frameworks on a flat surface, cramping them together, and marking in pencil the positions of the seating bearers. Remove the cramps holding the frames. Then fix the bearer onto the back frames. Glue and cramp it into position, then add screws for extra strength, counter-boring the holes to take wooden plugs. (**11**)

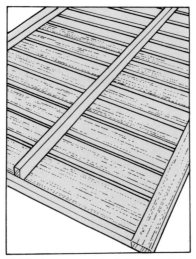

**11** *The batten on the back frame should be glued and screwed into position.*

Next, glue and screw the bearers onto the side frames. (**12**)

**12** *It is vital that the battens glued and screwed onto the inside edges of the frame line up accurately at the back corners.*

The bearers are not glued together at the corners as each frame is kept separate. The side frames are screwed to the back frame and the holes are counterbored to take 76mm (3ins) No. 10 screws. These must be done up very tight to hold the frames together.

The frames are held together at the front by a long, deep batten. This needs to be deeper than the other battens as it is the main support for the seating. Screw it to the side frames, and support it on the bottom of the frames with two short battens. (**13**)

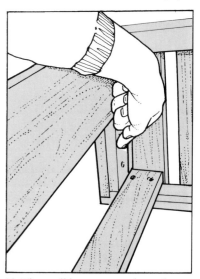

**13** *The small battens screwed onto the bottom of the frame give the front rail full support.*

## The front

All slats fixed to the front frames are sliding and all edges should be carefully checked for rough edges and corners. The front of the bed is made in exactly the same way as the side frame. This has to be strong rigid structure because it must support the foot of the bed when it is extended. Attach the front frame to the slats that allow it to be extended and retracted.

With so many slats, one sliding against the other, it is likely that one will bind on its neighbour. To avoid this, make sure the slats are not fitted too tightly against each other. There is also a danger that the unit will jam when it is being folded away. To prevent this, all the slats that slide towards the back need to be cut to a wedge shape. When the sliding slats reach the back, the wedge shape automatically prevents the slats fouling on the back batten.

Pencil in the wedge shape and smooth until the desired shape is achieved. (**14**)

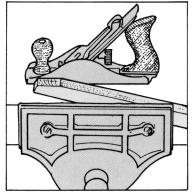

**14** *Use a smoothing plane to shape the slats.*

With a sheet of glasspaper, tidy up the ends and sides, making sure there are no sharp edges. The fixed slats also need to have their front edges cut to a wedge shape. (**15**)

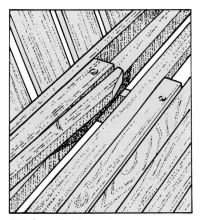

**15** *The wedge shape allows the front frame to slide easily into place.*

A long thin strip of timber should be placed on the top side of the battens that will slide out. (**16**) This is screwed to the first four sliding slats on each side. The remaining slats are secured to the lower tie bar. The front ends of all the slats are secured to the top of the front frame. In theory, it should be possible for slats of identical thickness to slide easily. However, it is best to plane each fitted slat just a little thinner than the sliding slats. If you find that a slat is binding, remove it and plane off a little timber. If you are not sure where the problem is, hold the batten up to the light and you will see a shiny surface where the wood is rubbing. A little candle wax rubbed on the surface will also ease the section when it slides.

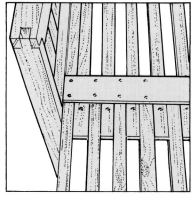

**16** *Fix a long, thin strip of wood to the top side of the battens that slide.*

### The arms
The arms should now be cut and shaped. They are then fixed to the side frames by glueing and counter-boring the screw holes to take wooden plugs.

Because the wood is fixed "end grain," it always shows if dowel rods are fitted into the counterbore holes. If you use a plug cutter, cut a circular piece of wood from the surface of the timber and this will, when fitted carefully, be almost invisible. Drill and counterbore holes in the arms to take the screws and plugs. (**17**)

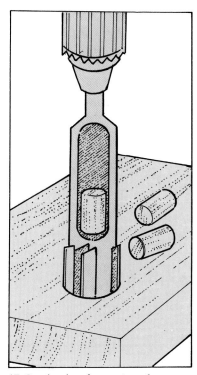

**17** *Cut the plugs from a piece of waste wood.*

Chamfer the ends of the plugs, as they will then fit in the holes with greater ease.

Now glue and screw the arms into the frames. "Inject" glue into the holes before carefully tapping in the plugs. (**18**)

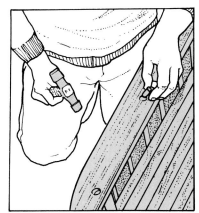

**18** *Use a hammer to gently tap the plugs into the holes in the arms.*

With a bevel edged chisel, cut off surplus wood at the top of the plugs. (**19**)

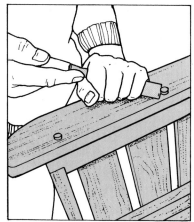

**19** *For the final cut, use the chisel with the bevel side face up.*

**Finishing off**
Use glasspaper to smooth the tops of the plugs. Then coat with clear acrylic varnish of the colour of your choice.

**20** *The finished bed settee.*

**BED SETTEE CUTTING LIST**

*Side frames*

| | | |
|---|---|---|
| Top & bottom rails | 4 off | 864 × 51 × 22mm (34 × 2 × ⁷/₈in) timber |
| Vertical rails | 4 off | 686 × 51 × 22mm (27 × 2 × ⁷/₈in) timber |
| Battens | 4 off | 820 × 32 × 22mm (32¼ × 1¼ × ⁷/₈in) timber |
| Arm | 2 off | 927 × 76 × 22mm (36½ × 3 × ⁷/₈in) timber |
| Seating bearer | 2 off | 842 × 70 × 22mm (33⅛ × 2¾ × ⁷/₈in) timber |
| Seating guide | 2 off | 820 × 32 × 22mm (32¼ × 1¼ × ⁷/₈in) timber |
| Vertical slats | 16 off | 642 × 76 × 20mm (25¼ × 3 × ¾in) timber |

*Rear panel*

| | | |
|---|---|---|
| Top & bottom rails | 2 off | 1,568 × 51 × 22mm (61¾ × 2 × ⁷/₈in) timber |
| Vertical rails | 2 off | 914 × 51 × 22mm (36 × 2 × ⁷/₈in) timber |
| Battens | 2 off | 1,524 × 32 × 22mm (60 × 1¼ × ⁷/₈in) timber |
| Seating bearer | 1 off | 1,524 × 70 × 22mm (60 × 2¾ × ⁷/₈in) timber |
| Vertical slats | 16 off | 870 × 76 × 20mm (34¼ × 3 × ¾in) timber |

*Front frame*

| | | |
|---|---|---|
| Top & bottom rails | 2 off | 1,524 × 51 × 22mm (60 × 2 × ⁷/₈in) timber |
| Vertical rails | 2 off | 356 × 51 × 22mm (14 × 2 × ⁷/₈in) timber |
| Battens | 2 off | 1,480 × 29 × 20mm (58¼ × 1⅛ × ¾in) timber |
| Vertical slats | 16 off | 312 × 70 × 22mm (12¼ × 1⅛ × ⁷/₈in) timber |
| Upper tie bar | 1 off | 1,524 × 73 × 6mm (60 × 2⁷/₈ × ¼in) timber |
| Lower tie bar | 1 off | 1,575 × 70 × 22mm (62 × 2¾ × ⁷/₈in) timber |
| Sliding slats | 22 off | 921 × 35 × 22mm (36¼ × 1⅜ × ⁷/₈in) timber |

*Front support assembly*

| | | |
|---|---|---|
| Cross piece | 1 off | 1,588 × 146 × 22mm (62½ × 5¾ × ⁷/₈in) timber |
| Support battens | 2 off | 116 × 28 × 22mm (6½ × 1⅛ × ⁷/₈in) timber |
| Bottom tie bar | 1 off | 1,588 × 73 × 22mm (62½ × 2⁷/₈ × ⁷/₈in) timber |
| Fixed slats | 21 off | 946 × 32 × 22mm (37¼ × 1¼ × ⁷/₈in) timber |

*The bed fully extended.*

*Remove and plane any battens that are preventing the bed from sliding easily.*

*The spokeshaved arm of the settee.*

*The chamferred edges soften the hard lines.*

*The back bottom corner showing counterbored holes which are not plugged so that the bed can be dismantled.*

**Left** *The settee, with the chamferred front edges visible.*

**Right** *Front view of the bed settee showing the arm and back support.*

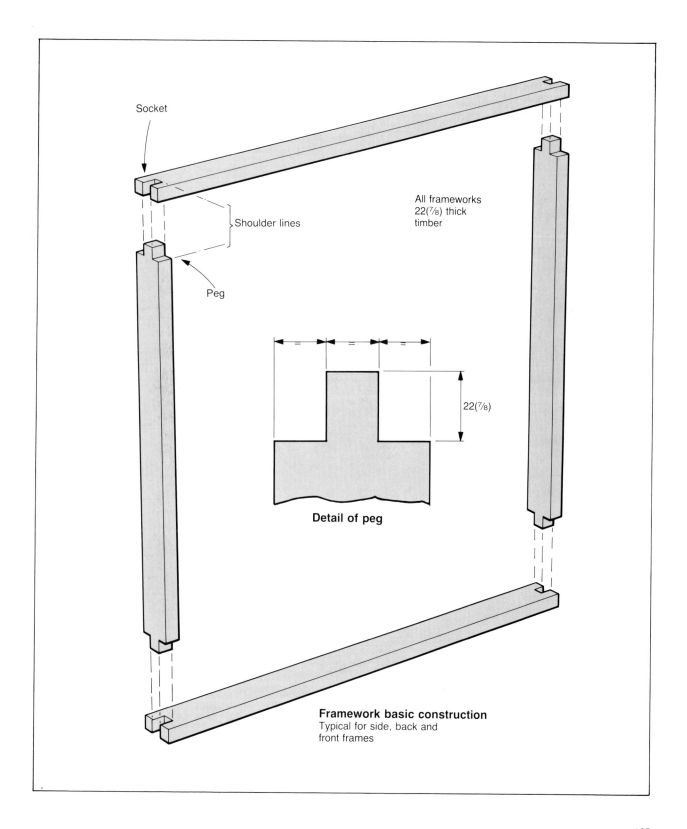

Socket

Shoulder lines

Peg

All frameworks
22(⁷⁄₈) thick
timber

$22(7/8)$

**Detail of peg**

**Framework basic construction**
Typical for side, back and
front frames

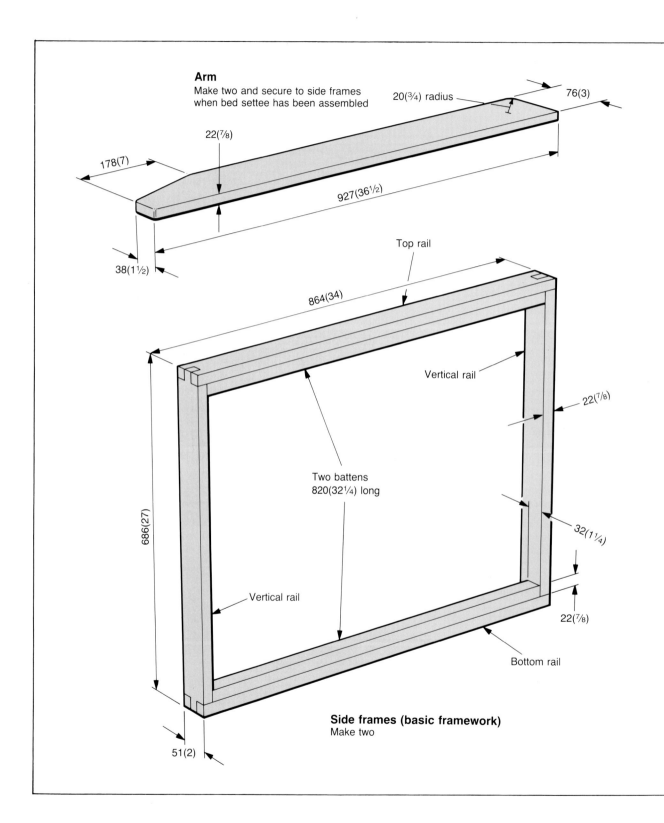

**Arm**
Make two and secure to side frames
when bed settee has been assembled

20(¾) radius

76(3)

22(⅞)

178(7)

927(36½)

38(1½)

Top rail

864(34)

Vertical rail

22(⅞)

Two battens
820(32¼) long

32(1¼)

686(27)

Vertical rail

22(⅞)

Bottom rail

**Side frames (basic framework)**
Make two

51(2)

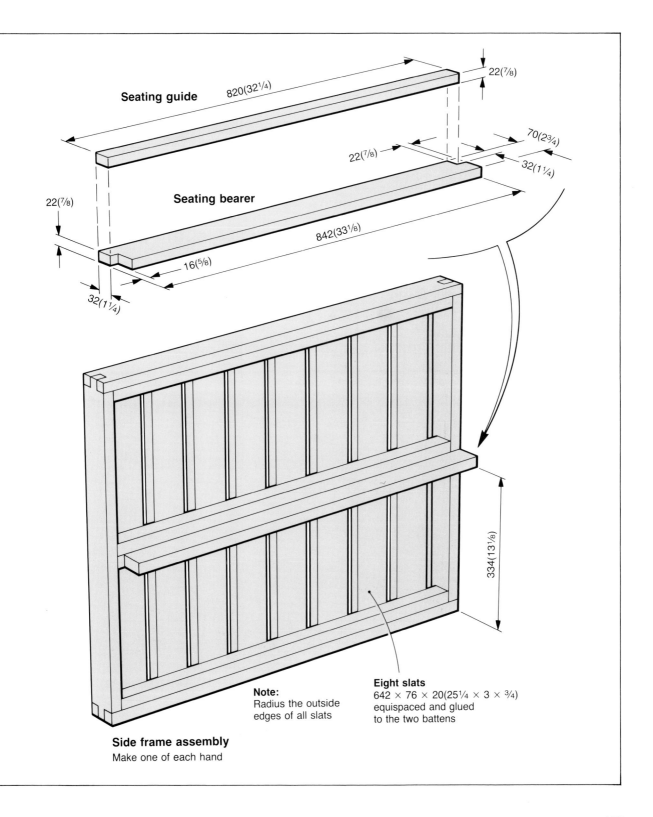

**Seating guide**

820(32¼)

22(⅞)

22(⅞)

70(2¾)

32(1¼)

**Seating bearer**

22(⅞)

842(33⅛)

16(⅝)

32(1¼)

334(13⅛)

**Note:**
Radius the outside
edges of all slats

**Eight slats**
642 × 76 × 20(25¼ × 3 × ¾)
equispaced and glued
to the two battens

**Side frame assembly**
Make one of each hand

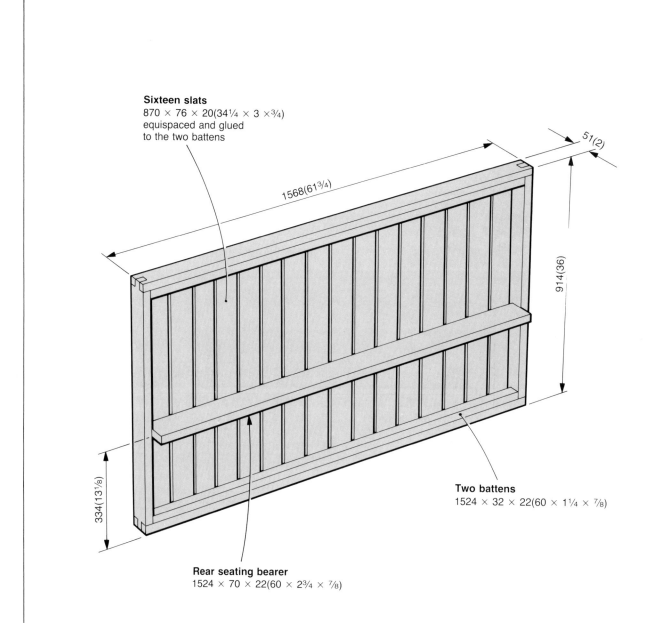

**Sixteen slats**
870 × 76 × 20(34¼ × 3 ×¾)
equispaced and glued
to the two battens

1568(61¾)

51(2)

914(36)

334(13⅛)

**Rear seating bearer**
1524 × 70 × 22(60 × 2¾ × ⅞)

**Two battens**
1524 × 32 × 22(60 × 1¼ × ⅞)

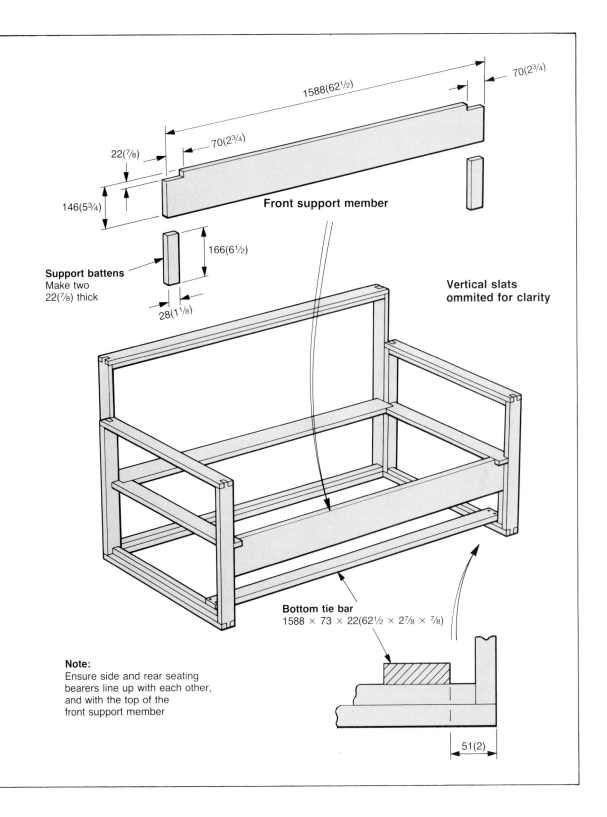

1588(62½)

70(2¾)

70(2¾)

22(⅞)

146(5¾)

**Front support member**

166(6½)

**Support battens**
Make two
22(⅞) thick

28(1⅛)

**Vertical slats
ommited for clarity**

**Bottom tie bar**
1588 × 73 × 22(62½ × 2⅞ × ⅞)

**Note:**
Ensure side and rear seating
bearers line up with each other,
and with the top of the
front support member

51(2)

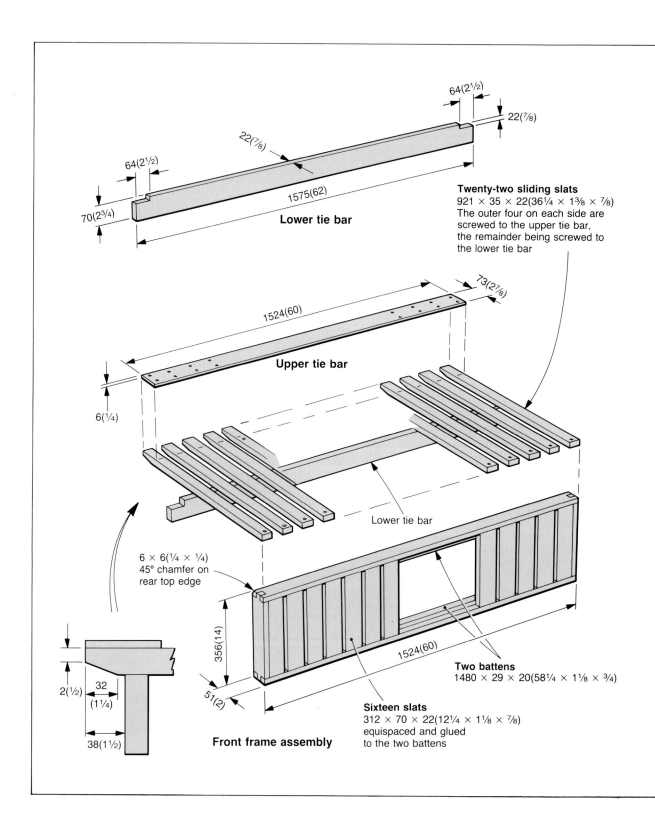

64(2¹/₂)

22(⁷/₈)

22(⁷/₈)

64(2¹/₂)

1575(62)

**Lower tie bar**

70(2³/₄)

**Twenty-two sliding slats**
921 × 35 × 22(36¹/₄ × 1³/₈ × ⁷/₈)
The outer four on each side are
screwed to the upper tie bar,
the remainder being screwed to
the lower tie bar

73(2⁷/₈)

1524(60)

**Upper tie bar**

6(¹/₄)

Lower tie bar

6 × 6(¹/₄ × ¹/₄)
45° chamfer on
rear top edge

356(14)

1524(60)

**Two battens**
1480 × 29 × 20(58¹/₄ × 1¹/₈ × ³/₄)

2(¹/₂)   32
(1¹/₄)

51(2)

**Sixteen slats**
312 × 70 × 22(12¹/₄ × 1¹/₈ × ⁷/₈)
equispaced and glued
to the two battens

38(1¹/₂)

**Front frame assembly**

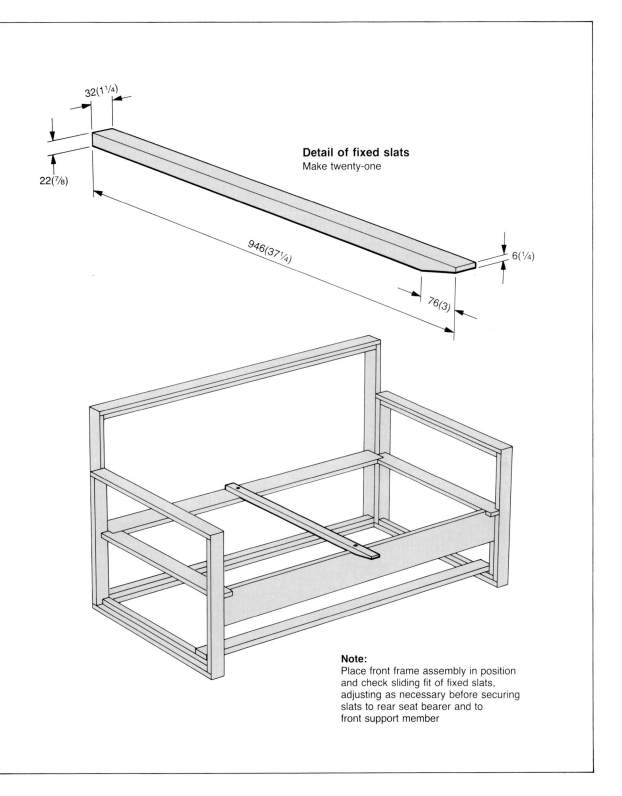

32(1¼)

22(⅞)

**Detail of fixed slats**
Make twenty-one

946(37¼)

6(¼)

76(3)

**Note:**
Place front frame assembly in position
and check sliding fit of fixed slats,
adjusting as necessary before securing
slats to rear seat bearer and to
front support member

# *Rocking cradle*

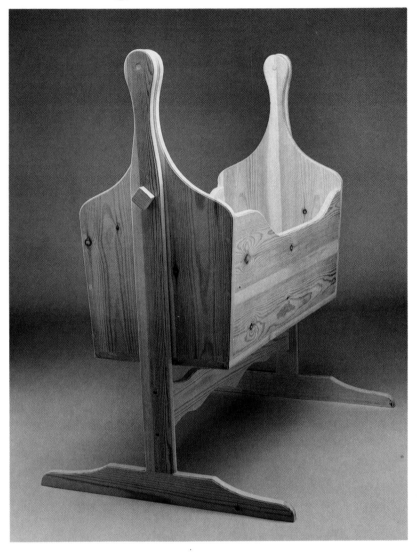

latter, as the ability to gently rock a baby helps to settle it down.

This particular design has a static framework, and the cradle is suspended from two pivot points. The cradle itself swings within the framework.

The wood used is Nordic redwood. This timber is available edge laminated (boards glued together) to provide sufficient width for this project. It is also possible to build the cradle from man-made boards – some of the blockboards and pine finished plywoods are particularly suitable.

This project has three jointing techniques to be mastered: jointing boards (you will not need to use this technique if you buy edge laminated boards), butt jointing boards, using screws and wooden pegs to cover screw heads; and wedged through mortice and tenons.

## Preparation

First select timber for the sides, ends and base. If you buy the ready prepared timber PSE (planed square edge) you will find it is still necessary to plane the edges that are to be jointed. This is done with a jointer plane which has a very long sole and smooths any unevenness in the timber. Jointer planes can be hired from tool hire shops. It is important that, as you plane the edges, the edge is at 90° to the face of the board.

---

**Essential tools**
Jointer plane
Belt sander
Spokeshave
Electric router
Plug cutter
Mortice gauge
Mortice chisel

There are few projects that give greater pleasure than making a cradle for your first child. Over the centuries a variety of both static and rocking cradle designs have been developed. However, my choice is always the

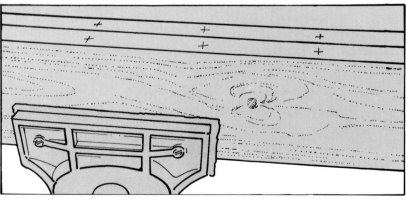

**1** *Mark out both planks together or the holes and dowel rods will not line up.*

Once the edges of both boards are prepared, mark along the edges where the dowel rods will go. Mark out both planks together or the holes and dowel rods will not line up.(**1**) You can buy ready-made fluted dowels for jointing. These are excellent as the fluted sides allow any glue trapped in the bottoms of the holes to escape. The ends of the dowel rods are also tapered, which helps when assembling the holes and dowels.

Apply a little glue to each hole and use a hammer to tap the dowels into the holes.(**2**) Now apply glue to the holes on the other plank and generously to the edges of the planks. Assemble the two planks; some initial adjustment is usually necessary to fit all the dowels into the holes.

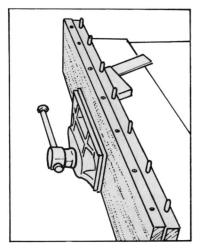

**2** *Prepare and mark the edges of both boards. Apply a little glue to each hole before tapping the dowels into place.*

Once the dowels are in place, use sash bar cramps to "pull up" the joint.(**3**) This procedure is repeated for all the boards that have to be jointed.

When the glue has cured, remove the cramps. However proficient you become at jointing boards, you will always have to plane them to remove the glue line in the middle. The skilled woodworker will use a jointer or a

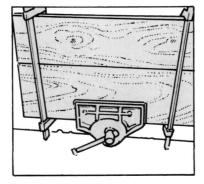

**3** *Make sure that the boards cramped together remain flat, and are not lifting in the middle or at the edges.*

jack plane for this task. However, if the joints have been well made, it is possible to use a belt sander.(**4**) This machine will tidy up the boards very quickly. Next, bore the holes for the pivots in the top of the ends before you do the shaping. The holes must be made in the exact centre of the boards, or the cradle will hang unevenly in the frame.

**Shaping**

When all the boards are prepared, start on the shaping. Make a full-size

cardboard template of the ends and sides; use this to pencil in the shapes.

Now, cut the ends and sides to shape with a jigsaw or coping saw. Remove the saw cuts with a spokeshave which, when well sharpened, will clean up the edges better than any orbital or palm sander. Spend time at this stage and get all the edges perfect.

One particularly attractive feature of this design is the small beading which is cut on the edges with a router. This has the important

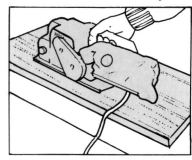

**4** *An electric belt sander fitted with a skirt or shoe will not dig in at the corners.*

function of removing any sharp edges on the sides of the cradle. You should

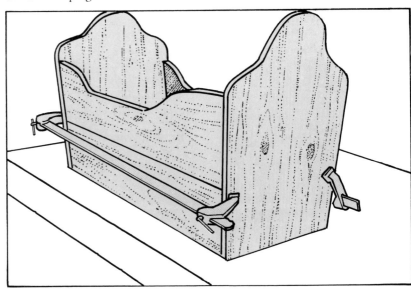

**5** *Cramp the sides of the cradle together and carefully mark in where the edges meet before preparing counterbore holes for the screws.*

cut the beadings before assembling the cradle. If you leave it until after glueing up, you will find it impossible to get the router into the inside corners. There is a great variety of cutters available, but the smaller cutters probably produce the best result. Some cutters have a small ball bearing on the base which prevents the pilot end burning the wood.

## Glueing up

The cradle is held together by screws and glue. However, as screws can look ugly, the heads are counterbored into the timber and wood plugs fitted over the top. This can be done in one operation with a combined drill and counterbore tool; the countersink is fully adjustable and makes light work of this job.(5)

It is a false economy to use dowel rods to cut and fit over the screw heads. The dowel rod will fill the hole, but its end grain will always show, as will the hole it fills. A plug cutter removes a plug of wood from the face of the timber, and if it is carefully glued and fitted, will almost completely disguise the hole. (6) The bottom of the cradle is fitted last.

6 *The plugs should stand proud of the holes. For almost complete invisibility, trim them flush with the surface using a very sharp chisel.*

## The stand

The stand consists of two uprights, a middle rail and two feet. The uprights are morticed and tenoned to the feet, and the central rail ties the uprights and feet together.

First mark out the uprights, feet and central rail with a pencil. Then, with a mortice chisel and mallet, chop the stopped mortice into the feet. Now cut the tenons on the ends of the upright and the long through mortice that takes the cross rail. Bore holes in the tops of the uprights to take the dowel rods on which the cradle swings. Do not forget the hole for the peg to stop the cradle rocking. Cut the tenons on the cross rail.

The legs and stand uprights are held together by the central rail. It is

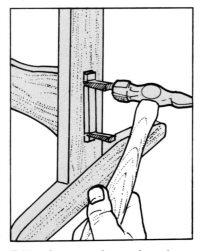

7 *Use a hammer to drive in the wedges.*

The legs and stand uprights are held together by the central rail. It is therefore vitally important that there is some method of tieing this rail securely to the two uprights. To achieve this the tenon comes right through the upright, and wedges are driven in on the outside edges.(7) The tenon is cut down at the top and bottom edges, so that the wedges can be inserted. The mortice hole is enlarged in the outer face only, allowing the tenon to be 'expanded' in the mortice and preventing the joint coming apart again.

I used a contrasting wood for the wedges as this gives a decorative effect. After the glue has dried, the wedges have to be cut off and planed flush.(8)

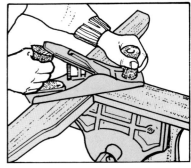

8 *Plane off the wedges and tenon with a smoothing plane.*

Finally, use candle wax on the dowel rods holding the cradle in the stand, or it will creak as it swings.

| ROCKING CRADLE CUTTING LIST | | |
|---|---|---|
| Cradle ends | 2 off | 714 × 413* × 22mm (28⅛ × 17* × ⅞in) timber |
| Cradle sides | 2 off | 826 × 349 × 22mm (32½ × 13¾* × ⅞in) timber |
| Cradle base | 1 off | 914 × 388* × 22mm (36 × 15¼* × ⅞in) timber |
| Leg uprights | 2 off | 1,073 × 83 × 22mm (42¼ × 3¼ × ⅞in) timber |
| Leg feet | 2 off | 737 × 83 × 22mm (29 × 3¼ × ⅞in) timber |
| Pivot pins | 2 off | 16 × 60mm (⅝ × 2⅜in) diam dowel |
| Washers | 2 off | 38 × 38 × 6mm (1½ × 1½ × ¼in) timber |
| Lock peg | 1 off | 16 × 76mm (⅝ × 3in) diam dowel |
| | 1 off | 41 × 41 × 22mm (1⅝ × 1⅝ × ⅞in) timber |
| Central tie bar | 1 off | 978 × 140 × 22mm (38½ × 5½ × ⅞in) timber |
| Wedges | 4 off | 9mm (³⁄₈in) thick timber off cuts |
| Jointing boards | make from | 5,000 × 12mm (192 × ½in) diam dowel |

\* Edge laminated or man made boards, or accumulative width if jointed boards

**Right** *Note the chamferred edges and the wood plugs down the side.*

**Left** *Detail of the wide leg that gives stability to the cradle.*

**Left** *Use a different coloured timber to make a feature of the wedged joint.*

**Right** *Detail of the rocking mechanism and locking peg arrangement.*

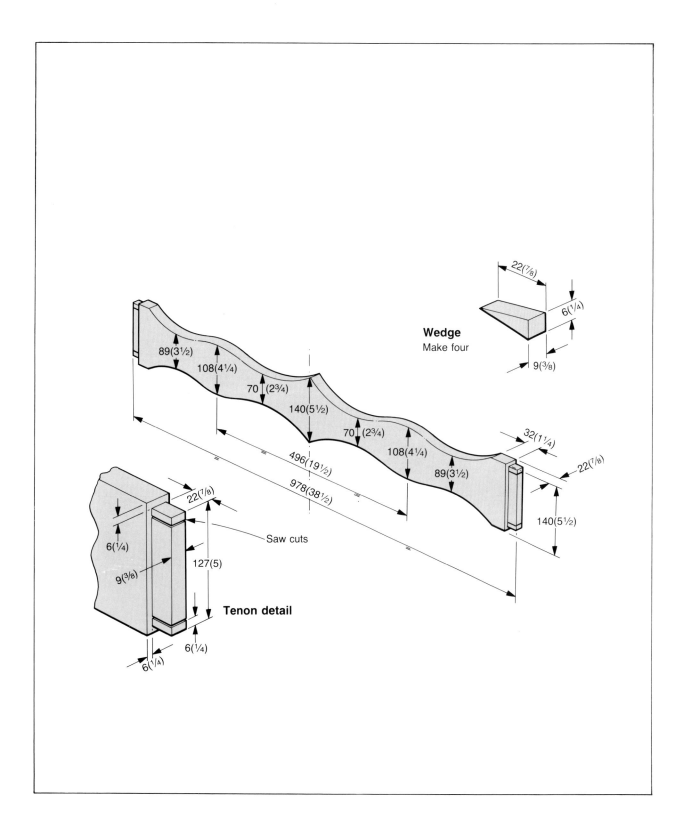

**Wedge**
Make four

22(⁷/₈)

6(¹/₄)

9(³/₈)

89(3¹/₂)

108(4¹/₄)

70 (2³/₄)

140(5¹/₂)

70 (2³/₄)

108(4¹/₄)

89(3¹/₂)

496(19¹/₂)

978(38¹/₂)

32(1¹/₄)

22(⁷/₈)

140(5¹/₂)

Saw cuts

22(⁷/₈)

6(¹/₄)

9(³/₈)

127(5)

**Tenon detail**

6(¹/₄)

6(¹/₄)

6(¹/₄)

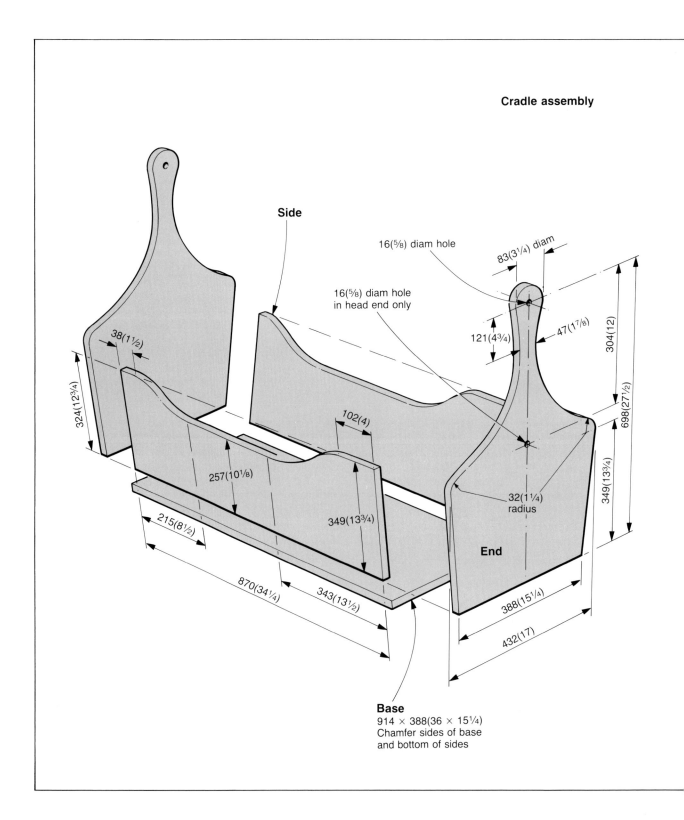

**Cradle assembly**

Side

16(⅝) diam hole

16(⅝) diam hole
in head end only

83(3¼) diam

38(1½)

304(12)

121(4¾)

47(1⅞)

324(12¾)

698(27½)

102(4)

349(13¾)

257(10⅛)

32(1¼)
radius

349(13¾)

215(8½)

**End**

870(34¼)

343(13½)

388(15¼)

432(17)

**Base**
914 × 388(36 × 15¼)
Chamfer sides of base
and bottom of sides

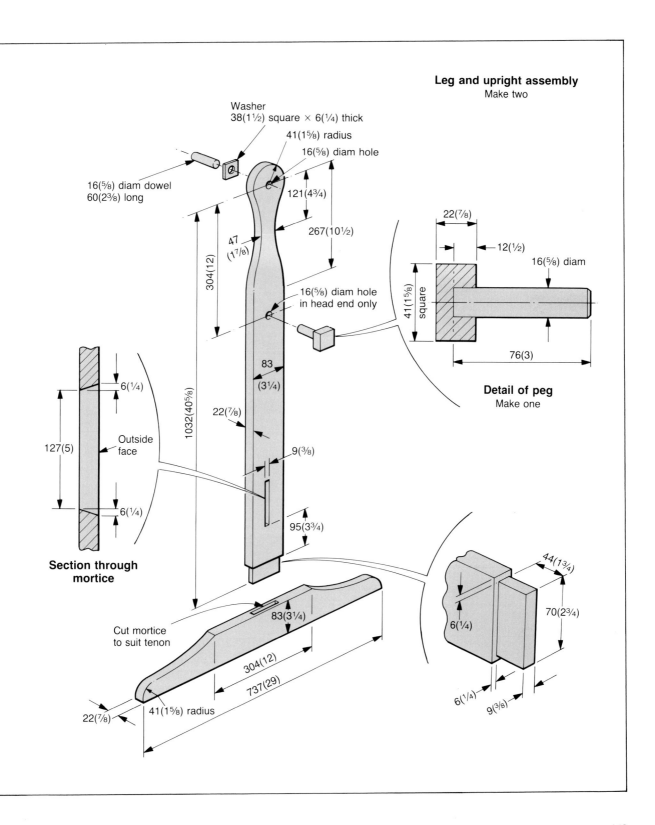

**Leg and upright assembly**
Make two

Washer
38(1½) square × 6(¼) thick

41(1⅝) radius

16(⅝) diam hole

16(⅝) diam dowel
60(2⅜) long

121(4¾)

267(10½)

47
(1⅞)

304(12)

16(⅝) diam hole
in head end only

22(⅞)

12(½)

16(⅝) diam

41(1⅝) square

76(3)

**Detail of peg**
Make one

83
(3¼)

6(¼)

127(5)

Outside
face

6(¼)

1032(40⅝)

22(⅞)

9(⅜)

95(3¾)

**Section through
mortice**

Cut mortice
to suit tenon

83(3¼)

44(1¾)

70(2¾)

6(¼)

304(12)

737(29)

22(⅞)

41(1⅝) radius

6(¼)

9(⅜)

# *Pine bed*

**Essential tools**
Electric router
Tenon saw
Mortice chisel
Mortice gauge
Spokeshave
Jigsaw or coping saw
Beading cutter

This bed was made in a redwood, but it would look equally well in hardwood. The joints used are mortice and tenon and there is a great deal of shaping involved for both the head and foot boards. The head board is of sufficient height to support a pillow for those fortunate enough to have the energy to lie in bed and read!

## Marking out

First mark out the legs. It is always important to pencil in both face side and face edge marks. Such marking is not only important for accuracy, it also helps to locate the sides and ends.

Once all the mortice holes are marked in and the tenons marked out, begin by cutting the mortices for the rails that will hold the sides and ends together. These differ from the others in that they meet in the middle. The mortice holes are chopped and meet each other at the back of the leg. The

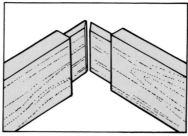

**1** *The long side rails and end cross rails, if chamferred and glued, give the framework great rigidity.*

tenons also meet up in the mortice holes.

Chamfer the ends of the tenons. (**1**) When the bed is assembled, the tenons are actually glued together. This gives a particularly strong joint.

The rails at the head and foot of the bed fit into stopped mortice and tenon holes. Make sure that you cut on the correct side of the legs. (**2**)

When all the mortices and tenons are chopped out, fit the joints together dry (without glue) to check that everything fits. (**3**) Do not glue the joints yet – there is the shaping to be done first.

## Shaping

Use a small beading cutter fitted on the router to cut a moulding onto the boards of the bed. This is best done before glueing because it would be impossible to get the router into the inside edge of the framework after.

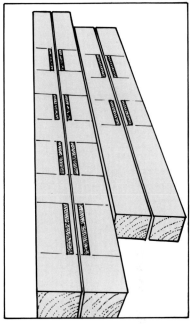

**2** *It is a good idea to cut out all the mortices in the legs at the same time.*

**3** *The tenons should fit neatly into the mortices, although they may need some adjustment.*

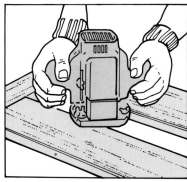

**4** *The beading cutter can be used on the outside edge of the boards after glueing.*

On the other hand, the outer edge *is* accessible to the router after glueing and curing. (**4**)

Unfortunately it is no longer possible to buy long paring chisels, so you will have to make do with a big bevel edge chisel. Pencil in the curved shape to be followed on both sides of the leg. Begin to pare away the wood from one side. (**5**) Only go halfway

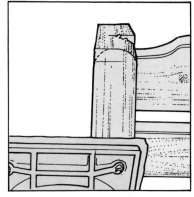

**5** *Begin to shape the top of the leg with the bevel edged chisel.*

across the top, or large chunks will be torn off. Then turn the leg round and work from the other side. (**6**) Make very shallow cuts and always try to even out any ridges as you work.

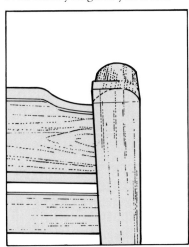

**6** *Remove any chippings, before turning the leg round and working from the other side.*

## Assembling

When the shaping is complete, check the fit of the long side rails. Mark with a pencil where the top and bottom edges of the rail fit onto the leg. Now use the router to complete the moulding round the top of the leg, making sure to stop when you reach the pencil mark.

The head and tail boards are now assembled. When the glue on these has cured, glue the head and tail boards to the long side rails. Check that the framework is square. It is necessary to fit extension bars to the average T bar cramps to get sufficient length to hold these boards in place. Sash bar cramps can be hired from tool shops.

The bed slats are supported at the top, bottom and sides by lengths of timber. As the timber used is fairly heavy, the holes are counterbored before the lengths of timber are screwed into the framework. (**7**)

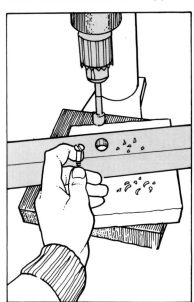

**7** *Allow plenty of room in the counterbore hole for the screw head to drop in.*

Notches are cut into the timber where it needs to fit round the legs of the bed. (**8**)

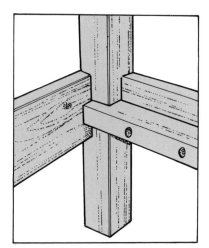

**8** *Cut notches in the timber to fit round the legs.*

Fit cross slats in the middle of the bed, supported by lengths of timber screwed to the inside edge of the long side rails. (**9**) Cut notches in the two outer slats to fit around the legs.

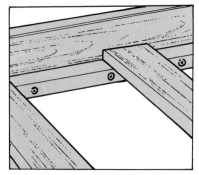

**9** *The cross slats go on top of the timber ledge screwed on the side rails.*

Now screw the full-length slats across the whole length of the bed. To avoid having to measure the gap between each slat, cut a batten of the equivalent size of the gap, and drop it in before fixing the next batten. (**10**)

**Finishing off**
Acrylic varnish has to be carefully brushed on and between all the slats. This is a tedious job but worth the effort. Care must be taken to avoid the varnish running.

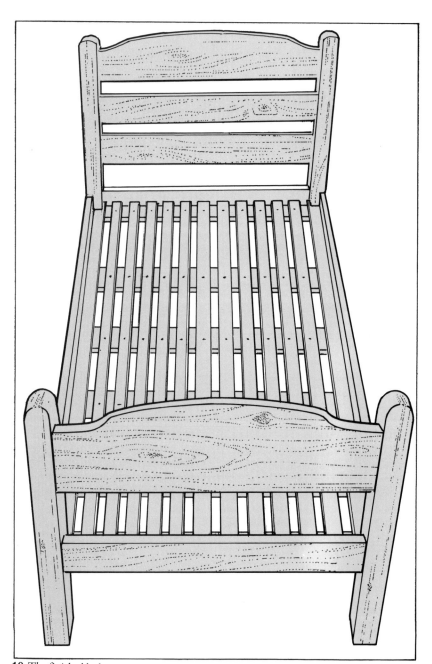

**10** *The finished bed.*

## PINE BED CUTTING LIST

| | | |
|---|---|---|
| Head board posts | 2 off | $918 \times 64 \times 64$mm ($36\frac{1}{4} \times 2\frac{1}{2} \times 2\frac{1}{2}$in) timber |
| Top rail | 1 off | $886 \times 168 \times 22$mm ($35 \times 6\frac{5}{8} \times \frac{7}{8}$in) timber |
| Centre boards | 2 off | $886 \times 124 \times 22$mm ($35 \times 4\frac{7}{8} \times \frac{7}{8}$in) timber |
| Cross tie bar | 1 off | $924 \times 124 \times 22$mm ($36\frac{1}{2} \times 4\frac{7}{8} \times \frac{7}{8}$in) timber |
| Support rail | 1 off | $894 \times 70 \times 32$mm ($35\frac{1}{4} \times 2\frac{3}{4} \times 1\frac{1}{4}$in) timber |
| Foot board posts | 2 off | $600 \times 64 \times 64$mm ($23\frac{5}{8} \times 2\frac{1}{2} \times 2\frac{1}{2}$in) timber |
| Top rail | 1 off | $886 \times 168 \times 22$mm ($35 \times 6\frac{5}{8} \times \frac{7}{8}$in) timber |
| Cross tie bar | 1 off | $924 \times 124 \times 22$mm ($36\frac{1}{2} \times 4\frac{7}{8} \times \frac{7}{8}$in) timber |
| Support rail | 1 off | $894 \times 70 \times 32$mm ($35\frac{1}{4} \times 2\frac{3}{4} \times 1\frac{1}{4}$in) timber |
| Side rails | 2 off | $2,044 \times 124 \times 22$mm ($80\frac{1}{2} \times 4\frac{7}{8} \times \frac{7}{8}$in) timber |
| Support batten | 2 off | $912 \times 32 \times 32$mm ($36 \times 1\frac{1}{4} \times 1\frac{1}{4}$in) timber |
| Cross slats | 4 off | $894 \times 79 \times 32$mm ($35\frac{1}{4} \times 3\frac{1}{8} \times 1\frac{1}{4}$in) timber |
| Longitudinal slats | 13 off | $2,013 \times 51 \times 22$mm ($79\frac{1}{4} \times 2 \times \frac{7}{8}$in) timber |

*The four cross slats give this bed great rigidity.*

**Above and right** *Two views of the shaped slats fixed to the support rail.*

*A detail of the headboard showing the chamferred edges.*

## Headboard assembly

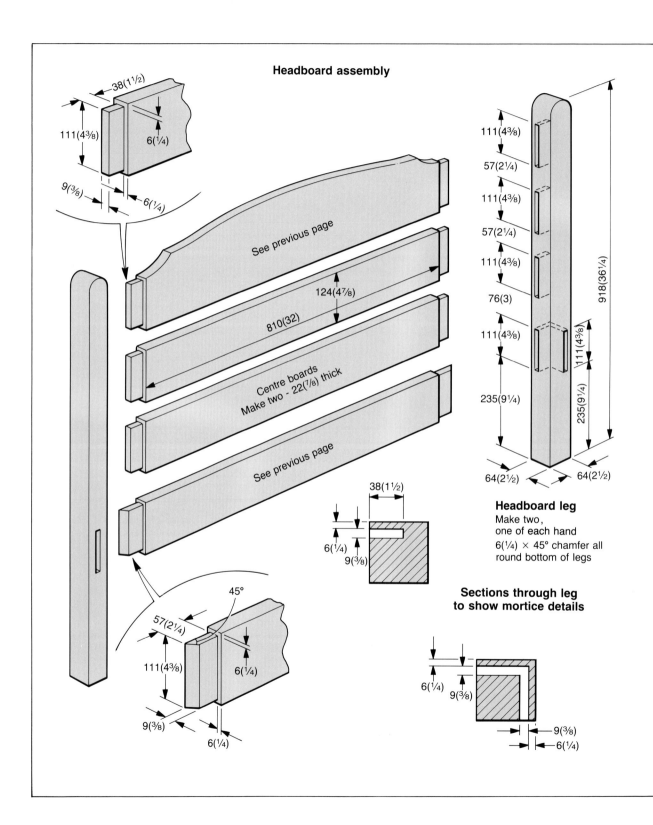

38(1½)

111(4⅜)

6(¼)

9(⅜)

6(¼)

See previous page

124(4⅞)

810(32)

Centre boards
Make two - 22(⅞) thick

See previous page

111(4⅜)

57(2¼)

111(4⅜)

57(2¼)

111(4⅜)

76(3)

111(4⅜)

111(4⅜)

918(36¼)

235(9¼)

235(9¼)

64(2½)

64(2½)

45°

57(2¼)

111(4⅜)

6(¼)

9(⅜)

6(¼)

38(1½)

6(¼)

9(⅜)

### Headboard leg
Make two,
one of each hand
6(¼) × 45° chamfer all
round bottom of legs

### Sections through leg
to show mortice details

6(¼)

9(⅜)

9(⅜)

6(¼)

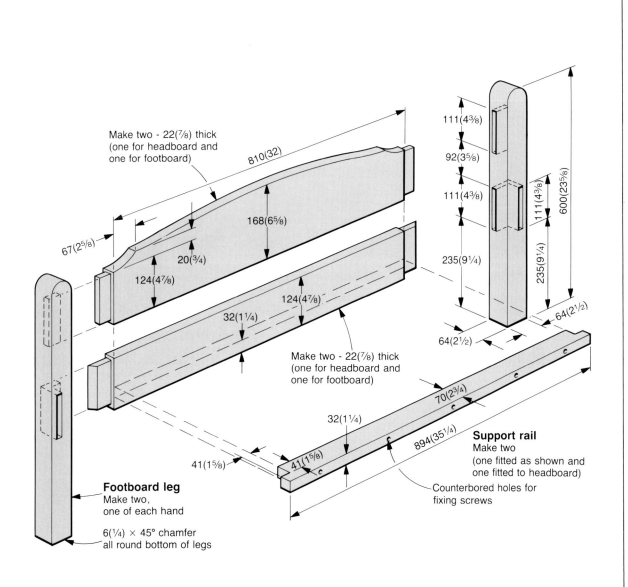

Make two - 22(⁷⁄₈) thick
(one for headboard and
one for footboard)

810(32)

168(6⁵⁄₈)

67(2⁵⁄₈)

20(³⁄₄)

124(4⁷⁄₈)

32(1¹⁄₄)

124(4⁷⁄₈)

Make two - 22(⁷⁄₈) thick
(one for headboard and
one for footboard)

111(4³⁄₈)

92(3⁵⁄₈)

111(4³⁄₈)

111(4³⁄₈)

600(23⁵⁄₈)

235(9¹⁄₄)

235(9¹⁄₄)

64(2¹⁄₂)

64(2¹⁄₂)

70(2³⁄₄)

32(1¹⁄₄)

894(35¹⁄₄)

**Support rail**
Make two
(one fitted as shown and
one fitted to headboard)

41(1⁵⁄₈)

41(1⁵⁄₈)

Counterbored holes for
fixing screws

**Footboard leg**
Make two,
one of each hand

6(¹⁄₄) × 45° chamfer
all round bottom of legs

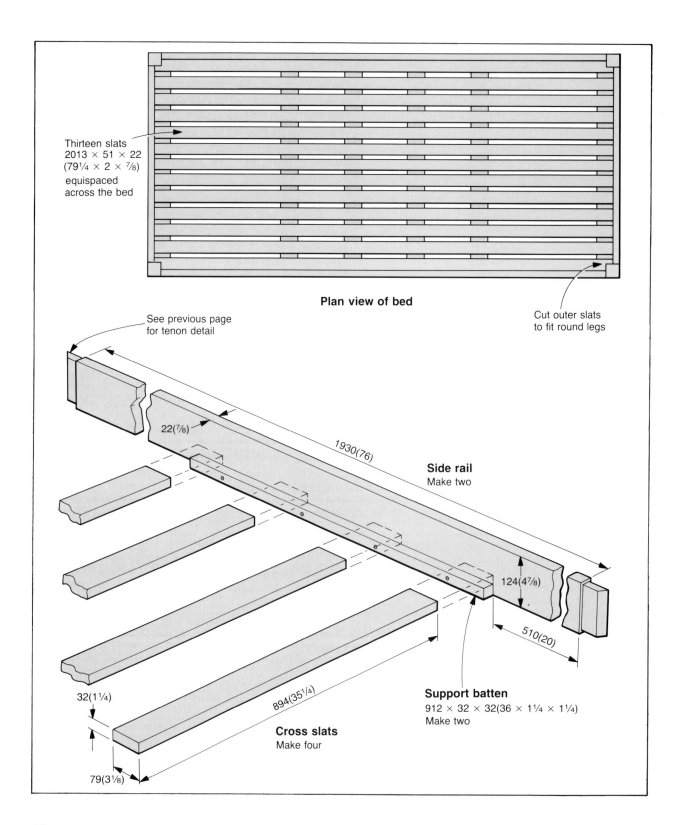

Thirteen slats
2013 × 51 × 22
(79¼ × 2 × ⅞)
equispaced
across the bed

**Plan view of bed**

Cut outer slats
to fit round legs

See previous page
for tenon detail

22(⅞)

1930(76)

**Side rail**
Make two

124(4⅞)

510(20)

32(1¼)

894(35¼)

**Support batten**
912 × 32 × 32(36 × 1¼ × 1¼)
Make two

**Cross slats**
Make four

79(3⅛)

# Garden table and benches

*Essential tools*
Marking gauges
Electric router
Tenon saw
Jigsaw
Moulding cutter

There is nothing more pleasant than sitting in your garden enjoying a meal with the family. Unfortunately, the cost of garden tables and benches tends to put such items out of the reach of many families, and some of the woodbuilding skills usually used to build the furniture are much too complicated.

In designing this table and its benches, I have purposely avoided the traditional square legs with the inevitable mortice and tenon joints. I have only used one joint and that is the halving joint. This can be cut with a

minimum of skill, and if you happen to have an electric router, then that can cut the joint for you!

The table and benches are made from Nordic whitewood, which is easily available from builders merchants. None of the dimensions are critical, apart from the height of the table and bench tops, so the overall dimension of the table and benches can be reduced.

As these pieces of furniture will spend a great deal of time outdoors it is essential to use waterproof glue. Ordinary steel screws will rust and leave ugly marks within the first week, so use zinc plated screws. It is also very important to treat the furniture with a good preservative. There are several beautiful ranges of colours available which will protect timber for many years.

## Marking out

Find a timber merchant that can supply you with timber that is planed all round (P.A.R.) or planed square edge (P.S.E.). All woodworking projects start with marking out. Pencil in face side and face edge marks on each piece. "G" cramp or tape together all the uprights for the table legs, and pencil in the shoulder lines for halving joints. (**1**) Tape together the cross pieces that hold the legs together, and mark in the position of the halving joints. On the bottom rails, pencil in the halving joint that takes the stretcher rail. This rail makes the legs stable at the bottom and prevents them flexing.

When you have pencilled in all the shoulder lines, check to see that all the measurements are correct. Now, with a Stanley knife, knife over all the

**1** *"G" cramp the wood for the table legs together and pencil in the shoulder lines. Now use a marking gauge to find the centre lines of the wood for the halving joints and pencil these in.*

pencil lines. This will ensure that when you come to cut the wood, the timber fibres will separate cleanly and leave a good tidy joint.

The next step is to use a marking gauge. Marking gauges provide the most accurate method of dividing the timber "in half". They also give the chisel a datum line to work down to when you start chiselling out the waste wood. Mark with a pencil where the point of the marking gauge has gone. It is good practice to pencil in all the parts that have to be cut away – there will be less chance of cutting out the wrong piece.

When all the marking out is completed, lay all the pieces on the bench or floor, and check to see that everything will fit together correctly when it has been cut out.

**Cutting out the halving joint**

The method for cutting out the halved angle joint at the corners is identical on all pieces. The stretcher rails have halved T joints as do the stretcher rails on the benches. The method is the same. As the halving joint for the stretcher rail is slightly more difficult, I will describe exactly how it is made.

Cramp the bottom rail in the vice or onto the bench top. With a tenon saw, cut carefully down the sides until you get to the bottom line (this is the one marked in by the marking gauge). (**2**)

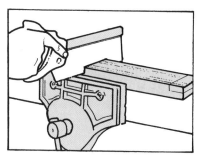

**2** *Clamp the wood firmly to the workbench, then cut carefully with a tenon saw down the sides until you reach the marking gauge line.*

Repeat on the other side.

Using a large chisel and a mallet, position yourself comfortably to one side of the joint and start chipping out the waste wood. (**3**) It is best to work from the top down; don't be tempted to try and cut it out all in one go. I usually angle my chisel up slightly to prevent any tearing out from the bottom of the joint.

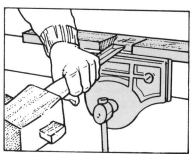

**3** *With a large sharp chisel and mallet, chip away the waste wood, working from the top down. The chisel should be angled slightly upwards to prevent the wood tearing. Halfway through, reverse the timber in the vice.*

Reverse the timber at about the halfway stage, and start from the other side. Finish off by cutting along the bottom marking gauge line. (**4**) Well pencilled marking gauge lines will greatly help this stage of the work. Check with a steel rule that there are no "high spots" in the middle. (**5**) Then tackle the halved

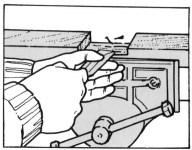

**4** *Finish off by cutting along the bottom marking line. For the last few cuts, use the chisel only, as shown.*

**5** *The finished halving joints. Check with a steel rule that there are no "high spots".*

joints on all the corners using the same method as above.

**Glueing up**

Cut out all the table and bench joints before you start to glue up. You will need some "G" cramps and two sash cramps to glue together the frames of both table and benches. Once the glue has been applied, cramp the framework. It is vital to have a flat area on which to lay all the pieces, otherwise accurate glueing will not be possible.

Use "G" cramps on the corners and check that all the shoulder lines are pulled up tight with the sash cramps. Sharpen a piece of waste wood at one end, and use this to check for the squareness of the framework. Place the waste wood across the diagonals, and make pencil marks. (**6**) If both pencil marks line up, then the framework is square. Repeat this

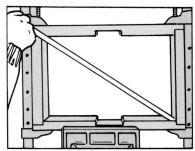

**6** *Check the diagonals are the same with a piece of sharpened waste wood.*

procedure for all the frames. Once the glue is cured (has dried), plane off any surplus glue and trim all edges.

I used a decorative cutter on the frames which gives them a more interesting and stylish shape. There are cutters available that have a small ball bearing on the bottom. This prevents any burring of the timber as you work, and makes it extremely simple to use, as the router is easily steered all around the frames. (**7**)

Now glue the stretcher rail between the two table frames.

**7** *A router fitted with a decorative cutter can give stylish shapes to all the edges.*

**Finishing off**

The table has two rails screwed onto the frames at the top. (**8**) First shape up the rails with a jigsaw, then plane off, or use glasspaper to smooth away, all the saw marks. Add a decorative edge using the router fitted with the same cutter as that used on the frames. To give the table top slats stability, two cross bearer rails are screwed into place. (**9**) Use a

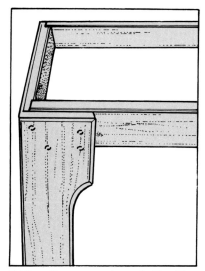

**8** *The rails are screwed to each side of the tops of the frames.*

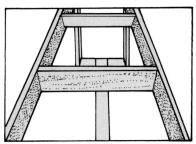

**9** *Two cross bearer rails will give the table top slats stability.*

countersink to ensure that all the heads of the screws are sunk below the surface of the wood.

Screw the slats for the table top into the framework, keeping the slats fairly close together. (**10**) Once they are in place, pencil in the curved ends. Use a jigsaw to shape the ends, and then work round the edges with a router. (**11**)

The stretcher rails are now glued onto the bench end frames.(**12**) Again, the edges are moulded with the router before the stretcher rails are fitted.

Fit rails at the top of the bench frames to give the slats support. The rails are screwed straight onto the frameworks. Screw a single cross

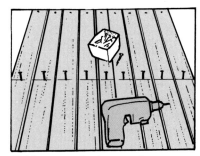

**10** *Now screw the slats onto the framework, using a countersink.*

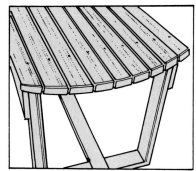

**11** *Shape the ends with a jigsaw; then mould the edges with the router and decorative cutter.*

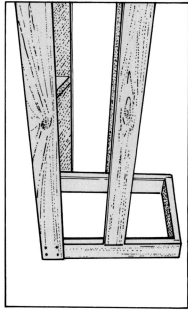

**12** *Now glue the stretcher rails onto the bench end frames, before screwing on the slats.*

161

bearer rail between the stretcher rails before screwing the bench slats onto each framework. Once this has been done, the router with the moulding cutter is used to work all around the slats, making them both attractive and comfortable.

Work over the table and benches with a fine glasspaper before applying wood preservative. (13)

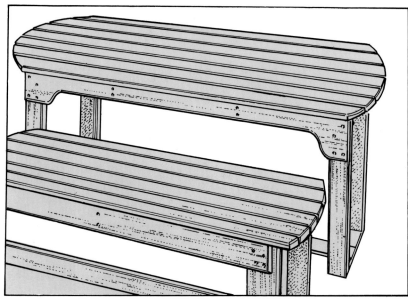

**13** *The finished table and one of the benches.*

### GARDEN TABLE CUTTING LIST

| | | |
|---|---|---|
| Table top | 9 off | 1,930 × 70 × 25mm (76 × 2¾ × 1in) timber |
| Top rail | 2 off | 1,677 × 146 × 25mm (66 × 5¾ × 1in) timber |
| Stretcher rail | 1 off | 1,689 × 86 × 32mm (66½ × 3⅜ × 1¼in) timber |
| Leg uprights | 4 off | 768 × 86 × 32mm (30¼ × 3⅜ × 1¼in) timber |
| Leg cross rails | 4 off | 603 × 86 × 32mm (23¾ × 3⅜ × 1¼in) timber |
| Cross bearer rails | 2 off | 635 × 83 × 32mm (25 × 3¼ × 1¼in) timber |

### GARDEN BENCH CUTTING LIST (numbers per bench)

| | | |
|---|---|---|
| Bench top | 5 off | 1,499 × 70 × 25mm (59 × 2¾ × 1in) timber |
| Support rail | 2 off | 1,359 × 73 × 25mm (53½ × 2⅞ × 1in) timber |
| Stretcher rail | 2 off | 1,371 × 86 × 32mm (54 × 3⅜ × 1¼in) timber |
| Leg uprights | 4 off | 508 × 86 × 32mm (20 × 3⅜ × 1¼in) timber |
| End frame cross rails | 4 off | 330 × 86 × 32mm (13 × 3⅜ × 1¼in) timber |
| Cross bearer rail | 1 off | 362 × 70 × 32mm (14¼ × 2¾ × 1¼in) timber |

*The front rail of the table has been cut away to give more leg room than normal.*

**Above and right** *The front stretcher rail and the table top slats are screwed onto the leg framework.*

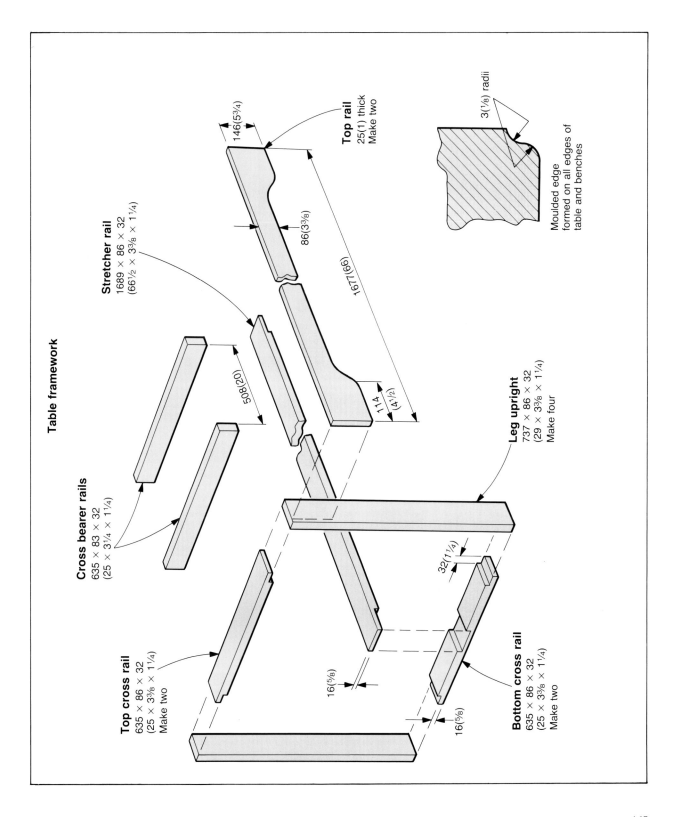

**Table framework**

**Top rail**
25(1) thick
Make two

146(5³/₄)

86(3³/₈)

1677(66)

114
(4¹/₂)

**Stretcher rail**
1689 × 86 × 32
(66¹/₂ × 3³/₈ × 1¹/₄)

508(20)

**Cross bearer rails**
635 × 83 × 32
(25 × 3¹/₄ × 1¹/₄)

**Leg upright**
737 × 86 × 32
(29 × 3³/₈ × 1¹/₄)
Make four

32(1¹/₄)

**Top cross rail**
635 × 86 × 32
(25 × 3³/₈ × 1¹/₄)
Make two

16(⁵/₈)

16(⁵/₈)

16(⁵/₈)

**Bottom cross rail**
635 × 86 × 32
(25 × 3³/₈ × 1¹/₄)
Make two

3(¹/₈) radii

Moulded edge
formed on all edges of
table and benches

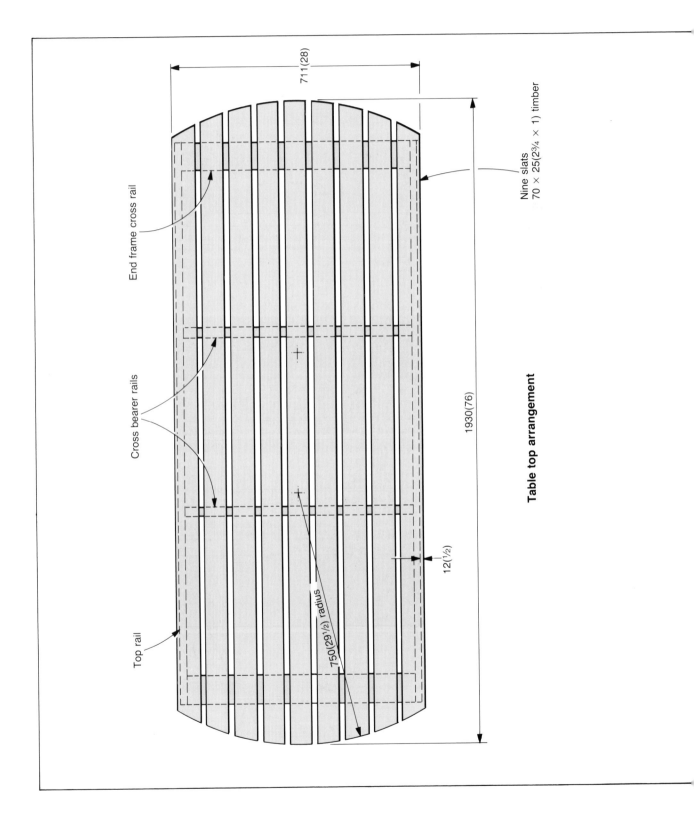

711(28)

Nine slats
70 × 25(2¾ × 1) timber

End frame cross rail

Cross bearer rails

1930(76)

Top rail

750(29½) radius

12(½)

**Table top arrangement**

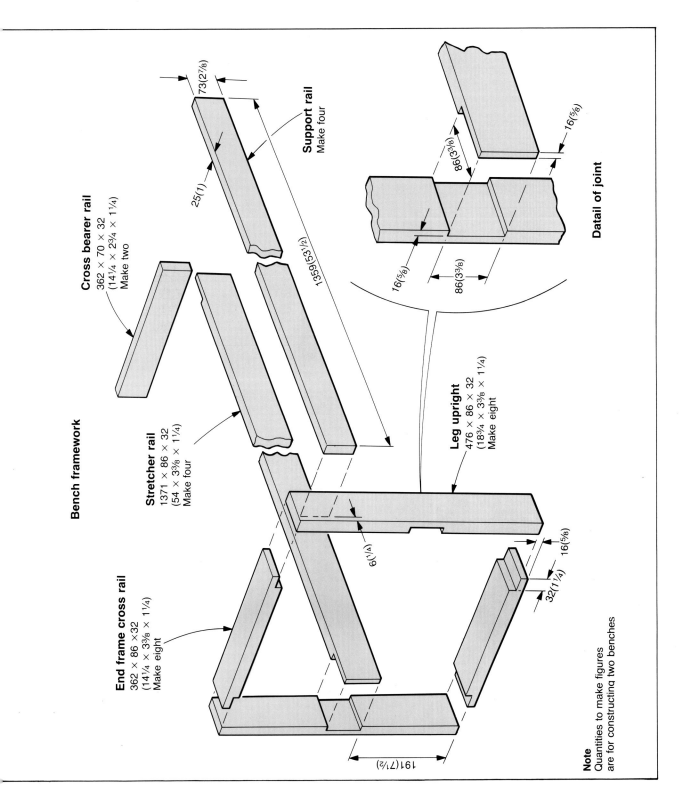

**Bench framework**

**Cross bearer rail**
362 × 70 × 32
(14¼ × 2¾ × 1¼)
Make two

**Stretcher rail**
1371 × 86 × 32
(54 × 3⅜ × 1¼)
Make four

**End frame cross rail**
362 × 86 ×32
(14¼ × 3⅜ × 1¼)
Make eight

**Support rail**
Make four

**Leg upright**
476 × 86 × 32
(18¾ × 3⅜ × 1¼)
Make eight

**Detail of joint**

73(2⅞)

25(1)

1359(53½)

86(3⅜)

16(⅝)

16(⅝)

86(3⅜)

6(¼)

16(⅝)

32(1¼)

191(7½)

**Note**
Quantities to make figures
are for constructing two benches

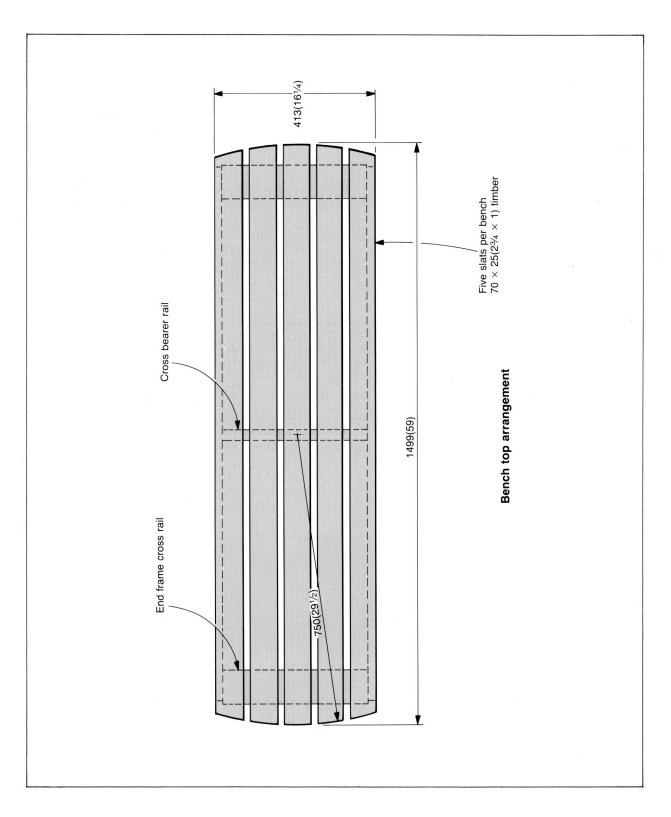

413(16¼)

Five slats per bench
70 × 25(2¾ × 1) timber

Cross bearer rail

End frame cross rail

1499(59)

750(29½)

**Bench top arrangement**

# Garden shed

*Essential tools*
Sliding bevel gauge
Claw hammer
Electric screwdriver
Panel saw
Mastic gun

Acquiring a garden shed has become a major investment in recent years, and frequently the purchaser wants a shed of a particular size which is not available commercially. The alternative is to build one yourself. This may seem at first glance rather daunting. However, providing that you master some basic woodworking techniques, the job is well within the scope of the D.I.Y. enthusiast.

This shed was constructed with Nordic whitewood and I used sawn timber throughout, except for the door which was made from tongued and grooved boards. The door framework timbers were made from planed square edge timber (sold in the UK as P.S.E.).

To reduce costs, I used weather-board sawn in a wedge shape. The sawn grade is fairly inexpensive, and the sawn timbers hold the wood preservative far better than a planed surface would. As an alternative you can buy shiplap board which comes ready planed. In Scandinavian countries, sawn timber is preferred for this type of project.

External grade plywood was used for the floor and roof. However,

"shuttering" grade plywood – which has only one good surface – is much cheaper and is ideal for this type of construction.

The roof was covered in a medium weight felt. The windows were glazed with perspex, which is easily cut to size and fitted; it is also safer to have this shatterproof glazing material in a garden shed.

It is vital that a method of construction is used that ensures that the frames that make up the shed are square and of a uniform size. When mass produced, these sheds are built in large jigs, or guide frameworks, a process that ensures accuracy. In the home workshop, garage or even driveway, this is not possible. So a D.I.Y. method is necessary.

## The framework

The first task is to make the temporary jig around which you can nail together the framework of the shed. To do this, form two triangular shapes with one 90° angle each from plywood offcuts. Screw the triangles onto the sheet of plywood that will be used for the floor of the shed. (1)

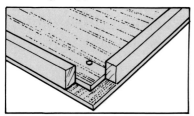

**1** *Screw triangles onto the plywood that form the shed floor.*

In order to ensure that each triangle is placed accurately with the 90° angle into the corner, place two pieces of batten against the edges of the plywood sheets. Their inner edges should butt tightly with the sides of the triangles. (2)

**2** *Use battens to check that the edges are correctly placed.*

Now cut the battens for the framework to length. Cut all the side lengths together to ensure accuracy. The ends should be cut cleanly and square, as these "butt up" to form the corners. (3)

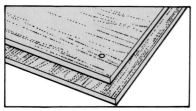

**3** *The batten edges should butt up to form the corners.*

For all those who have had the unfortunate experience of nailing wood only to see it split, the following technique will be a great help. Position the end and upright of one side onto the jig and cramp one side firmly in place. Use a small drill bit to make a hole right through both pieces of timber. (4) Drilling this hole will prevent the wood from splitting, but it will not stop the grip the nail has on the timber.

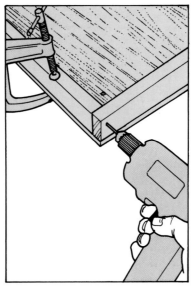

**4** *It is crucial that the holes drilled are small so that the nail will end up in a very tight fit.*

Once the main holes are bored, the nails are driven in. (5) This method of fixing corners for a shed construction is very strong. The nail is an iron dowel, and if used correctly makes a very strong jointing method. The corner can be further strengthened by screwing plywood triangles onto it. (6)

Now make the other three corners. The frames need to be strengthened by cross pieces. These firm up the frames and provide fixing points for the weather boarding to be nailed onto the frames later. The cross pieces are all fixed by the same method. (7)

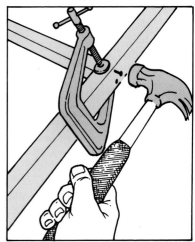

**5** *Now drive a nail through the holes made by the drill.*

**6** *Plywood triangles screwed onto the corners will strengthen them.*

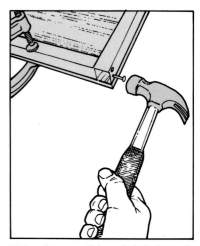

**7** *Use a "G" cramp to hold each cross piece as the nails are driven home.*

The front frame is shorter than the back, and has spacers fixed to take the four windows while the back is windowless. The side frames are fairly straightforward to make. They differ slightly and you have to remember that one end is blank, and the other takes the door. Also, the upper rail must be fixed at the top of each frame at an angle that will accommodate the slope of the roof.

The angle or slope is the difference between the height of the back panel and the front. Carefully measure out the different lengths needed for the side frame members. Place a batten between the two frames and pencil in the angle that has to be cut on the frame. Use a bevel gauge to transfer the angle on both sides of the frame. Knife in the angle and then cut it into the end frame with a tenon saw. (**8**)

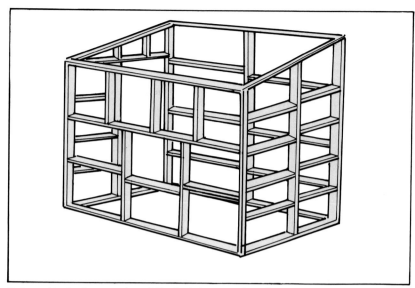

**9** *Assemble the frames and carefully check that everything fits together.*

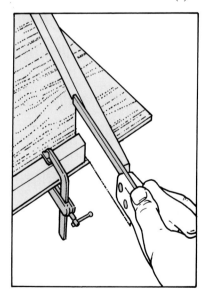

**8** *Carefully cut the angle onto the end of the frame.*

Nail up the four frames and the cross pieces together. Use plenty of nails.

When all the frames have been made, assemble them temporarily, holding the corners with "G" cramps. (**9**) Check that the ends and sloping

sides line up. When the fit has been checked, it is time to clad the frames with feather edge weather board.

**The cladding**

Weather boarding "sawn" is the cheapest form of cladding for a shed. If you prefer, shiplap board can be used instead and comes ready planed.

Work the back panel first as this is a straightforward "planking in" job. Start cladding the frames at the bottom edge. (**10**) This will make any rain running down drop off below the floor. Now fix the second board in place. (**11**)

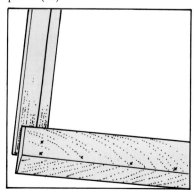

**10** *Leave a good overlap at the bottom edge of the frames.*

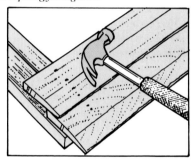

**11** *Allow sufficient overlap of one board over the next .*

As you place each board on top of the other, use a "spacing stick". Simply drop the spacing stick onto the top of the board that is in place, and pencil in where the next board will go. (**12**) This ensures that the boards are fixed uniformly on all four panels.

The front panel is a little different when you reach the bottom of the windows. A sill made from weather board has to be fitted. The sawn angle of the board makes it ideal for this purpose. Cut it so that it fits around the window bar uprights. (**13**) This leaves less corners for water to penetrate; if water is allowed to stand on the surface of timber, it will start to rot. Always try to make sure that water is "led" off and that air can get in to dry the timber.

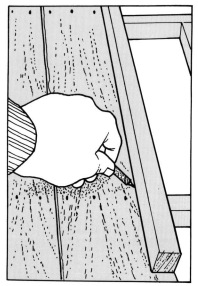

**12** *The use of a spacing stick will make the job quicker and eliminates the need to measure each board individually.*

**13** *The window board should fit snugly round the window bar uprights.*

When you reach the top of the door frame on the front panel, it is necessary to add an additional batten of timber along the top of the door. The batten will support the bottom edge of the next board. (**14**) The next board is added across the full length of the panel. (**15**)

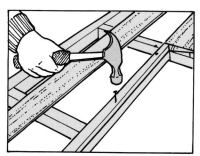

**14** *The extra batten lines up with the feather edged board on the right hand side of the door frame.*

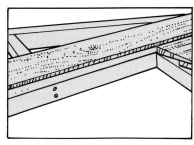

**15** *Place the next board across the full length of the frame .*

## The windows

The windows of the shed are made with perspex. This is available in sheet form from D.I.Y. stores and builders merchants. The manufacturer usually provides advice on cutting it. I always find a fine-toothed saw works well. However, it is vital to support the material as you cut it, or it may shatter at the corners.

The windows are held in place inside the shed by small wooden strips nailed all round the frames. (**16**)

**16** *Nail small wooden strips round the inside of the window frames.*

Then use a mastic gun to apply silicone sealant, which doubles as a putty and sticks the windows in place. (**17**)

**17** *Run a seam of silicone round the window frame.*

Push the ready-cut perspex windows into place and run a further seam of sealant along the front edges of the perspex. (**18**) If the seam does not run perfectly straight first time, wet your finger and run it along to smooth out the seam.

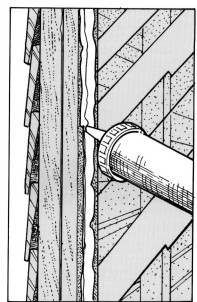

**18** *When the perspex windows are in place, run a further seam of silicone along the front edges of the perspex.*

## The door

The boards used for the door are tongued and grooved and the framework on the back is planed timber. There are no joints on the door; it is all held together with screws.

Begin by cutting the T&G boards to length. It is important to use sash cramps to pull the boards tightly together before you put in any of the screws. Place battens on the back of the door. Pencil in on the front edge the position of the battens and screw the T&G boards to the battens. (**19**)

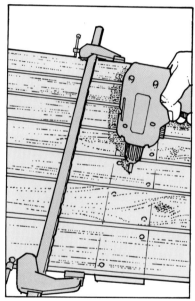

**19** *The boards are pulled together with sash cramps and the battens are screwed in to the back of the door.*

This type of door must have diagonal braces fitted to make it stable. (**20**) It is vital that the braces are angled in relation to the side the door will be hinged. If not, the stresses in the door as it is opened and closed will distort it.

Water will run down the door into the shed unless a weather bar is fitted. Weather bar is available from D.I.Y. shops and builders merchants. It is important that the bar is sealed onto

the door, so mastic is used behind the door *before* the bar is fitted. The grooves in the boards will make a natural channel for the water, so a seam of mastic is also applied to the top of the weather board.

**20** *Place the braces on to the cross pieces and pencil in the extra wood to be cut off. The braces are fitted this way when the hinge is to be on the left hand side of the door (seen from the front).*

The door is fitted to the frame using T hinges. I used three hinges and round head screws. (**21**) A small bolt is also fitted to prevent the door blowing open.

**21** *The T hinges and round head screws must all be black japanned to prevent rust.*

## The floor

The floor is made from a single sheet of external grade plywood with battens fitted on all the outside edges. The first battens are screwed onto the back of the plywood from the face side, and cross battens are nailed in place. (**22**) This will provide a rigid floor structure.

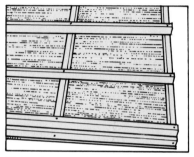

**22** *Fix battens to the plywood to give it rigidity.*

## Assembling the frames

Apply a good quality wood preservative to the underside of the floor, and the inside and edges of the frames, before assembling the shed. You will need help with the assembly – someone to hold two panels, while you drive in screws to hold the corners together from the inside.

The feather edge board is overlapped at the bottom, so it will butt up against the base very easily. (**23**) Do not drive in more than three screws at this stage. Now "bolt on" the other panels.

## The roof

This is made from external grade plywood, like the floor. To achieve generous roof overhangs, it is necessary to buy two sheets. The joint in the plywood is arranged so that it falls in the middle. A batten of wood is screwed to the underside to hold the two pieces together. Fix battens tight against the shed ends and drive screws through to hold on the roof. (**24**)

Along the back and front edges,

**23** *Make sure that the sides butt up against the base.*

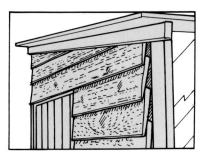

**24** *The battens have to fit tight against the sides of the shed, and are screwed into place.*

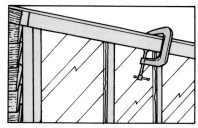

**25** *Clamp and screw battens onto the back and front edges of the roof.*

battens are screwed to the plywood. (**25**) This makes the shed roof look much more substantial.

The roof is now screwed to the framework from the top side. Cut and fix a medium weight felt to the plywood. Use galvanised felt tacks and plenty of them – remember the spring gales!

**The final touches**

Now secure all corners with extra screws as needed. A gutter downpipe and a water butt would be useful additions.

It is advisable to stand the base on concrete blocks, just off the ground. Make sure that air can circulate underneath it. Treat the outside of the shed with the wood preservative of your choice. (**26**)

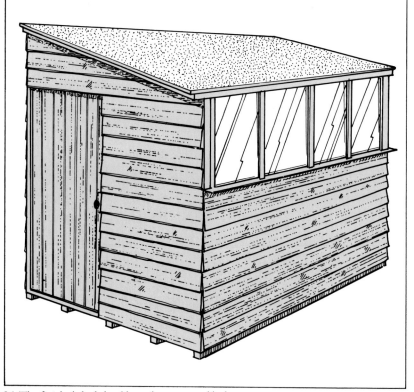

**26** *The finished shed should stand on concrete blocks.*

## GARDEN SHED CUTTING LIST

| | | |
|---|---|---|
| Back wall assembly | 5 off | 2,133 × 51 × 25mm (84 × 2 × 1in) timber |
| | 6 off | 1,029 × 51 × 25mm (40½ × 2 × 1in) timber |
| Cladding | 22 off | 2,235 × 127mm (88 × 5in) weather board |
| Right hand side wall assembly | 1 off | 2,133 × 51 × 25mm (84 × 2 × 1in) timber |
| | 1 off | 2,007 × 51 × 25mm (79 × 2 × 1in) timber |
| | 1 off | 1,880 × 51 × 25mm (74 × 2 × 1in) timber |
| | 1 off | 1,207 × 51 × 25mm (47½ × 2 × 1in) timber |
| | 1 off | 1,168 × 51 × 25mm (46 × 2 × 1in) timber |
| | 8 off | 546 × 51 × 25mm (21½ × 2 × 1in) timber |
| Cladding | 22 off | 1,168 × 127mm (46 × 5in) weather board |
| Left hand side wall assembly | 1 off | 2,133 × 51 × 25mm (84 × 2 × 1in) timber |
| | 1 off | 1,880 × 51 × 25mm (74 × 2 × 1in) timber |
| | 1 off | 1,812 × 51 × 25mm (71⅜ × 2 × 1in) timber |
| | 1 off | 1,812 × 51 × 9mm (71⅜ × 2 × ⅜in) timber |
| | 1 off | 1,864 × 51 × 25mm (73⅜ × 2 × 1in) timber |
| | 1 off | 1,207 × 51 × 25mm (47½ × 2 × 1in) timber |
| | 1 off | 1,168 × 51 × 25mm (46 × 2 × 1in) timber |
| | 1 off | 1,118 × 51 × 25mm (44 × 2 × 1in) timber |
| | 3 off | 435 × 51 × 25mm (17⅛ × 2 × 1in) timber |
| | 1 off | 229 × 51 × 25mm (9 × 2 × 1in) timber |
| | 1 off | 152 × 51 × 25mm (6 × 2 × 1in) timber |
| Cladding | 3 off | 1,168 × 127mm (46 × 5in) weather board |
| | 19 off | 495 × 127mm (19½ × 5in) weather board |
| Door Assembly | 7 off | 1,803 × 89 × 16mm (71 × 3½ × ⅝in) tongued and grooved board |
| | 3 off | 632 × 64 × 32mm (24⅞ × 2½ × 1¼in) timber |
| | 2 off | 927 × 64 × 32mm (36½ × 2½ × 1¼in) timber |
| | 1 off | 632 × 70 × 48mm (24⅞ × 2¾ × 1⅞in) weather board |
| Front wall assembly | 2 off | 2,133 × 51 × 25mm (84 × 2 × 1in) timber |
| | 2 off | 1,880 × 51 × 25mm (74 × 2 × 1in) timber |
| | 1 off | 2,083 × 51 × 25mm (82 × 2 × 1in) timber |
| | 2 off | 1,168 × 51 × 25mm (46 × 2 × 1in) timber |
| | 2 off | 686 × 51 × 25mm (27 × 2 × 1in) timber |
| | 1 off | 660 × 51 × 25mm (26 × 2 × 1in) timber |
| Window dividers | 3 off | 686 × 51 × 25mm (27 × 2 × 1in) timber |
| Window sill | 1 off | 2,235 × 127mm (88 × 5in) weather board |
| Window strip horizontals | 8 off | 502 × 20 × 9mm (19¾ × ¾ × ⅜in) timber |
| Window strip verticals | 8 off | 651 × 20 × 9mm (25⅝ × ¾ × ⅜in) timber |
| Cladding | 12 off | 2,235 × 127mm (88 × 5in) weather board |
| Roof assembly | 2 off | 2,300 × 51 × 25mm (90½ × 2 × 1in) timber |
| | 2 off | 1,397 × 51 × 25mm (55 × 2 × 1in) timber |
| | 1 off | 1,092 × 51 × 25mm (43 × 2 × 1in) timber |
| | 2 off | 1,397 × 1,220 × 9mm (55 × 48 × ⅜in) plywood |
| Floor | 1 off | 2,235 × 1,168 × 12mm (88 × 46 × ½in) plywood |
| Underfloor frame | 2 off | 2,235 × 51 × 25mm (88 × 2 × 1in) timber |
| | 5 off | 1,118 × 51 × 25mm (44 × 2 × 1in) timber |
| Optional air spacers | 5 off | 2,235 × 51 × 25mm (88 × 2 × 1in) timber |

Ancillaries

Roofing felt (medium weight)
Door hinges & lock assembly
Clear plastic windows 4 off  670 × 502 × 3mm (26⅜ × 19¾ × ⅛in)
Tube of silicone sealant

*Accurate measuring will ensure that the frames will butt up correctly.*

**Left and below** *Two views of the inside of the shed.*

**Left** *The roof is screwed to the shed framework from the outside.*

**Right** *The medium weight felt is fixed to the roof by galvanised felt tacks.*

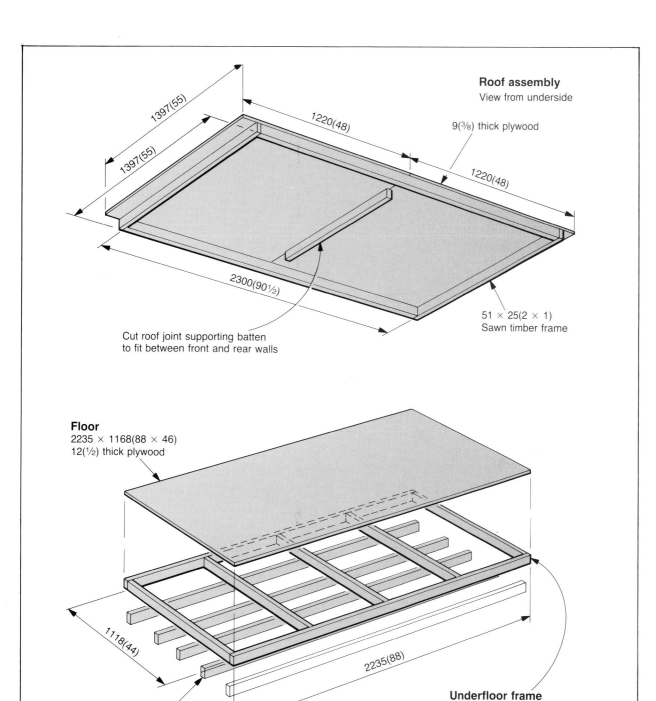

**Roof assembly**
View from underside

1397(55)

1220(48)

9(3/8) thick plywood

1397(55)

1220(48)

2300(90½)

Cut roof joint supporting batten
to fit between front and rear walls

51 × 25(2 × 1)
Sawn timber frame

**Floor**
2235 × 1168(88 × 46)
12(½) thick plywood

1118(44)

2235(88)

**Underfloor frame**
51 × 25(2 × 1) sawn timber

**Optional;**
2235(88) lengths of
51 × 25(2 × 1) sawn timber
to lift shed clear of ground and
allow an airflow beneath the floor

**Back assembly**

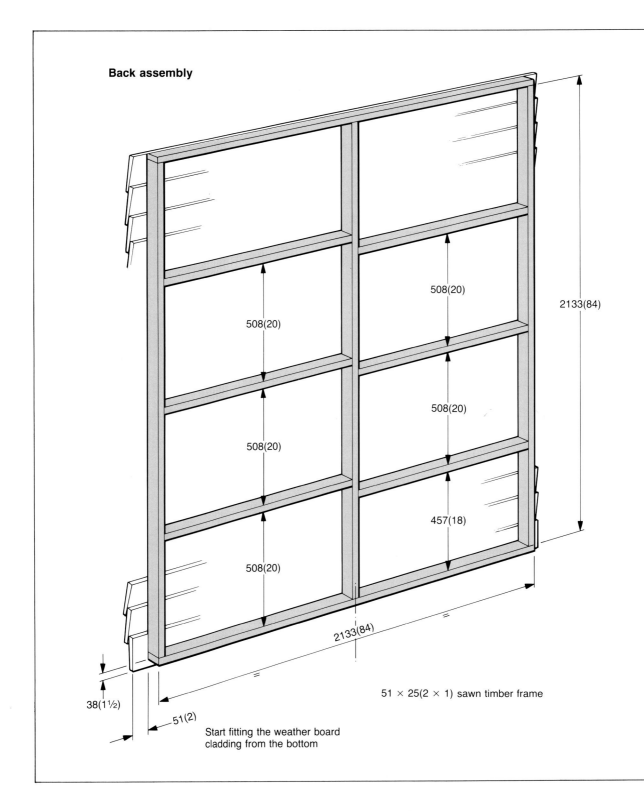

2133(84)

508(20)

508(20)

508(20)

508(20)

508(20)

457(18)

2133(84)

51 × 25(2 × 1) sawn timber frame

38(1½)

51(2)

Start fitting the weather board
cladding from the bottom

**Right hand side wall**

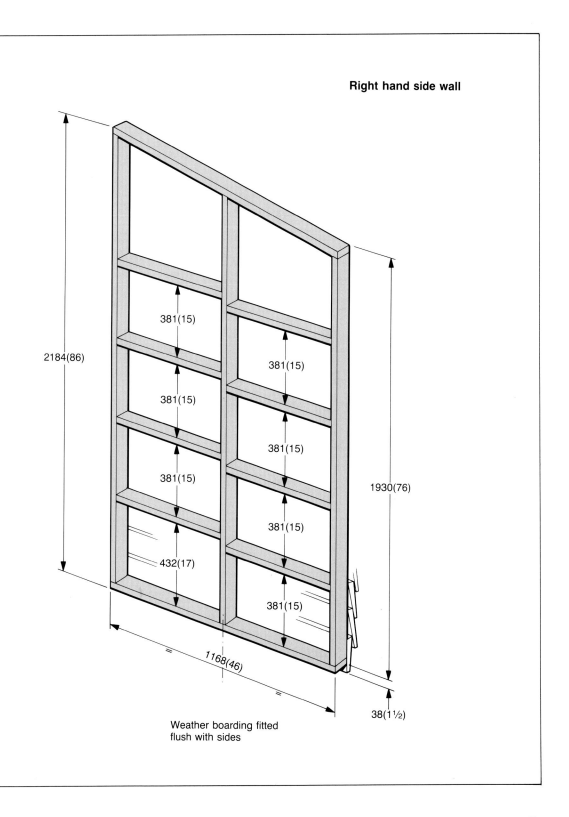

2184(86)

381(15)

381(15)

381(15)

381(15)

381(15)

381(15)

381(15)

432(17)

381(15)

1930(76)

1168(46)

38(1½)

Weather boarding fitted
flush with sides

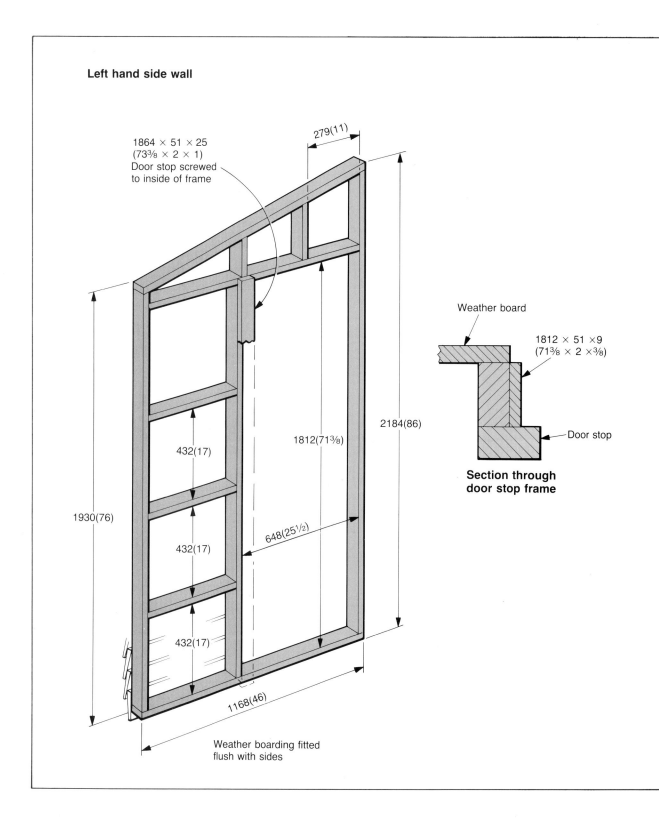

Left hand side wall

1864 × 51 × 25
(73³⁄₈ × 2 × 1)
Door stop screwed
to inside of frame

279(11)

Weather board

1812 × 51 ×9
(71³⁄₈ × 2 ×³⁄₈)

Door stop

**Section through
door stop frame**

2184(86)

1812(71³⁄₈)

432(17)

1930(76)

432(17)

648(25¹⁄₂)

432(17)

1168(46)

Weather boarding fitted
flush with sides

**Front assembly**

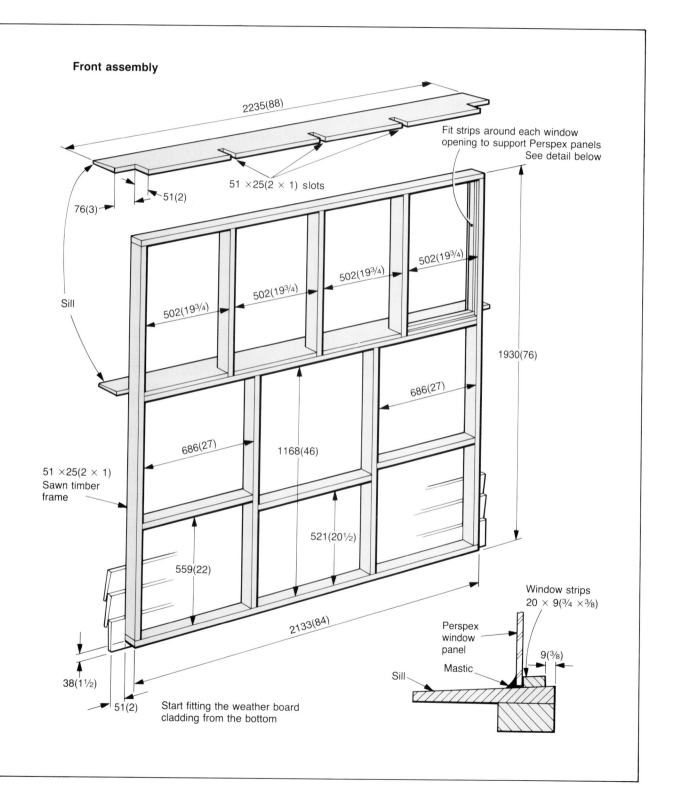

2235(88)

Fit strips around each window opening to support Perspex panels
See detail below

51 ×25(2 × 1) slots

51(2)

76(3)

Sill

502(19¾)

502(19¾)

502(19¾)

502(19¾)

1930(76)

686(27)

51 ×25(2 × 1)
Sawn timber
frame

686(27)

1168(46)

521(20½)

559(22)

2133(84)

38(1½)

51(2)

Start fitting the weather board
cladding from the bottom

Window strips
20 × 9(¾ ×⅜)

Perspex
window
panel

9(⅜)

Mastic

Sill

**Door assembly**

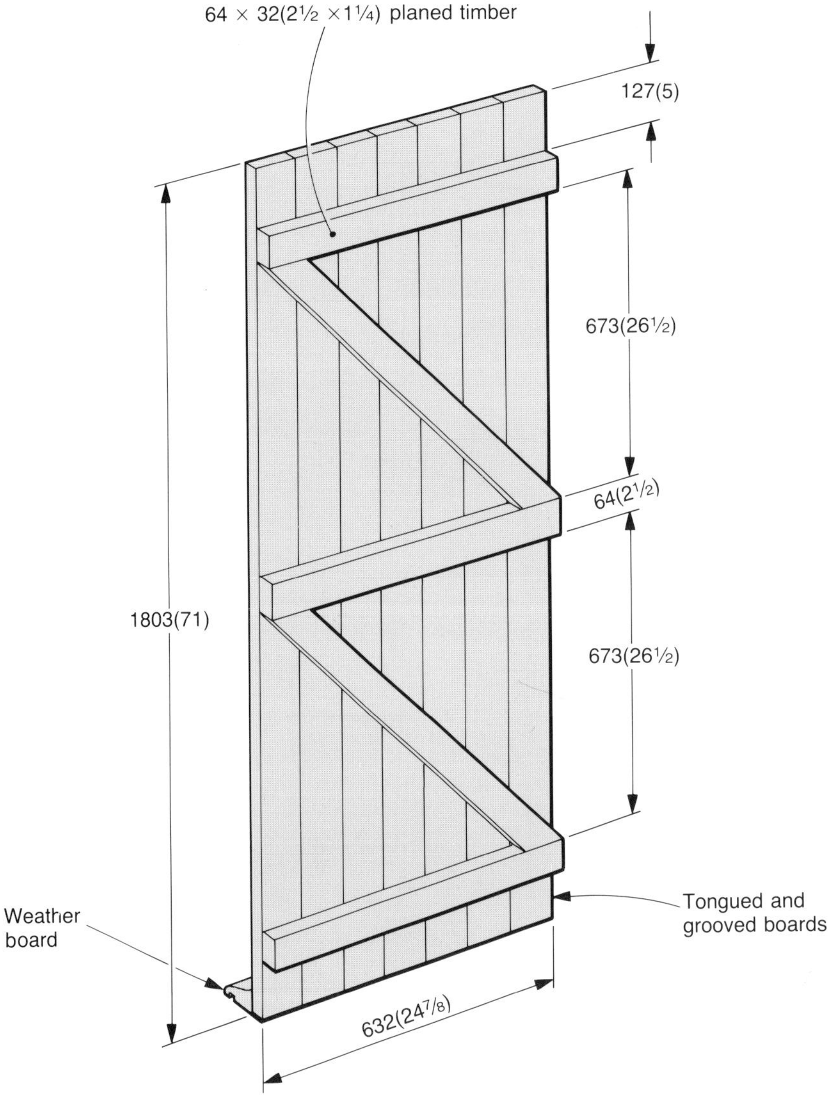

$64 \times 32(2\frac{1}{2} \times 1\frac{1}{4})$ planed timber

127(5)

673(26$\frac{1}{2}$)

64(2$\frac{1}{2}$)

673(26$\frac{1}{2}$)

1803(71)

Tongued and
grooved boards

Weather
board

632(24$\frac{7}{8}$)

Fit Hinges on outside face of door,
in line with the framework horizontals

# Gazebo

**Essential tools**
Jigsaw
Spokeshave
Sliding bevel gauge
Electric screwdriver
Bevel edged chisel

The past twenty years have seen a tremendous revival of interest in gardens. Throughout the country, garden centres have sprung up, able to supply everything from everlasting rhubarb to rotating summer houses!

However, mention the word "gazebo" and you may well be asked what to feed it on! Many of our Victorian ancestors had one of these in their gardens. A large gazebo gave them somewhere to sit in the heat of the summer, and the roses trained up the sides would have filled the air inside with a beautiful fragrance.

This design is for a small gazebo, intended to fit into a small garden. Making it eight-sided means that there is the opportunity to have four entrances to allow a walk through at the junction of garden paths. Four trellises support the roof. Although complicated, the roof timbers are not difficult to cut and fit.

The base and circular dome are cut from one sheet of exterior grade plywood, and the timber is Nordic whitewood battens. Some timber merchants keep a good substantial batten in stock that when planed up makes an excellent trellis.

The project is designed around the use of the jigsaw, which is perhaps the most useful and certainly the most versatile cutting tool available.

## The floor

Make a start by cutting a sheet of plywood in half. Use exterior grade plywood – a "shuttering" grade plywood which has one good face is ideal for the job. Then mark the octagonal shape of the floor of the gazebo on one half of the plywood sheet, using a rule, batten and pencil.

The floor needs to be strengthened. This is done by fastening battens on the underside. Use sawn timber to make the battens; wood preservative adheres to this type of surface better than it does to a planed surface. The simplest method of fixing the battens is to pencil in their positions, cramp them in place, drill pilot holes, countersink them, and then drive in the screws.(**1**)

Screw in the battens across the full width of the base first, then work around the edges fixing the battens

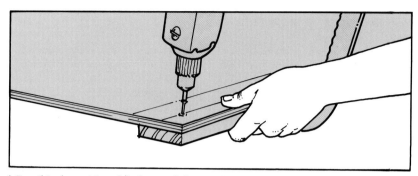

*1 Pencil in the position of the batten, drill a pilot hole and then drive in the screw.*

there. The angles at the junctions need to be carefully marked and cut with a tenon saw.(**2**) Use a sliding bevel gauge to mark the timber all the way round before beginning to cut. The bevel gauge ensures that you can cut out all the angles accurately.

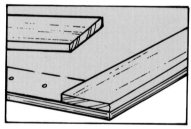

*2 Cut the corner joints with a tenon saw.*

Once the first round of battens have been fixed, fix a second round of battens across the first.(**3**) Screwing battens on in this way braces the floor and prevents it flexing.

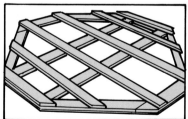

*3 The second round of battens is screwed on at right angles to the first round, in order to brace the floor.*

## The trellises
The battens for the trellises must be planed. Ideally, a gazebo should be

painted white, and if you try to paint sawn timber white it looks dreadful. If you have bought sawn batten for the base, a hand held power plane will very quickly provide you with clean planed battens. There is no reason why you should not use a jack plane – it will just take a little longer.

The trellises for this project are identical in size, so to save time cut all the long battens and cross in one go.

First drill pilot holes in the cross battens. Fix the top and bottom battens first and, holding a length of dowel rod across the diagonals, check that the trellis is square.(**4**) Now screw the other battens in place.(**5**)

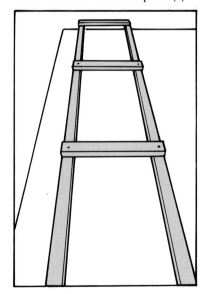

*4 Fix the top and bottom battens of the trellis in place first.*

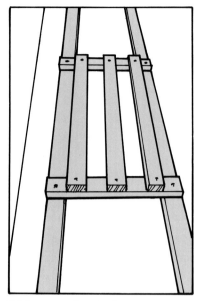

*5 Now screw the other battens on top.*

## The roof
Take the other half of the plywood sheet and mark the centre. Attach a length of cord to a drawing pin and with a pencil attached to the other end scribe a circle.(**6**)

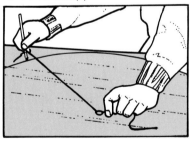

*6 Scribe first an outer, and then an inner circle on the plywood.*

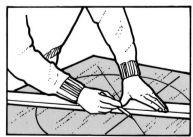

*7 Mark the sections of the roof and the curved areas.*

Mark an inner circle. Next, with a pencil and rule, divide the circle into eight equal segments, and mark where the curved sections will go.(**7**) It is much easier if you pencil in the curved areas at this early stage.

Now cut out the inner circle with the jigsaw. The technique is called sabre sawing. If you look carefully at the sole plate of most jigsaws, you will see that the front end is curved. Switch the saw on and allow it to run up to full speed, then carefully "rock" the saw into the wood. As the cutting continues, the blade will begin to eat into the wood.(**8**)

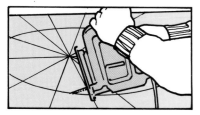

**8** *Allow the saw to run up to full speed before applying it to the wood. As you cut, the saw blade will gradually eat into the wood. Remember to use a firm, even pressure at all times.*

Eventually, the saw blade will go right through the wood, allowing the sole of the jigsaw to end up flat on the plywood. (**9**) The cutting of the curve can now be completed. Apply the same technique to the outer circle.

**9** *The saw blade will go right through the wood and the circle can be cut and lifted out carefully.*

Now mark out the curved sections for the circular dome. First trace the shape full size onto tracing paper, and then transfer the shape onto a piece of hardboard. This will ensure that each curved section is accurately sized.

Cramp the plywood firmly to the bench top before cutting and shaping the curved sections.(**10**)

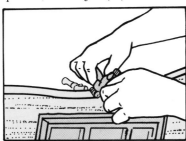

**10** *The jigsaw is the ideal tool to shape the curved roof section.*

After cutting has been completed, the saw marks can be removed with glasspaper, but a spokeshave will do a quicker, cleaner job.(**11**)

**11** *Use a spokeshave to remove the saw cuts before cleaning up the sections.*

When all the roof sections have been cleaned up, glue and screw each section into the circular plywood base.(**12**) The lines pencilled in at the earlier stage make assembling the roof much easier.

The first two sections should be fixed across the roof area.(**13**) To fit the second four sections, it is necessary to trim the edge of the timber to an apex on each one. Using a sliding bevel gauge, "take off" the angle and transfer it onto the timber.

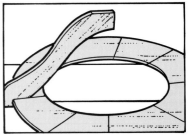

**12** *Screw the sections of the roof into place from the underside.*

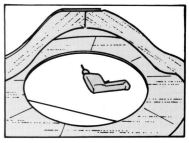

**13** *It may be necessary to make slight adjustments to get the sections to meet exactly in the middle.*

Then with a bevel edged chisel and a plane, alternately chisel and plane the angle.(**14**) Glue and screw the second four sections into position.(**15**)

**14** *Use a bevel edged chisel to cut the angle and then a plane to smooth both edges.*

**15** *An individual fitting will be necessary for each timber.*

To make the top of the gazebo, cut a circle from a piece of waste plywood and cut and shape four pieces of wood from the waste timber.(**16**) Glue and screw the four pieces of wood onto the plywood base, and screw the whole thing onto the top of the gazebo.(**17**)

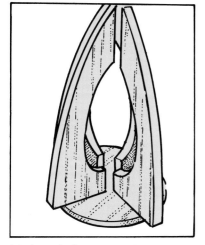

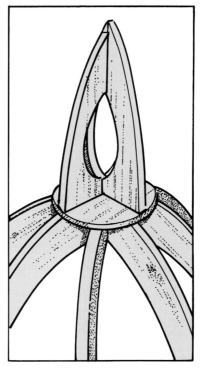

*16 Shape the four sections of the crown of the gazebo with a jigsaw.*

*17 Screw the crown onto the roof of the gazebo.*

*18 The finished gazebo.*

## Assembling

The base is placed on a flat surface and, with the help of an assistant, the four trellises are screwed onto the top of the base with three large screws each. A batten is screwed onto the top of each trellis to give stability.

The top is now screwed onto the trellis and battens. Work all over the structure with fine glasspaper. Give the wood a coat of primer and then undercoat. The undercoat needs to be carefully rubbed down. This is rather a tedious job because it takes some time to work round each batten, but it is worth the effort. Finally, apply a top coat of brilliant white gloss.(**18**)

### GAZEBO CUTTING LIST

| Part | Quantity | Dimensions |
|---|---|---|
| Roof base | 1 off | 1,220 × 1,220 × 12mm (48 × 48 × ½in) plywood |
| Roof sections | 8 off | 813 × 114 × 22mm (32 × 4½ × 7/8in) timber |
| Trellis | 8 off | 2,058 × 51 × 25mm (81 × 2 × 1in) timber |
| | 16 off | 356 × 51 × 25mm (14 × 2 × 1in) timber |
| | 16 off | 711 × 51 × 25mm (28 × 2 × 1in) timber |
| | 12 off | 737 × 51 × 25mm (29 × 2 × 1in) timber |
| Bracing struts | 4 off | 660 × 51 × 25mm (26 × 2 × 1in) timber |
| Base | 1 off | 1,220 × 1,220 × 12mm (48 × 48 × ½in) plywood |
| Battens 1st round | 2 off | 1,372 × 51 × 25mm (54 × 2 × 1in) timber |
| | 2 off | 254 × 51 × 25mm (10 × 2 × 1in) timber |
| | 2 off | 457 × 51 × 25mm (18 × 2 × 1in) timber |
| | 4 off | 692 × 51 × 25mm (27¼ × 2 × 1in) timber |
| Battens 2nd round | 2 off | 1,372 × 51 × 25mm (54 × 2 × 1in) timber |
| | 2 off | 965 × 51 × 25mm (38 × 2 × 1in) timber |
| | 2 off | 457 × 51 × 25mm (18 × 2 × 1in) timber |
| Crown base | 1 off | 279 × 279 × 9mm (11 × 11 × 3/8in) plywood |
| Crown sections | 2 off | 368 × 127 × 22mm (14½ × 5 × 7/8in) timber |
| | 2 off | 343 × 116 × 22mm (13½ × 4 9/16 × 7/8in) timber |

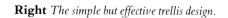

**Right** *The simple but effective trellis design.*

*The top structure of the gazebo before final assembly.*

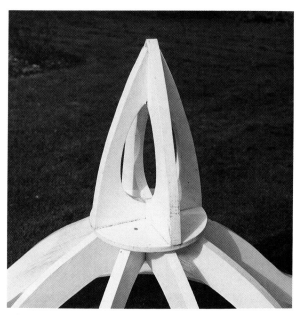

*The crown screwed onto the very top.*

*The top structure of the gazebo assembled.*

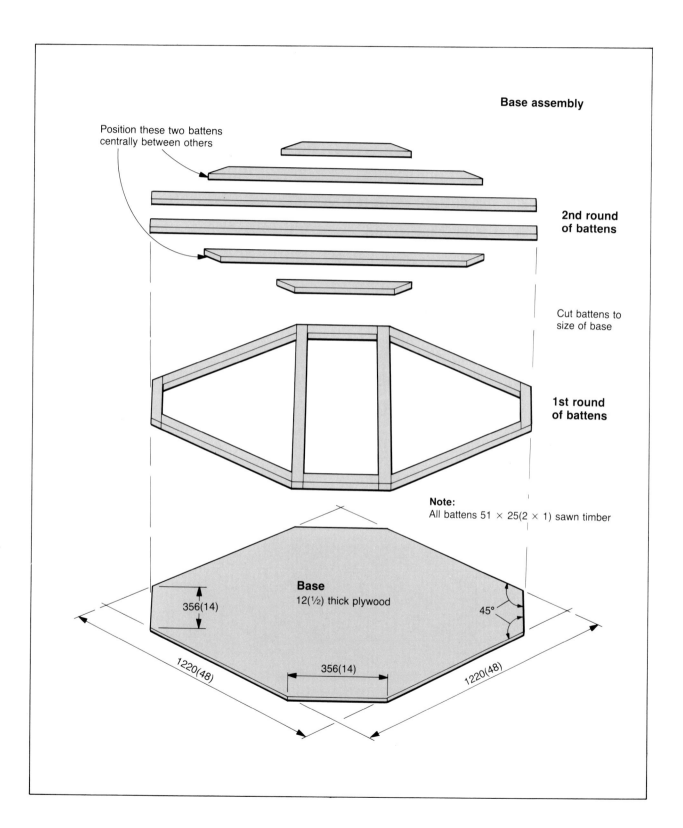

**Base assembly**

Position these two battens
centrally between others

**2nd round
of battens**

Cut battens to
size of base

**1st round
of battens**

**Note:**
All battens 51 × 25(2 × 1) sawn timber

**Base**
12(½) thick plywood

356(14)

45°

1220(48)

356(14)

1220(48)

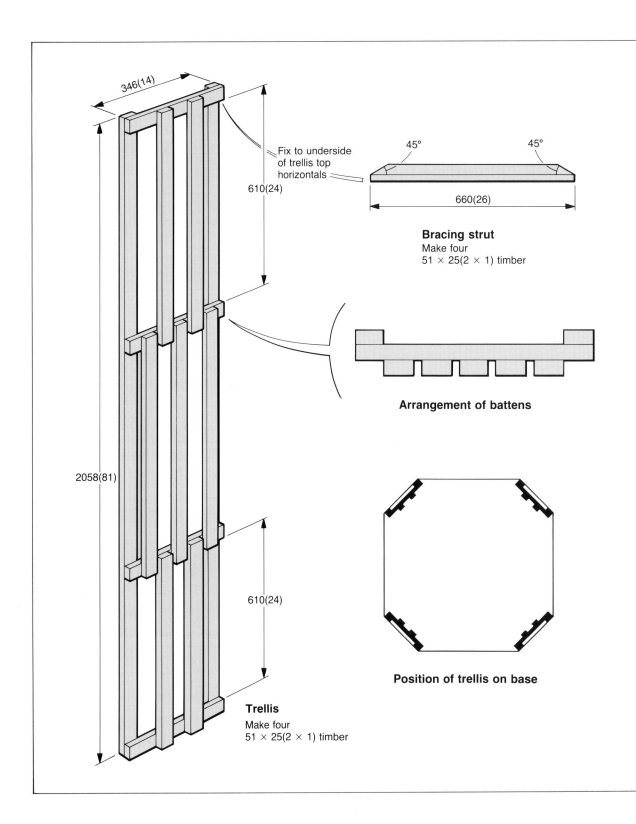

346(14)

Fix to underside
of trellis top
horizontals

610(24)

45°          45°

660(26)

**Bracing strut**
Make four
51 × 25(2 × 1) timber

**Arrangement of battens**

2058(81)

610(24)

**Position of trellis on base**

**Trellis**
Make four
51 × 25(2 × 1) timber

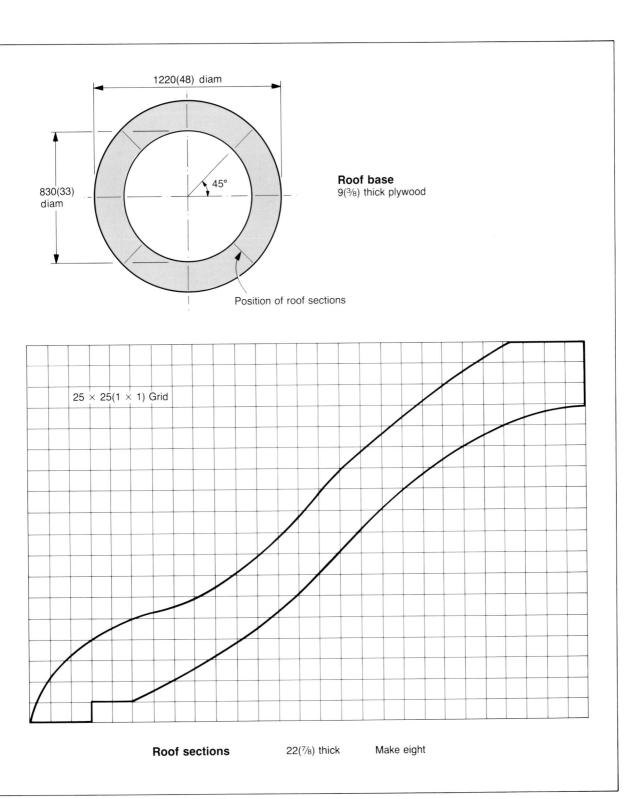

1220(48) diam

830(33) diam

45°

**Roof base**
9(3/8) thick plywood

Position of roof sections

25 × 25(1 × 1) Grid

**Roof sections**   22(7/8) thick   Make eight

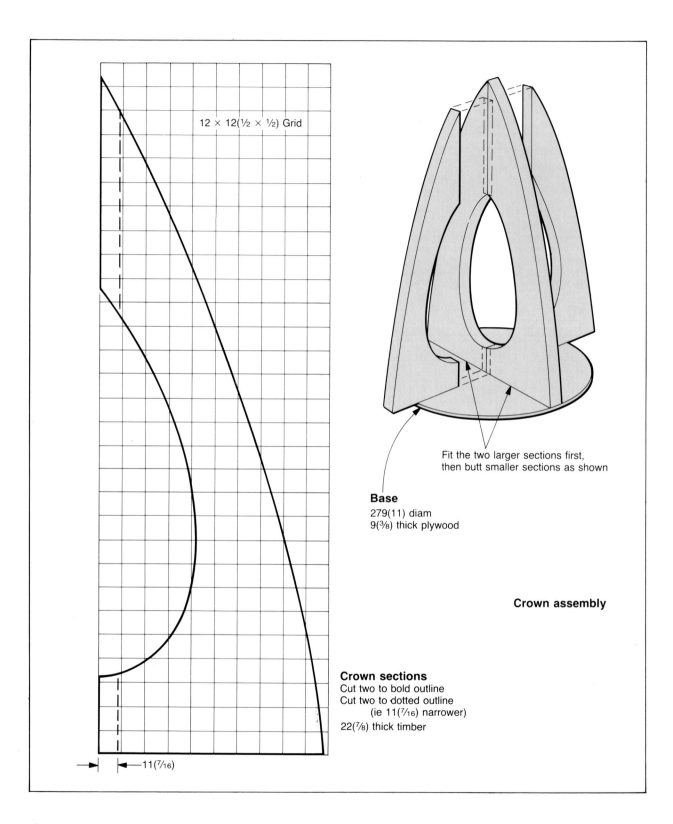

12 × 12(½ × ½) Grid

Fit the two larger sections first,
then butt smaller sections as shown

**Base**
279(11) diam
9(³⁄₈) thick plywood

**Crown assembly**

**Crown sections**
Cut two to bold outline
Cut two to dotted outline
   (ie 11(⁷⁄₁₆) narrower)
22(⁷⁄₈) thick timber

11(⁷⁄₁₆)

# Tools and materials

Buying your own tools is always a good investment. Chisels, marking gauges, planes and cramps can all be bought individually, and over the years you can build up a comprehensive tool box. However, you only get what you pay for, so buy the very best in both hand and electric power tools.

It is false economy to buy cheap foreign imports, particularly chisels or hammers. These cheap tools will not last and can be dangerous to use; it is not unknown for the head of a hammer to shatter in use. Buy a tool with a good brand name – that is, toolmakers who forge and temper their tools correctly.

## A place to work

It is a great advantage to have somewhere to keep everything. Many people work in the garage, but this is not ideal as things often get moved while you are working. A purpose-built shed, insulated and racked to take all your tools, is ideal. Such a building can be kept at a uniform temperature, and this will prevent the tools and the on-going work from deteriorating.

There are many ready-built kit sheds on the market, and it is worth insulating and then lining the interior of a shed with plywood. The safest way to heat the workshop is with a small thermostatically controlled convector heater. In winter, it is very important to keep the workshop and its contents at a low, even temperature. Variations in temperature will cause condensation to form on the cold surface of tools.

Timber absorbs water and if your work is to remain undamaged, it must also be kept at an even temperature. If you intend to do fine cabinet work, cutting dovetails and mitre joints, then constant temperature is essential.

## Hand tools

Electrically powered battery and mains powered hand tools are playing an ever-increasing role in the home workshop. The battery powered drill/screwdriver must be one of the most useful tools to emerge in the past ten years. Some have twin speeds, plus a variety of torque settings. The range of battery tools available is excellent and includes jigsaws and circular saws. The great advantage of the battery tool is that it is cordless and allows you to move about much more freely in the workshop and "on site" as it does not need a power point.

The mains powered electric tools are of tremendous assistance when you want to work quickly. There are few jobs that the traditional hand tools and saws cannot do, but electric power tools speed the work along.

## Timber

Today, great concern is being expressed for the survival of the rain forests, so to avoid contributing to the destruction of so many animals and exotic plants, it is important to only buy hardwoods when you are sure of the source of the timber. Hardwood suppliers are a little thinner on the ground than they used to be, but addresses can be found in the pages of specialised woodworking magazines. Some companies even operate a mail order service.

Some excellent pine is available. All the projects in this book are made using either Nordic redwood or whitewood. The Nordic redwoods are easily worked and give an excellent finish. The Swedish and Finnish forests have been managed for 200 years and more timber is grown annually than is cut. There are also some good whitewoods, although whitewood does not work as easily as redwood, and there is a tendency for it to have lots of tiny resinous pockets. There are also very plentiful supplies of Russian softwoods. These are usually of a very high quality, but they have a higher level of resin than the Nordic timbers.

Whatever you buy, make sure it comes from a covered area of the timber yard. If the timber is very wet, you will not be able to work with it. Do not be fooled by merchants who tell you that the timber is outside because it has just arrived!

Local road widening schemes usually involve the felling of trees, and frequently the trees are cut up on site with a small chain mill. It is quite easy to bargain for timber by the plank and a wonderful way to buy some very rare timbers. Obviously green planks require stacking and seasoning, so you need to have storage space; but it is well worth the time and effort that this requires.

Another good source of timber is the auction room. Sometimes huge wardrobes go for very reasonable prices. Frequently a bank or shop will be having a refit, and provide an excellent source for teak and mahogany.

Check recycled timber very carefully. Work over the timber with a battery powered metal detector, and remove all nails, screws etc. The most difficult pieces of metal to detect and remove are small panel pins. It is important to do this job thoroughly; as many powered tools are used in woodworking, any pieces of metal that are found in the timber will damage the cutting surfaces of the tools. *Always* use eye protectors while doing this type of work.

Man-made boards come in an enormous variety of materials. Plywood is one that most people know, but there are also chip board, hardboard, royal board, fibre board and the medium density fibre board. There are quite literally dozens of colours available in melamine boards. These are best cut with the new "hard point" teeth that many screw makers now favour. Cut the boards using a power saw with a blade that has tungsten carbide teeth, or the blade will blunt off very quickly.

# Tools

**Square** This tool is used to mark out all shoulder lines. The best squares have brass-tipped sides to prevent wear. Avoid dropping as the shock may cause it to go out of square.

**Bevel gauge** The bevel gauge is used for setting out all shoulder lines that are at an angle. Once the angle of the shoulder line is determined, all the rails are marked out without the angle being altered. The best gauges have brass-tipped edges and a wing nut to adjust the tension.

**Gauge** The tool illustrated "doubles up" as a marking and mortice gauge. The side with the single spur is the marking gauge and the twin spur the mortice gauge. A brass knob adjusts one of the spurs to allow for different widths of mortice chisel to be accommodated. The fence stock is fully adjustable.

**Punches** These drive the nail head below the surface of the wood, allowing for filler to be applied before painting. **Pin punches** function in the same way, except that they have a much smaller driving point.

**Bradawl** An invaluable aid for "starting off" screws and making small holes.

**Expanding rule** Also known as a steel tape, this is essential for measuring board and timber. A hook at the end of the rule and a locking button to keep the rule expanded are great advantages.

3m 10ft

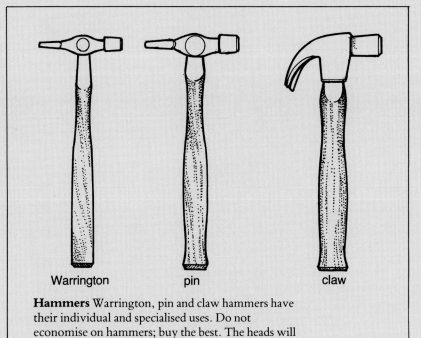

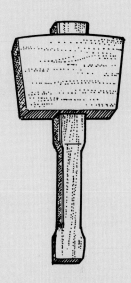

**Hammers** Warrington, pin and claw hammers have their individual and specialised uses. Do not economise on hammers; buy the best. The heads will stay on the ends of the shafts and the hammer head will not shatter.

**Mallet** For all work with chisels, a mallet is the best tool. *Never* hit a chisel head with a hammer.

**Bench hook** Essential for holding timber while it is being sawn on the bench. Typically, the bench hook is used to hold smaller pieces of wood while the shoulders of tenons are cut off. The bench blocks also prevents saw cuts marking the bench top.

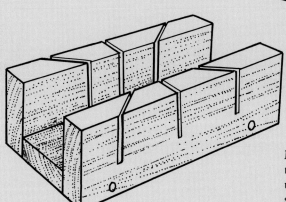

**Mitre block** Timber is held in the "well" of the mitre block while a tenon saw is being used to cut the desired angle. The slots in the sides of the mitre block guide the blade. The best mitre blocks have brass "lugs" at the tops of the slots to prevent wear.

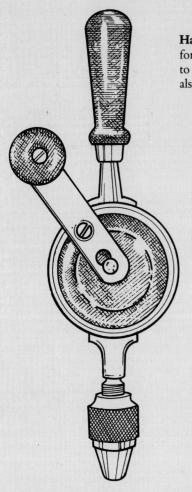

**Hand drill** Despite the electrification of the woodwork bench, there is still a place for this tool. The better hand drills have a twin pinion drive. The hand drill is used to bore a variety of holes, although today increasingly the smaller holes, and it is also used with a countersink.

**Countersink** No tool box is complete without one of these. Used for countersinking holes for all countersunk screws.

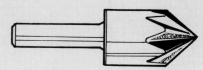

**Screw sink** A useful addition to the tool box and for all counterboring. The screw sink not only drills the hole but bores the hole to take the screw head.

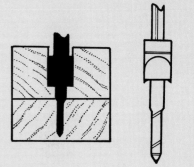

**Plug cutter** Frequently, after using a screw sink, the hole needs to be filled. A plug cutter, as its name implies, cuts a plug to fill a hole. The cut plugs give a much better finish than if a dowel rod was used.

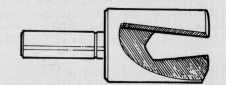

**Firmer chisel** With its square sides, this was traditionally the workhorse of the bench. A firmer chisel is stronger than a bevel edged chisel.

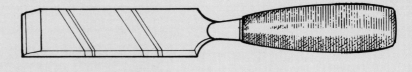

**Bevel edged chisel** This was initially designed for cutting out dovetail slots, and the bevel on the back of the chisel prevented it from damaging the edge of the dovetail. Today, the blade of the chisel has been strengthened and it is used more generally in woodworking.

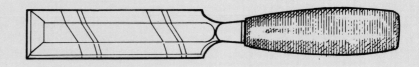

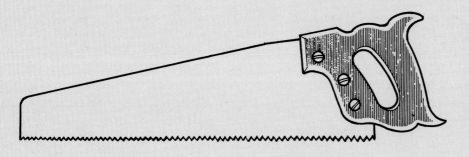

**Handsaw** The handsaw has seen considerable changes in the past five years. The introduction of the hardened tooth has been revolutionary. Handsaws with fleam teeth are capable of cutting on both forward and backward strokes.

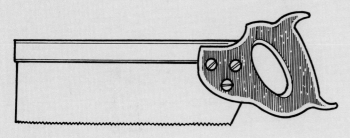

**Backsaw** or **tenon saw** This has a hardened steel or brass back. Its purpose – as one of its names suggests – is to cut tenons or indeed any piece of wood that needs to be jointed accurately. The brass or steel back stiffens the blade and makes for accurate cuts in timber.

**Gent's saw** This little saw is very useful for cutting dovetails, mitres etc. It is really a lightweight version of the tenon saw.

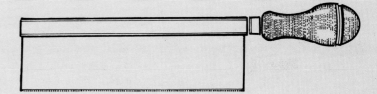

**Coping saw** A most versatile member of the saw family. It is capable of making intricate curved cuts and has the added advantage of a blade that can be rotated within the frame.

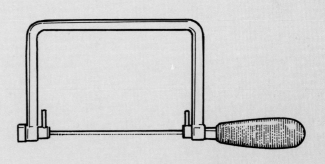

**Multihole saw** This gives the woodworker the ability to bore a variety of holes. The tool comes complete with a range of hole saws of different diameters.

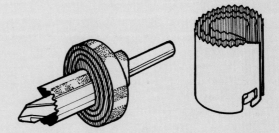

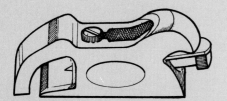

**Shoulder plane** As its name implies, this tool was developed to trim the shoulders of tenons. Sometimes with very large tenons it is useful to have the ability to trim a fraction off the tenon shoulder. The plane's blade is flush with the side of the plane body.

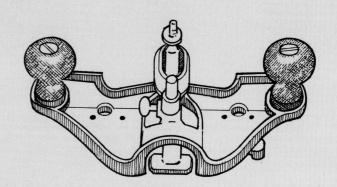

**Hand router** This traditional tool (available long before the advantage of electric routers) was used for producing a uniform depth at the bottom of housing joints. The tool normally has three different-sized cutters, which are all adjustable for depth of cut.

**Spokeshave** A lovely tool to use. A well-sharpened "shave" will produce a bench full of shavings in minutes. It is wonderfully quick in removing saw cuts from curved surfaces. Spokeshaves are available with a choice of soles – convex or concave.

**Surform tools** These are available for a whole range of smoothing operations. The cutting action is carried out by rows of small sharpened teeth. A very useful addition to any tool box.

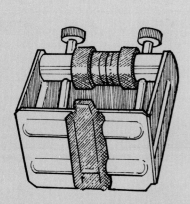

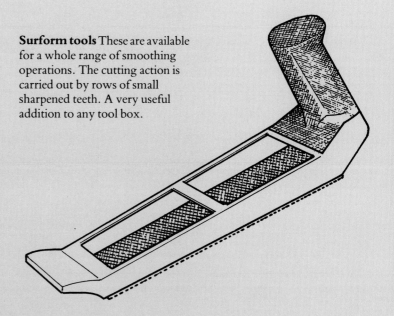

**Honing guide** An absolute must for all chisel and plane blades. The wing clamp nuts hold the blade firmly at the correct angle, and a set of rollers support the tool as it glides to and fro on the oilstone.

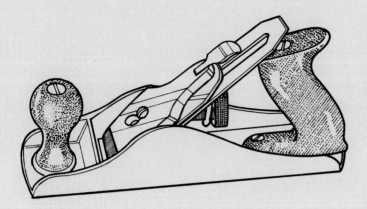

**Smoothing plane** No woodworking of any real quality can be carried out without a smoothing plane. A good smoothing plane will last a lifetime. These tools have a variety of adjustments, shaving thickness, width of mouth and horizontal adjustment of the blade.

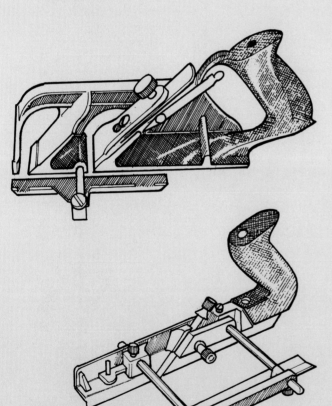

**Rebate plane** This is specifically designed to cut rebate joints on the edges of boards. The blade is flush with the side of the tool. A fence and depth gauge are provided. For cutting across the grain a small "spur" tooth is fitted in order to cut the grain fibres and prevent the blade "tearing out" the wood.

**Plough plane** Used to cut a variety of different-sized grooves. The width of the groove is governed by the cutter. The fence and depth gauge are both fully adjustable. The plane is supplied with a range of different cutters.

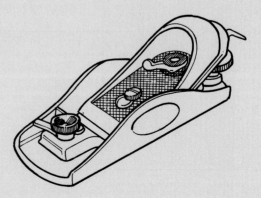

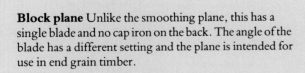

**Block plane** Unlike the smoothing plane, this has a single blade and no cap iron on the back. The angle of the blade has a different setting and the plane is intended for use in end grain timber.

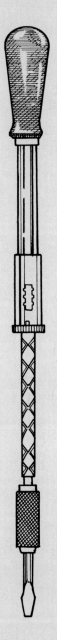

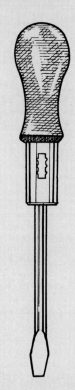

**Spiral "Yankee" ratchet screwdriver** Capable of driving screws in at tremendous rate. If you have a repetitive job to do, then this is the ideal tool.

**Traditional screwdriver** Evolved over hundreds of years, this is still a joy to use. It is important to use the correct size blade for each screw.

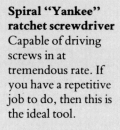

**Ratchet screwdriver** For those who do not usually use a screwdriver, this will prevent a blistered palm!

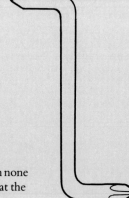

**90° bend screwdriver** There are some occasions when none of the usual screwdrivers will do. It is at such a time that the 90° bend screwdriver comes to the rescue.

**Commonly used screwheads**

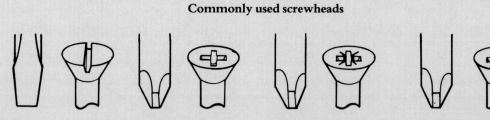

# Electric tools

**Hammer drill** A first rate 12mm (½in) drill capable of coping with hole drilling in a variety of materials is invaluable – a drill with percussion action, backward/forward rotation and fully adjustable for speed even more so. A trigger with a "slow start" facility is ideal for attaining an accurate start.

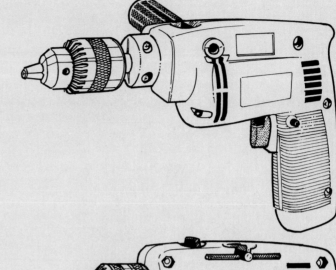

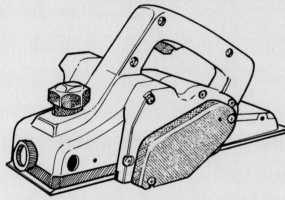

**Power planer** This is very useful for rapidly "shaping up" sawn timber. The Makita plane has the ability to rebate with its sharp blades and correct the rate of feed.

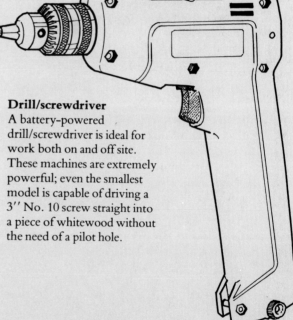

**Drill/screwdriver**
A battery-powered drill/screwdriver is ideal for work both on and off site. These machines are extremely powerful; even the smallest model is capable of driving a 3″ No. 10 screw straight into a piece of whitewood without the need of a pilot hole.

**Belt sander** This is capable of removing large quantities of "stock" very rapidly. Some belt sanders can be fitted with a "shoe frame" that prevents them digging into the wood, leaving a perfectly flat surface.

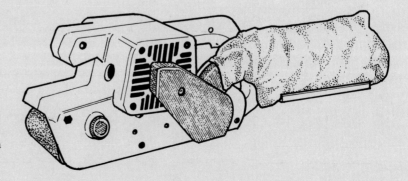

**Plunge router** In the past ten years, no other tool has changed the face of woodworking so much. These machines have made it possible for the novice woodworker to perform operations that before only a skilled craftsman could do.

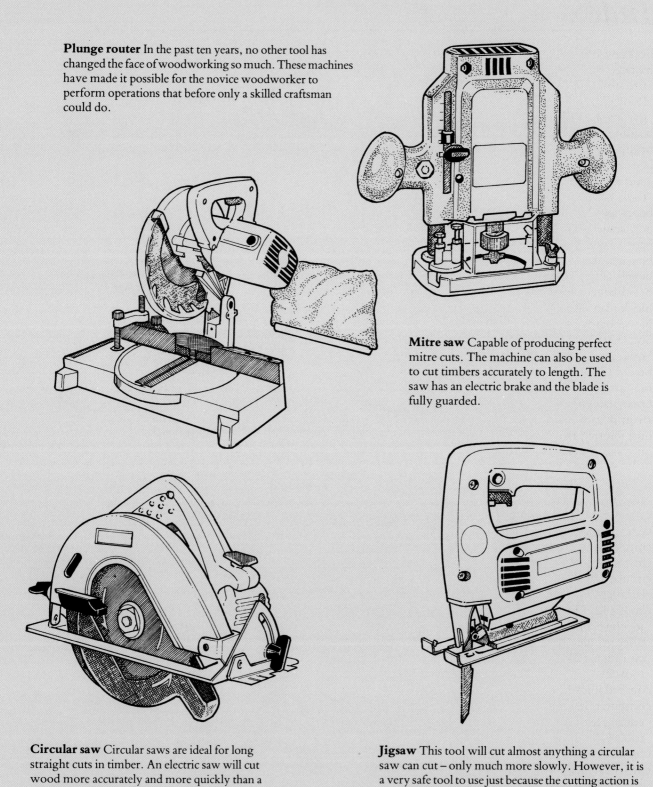

**Mitre saw** Capable of producing perfect mitre cuts. The machine can also be used to cut timbers accurately to length. The saw has an electric brake and the blade is fully guarded.

**Circular saw** Circular saws are ideal for long straight cuts in timber. An electric saw will cut wood more accurately and more quickly than a hand held saw.

**Jigsaw** This tool will cut almost anything a circular saw can cut – only much more slowly. However, it is a very safe tool to use just because the cutting action is much slower than that of the circular saw.

# Index